## *Praise for*
## *Witnesses of Christ*

"Jerry Houck's *Witnesses of Christ* was first written to give tour guides high-quality biographical information to be used in describing the painted portraits of deceased Apostles hanging in the Conference Center in Salt Lake City. Carefully researched and written, the work provides concise but meaningful accounts of the lives of each man who has served as an Apostle in this dispensation. It's an important resource for LDS scholars, teachers, and students. I'd recommend it to anyone seeking rudimentary biographical material in a single volume regarding the men who have held the office of Apostle in The Church of Jesus Christ of Latter-day Saints."

— *John A. Peterson*, author of *Utah's Blackhawk War*

"Jerry's compilation is a great place to begin investigating the lives of some of the most influential people in The Church of Jesus Christ of Latter-day Saints. It's a rare quality to write both concisely and insightfully; Jerry achieves this in a delightful style. He gives you just enough insight into each of the Apostles' lives that you feel you know them a little more intimately and, at the same time, you are filled with a desire to learn more. And once you get started, it's hard to stop at just one."

— *David B. Marsh*, religious educator, curriculum developer

"Recently, Jerry shared a draft copy of his book, *Witnesses of Christ*, concerning the lives of the Apostles of the dispensation of the fulness of times. As my wife and I read it, we were amazed at the stories of these men. There were many whose names we knew, but their life stories were unknown to us. There were others that we did not know, and we were excited to learn about their lives and missions. It was inviting to read the brief digests of each Apostle. To get a glimpse into the achievements and character of each man was inspiring. Their life stories tell the major event of the Restoration and the difficult times they lived in. I heartily endorse this book to anyone desiring to learn more about the great men of this dispensation that lead The Church of Jesus Christ of Latter-day Saints."

— *Josiah W. Douglas*, religious educator, curriculum developer

# WITNESSES

## *of*

# CHRIST

## PROPHETS *and* APOSTLES
## ❖ *of Our* DISPENSATION ❖

# JERRY H. HOUCK

CFI
An Imprint of Cedar Fort, Inc.
Springville, Utah

This is not an official publication of The Church of Jesus Christ of Latter-day Saints. The opinions and views expressed herein belong solely to the author and do not necessarily represent the opinions or views of Cedar Fort, Inc. Permission for the use of sources, graphics, and photos is also solely the responsibility of the author.

ISBN 13: 978-1-4621-1550-1

Published by CFI, an imprint of Cedar Fort, Inc.
2373 W. 700 S., Springville, UT 84663
Distributed by Cedar Fort, Inc., www.cedarfort.com

Library of Congress Cataloging-in-Publication Data

Houck, Jerry, 1940- author.
Witnesses of Christ / Jerry Houck.
     pages cm
Includes bibliographical references and index.
Summary: Biographical sketches of 82 men who have served in the Council of the Twelve Apostles of the Church of Jesus Christ of Latter-day Saints.
ISBN 978-1-4621-1550-1 (alk. paper)
1. Council of the Twelve Apostles (Church of Jesus Christ of Latter-day Saints)--Biography.
2. Mormon Church--Apostles--Biography.  I. Title.

BX8693.H68 2015
289.3'320922--dc23
[B]

                                    2015006831

Cover design by Shawnda T. Craig
Cover design © 2015 Lyle Mortimer
Edited and typeset by Mary-Celeste Ricks and Kevin Haws

Printed in the United States of America

10  9  8  7  6  5  4  3  2  1

Printed on acid-free paper

# Contents

# Contents

# *Introduction*

I should first acknowledge that this book wasn't originally written with the intent of publication. It was written for a special audience and has been published only at that audience's insistence—and yes, nagging.

For three years (2008–2011), my wife, Wendy, and I served as assistant supervisors over the approximately five hundred hosts and hostesses (tour guides), who serve voluntarily at the Church Conference Center. On the third floor of the Center is displayed the painted portraits of all the deceased members of the Quorum of the Twelve Apostles who have lived in this dispensation.

Our hosts and hostesses walk past these portraits and gaze upon them every day. Some of these Brethren are familiar names in the Church, like Heber C. Kimball, James E. Talmage, and Neal A. Maxwell. But unfortunately, many of these names are virtually unknown to the general membership of the Church today, such as Albert Carrington, Marriner Merrill, and Charles A. Callis. Speaking at the April 2006 general conference, President Gordon B. Hinckley reminisced about some of his experiences with general authorities who had since passed from this life. He observed, "The old, wise heads are passing on. They were my friends. In my brief time I have seen many of the great men of the Church come and go. Most of them I have worked with and known intimately. Time has a way of erasing their memory. Another five years and such names as Merrill, Widtsoe, Bowen—all powerful figures—will be forgotten by all but a few."

These brief biographical sketches were written in the hope of preventing that forgetfulness and keeping alive the memory of these great men in the hearts and minds of our hosts and hostesses. Obviously, the lives of any of these Brethren could occupy a large volume of work. The intent here is to give only a brief glimpse or insight into their characters and accomplishments. The segments included in each of the sketches have been chosen to give the reader a feel for the Apostles' personalities, their strengths—and in some cases, their weaknesses— their unique experiences and contributions to the Church.

Most importantly, it is hoped that the readers will feel a greater sense of familiarity with these Church leaders of the past and be able to learn from and apply their life lessons. In essence, these are neither biographies nor histories—space did not allow. Rather, they are brief introductions into the personalities of our past leaders.

## Thomas B. Marsh

Born: November 1, 1799, Acton, Massachusetts
Ordained Apostle: April 26, 1835
Sustained President of the Quorum of the Twelve: May 2, 1835
Excommunicated: March 17, 1839
Rebaptized: July 16, 1857
Died: January 1866, Ogden, Utah, at age 66

At the time the Book of Mormon was being published, many rumors were circulating concerning Joseph Smith and his golden bible. Thomas B. Marsh, his curiosity raised over these rumors, traveled to Palmyra, where he met Martin Harris at the Grandin printing shop. Martin gave Thomas proof sheets of the first sixteen pages of the Book of Mormon and then took him to the Smith home. There, over the next two days, Oliver Cowdery taught him about Joseph and the Restoration. Thomas then returned to his home in Massachusetts, where he showed the pages to his wife and told her of the things he had learned. Both believed. When Thomas heard that the Church had been organized, he moved his family to Palmyra and was baptized by David Whitmer in September 1830. Shortly thereafter he was called on a mission.

In 1832 Thomas led a company of Saints to Jackson County, Missouri. In 1835 he was called as one of the original Twelve Apostles. When the Quorum of the Twelve was organized, Joseph Smith established member seniority by age. Thomas, being the oldest, became president of the quorum. In 1837 he accompanied Joseph Smith and Sidney Rigdon on a mission to Canada. The following year he and David W. Patten were appointed as temporary presidents over the Saints in Missouri until such time as the Prophet Joseph could arrive.

In 1838, when the spirit of apostasy took hold in the Church, Elder Marsh fell away and turned traitor against the Saints. An incident occurred in February of that year that has become well-known in Church history. As told by Elder George A. Smith, Thomas's wife, Elizabeth, and Lucinda Harris both wanted to make a cheese, but neither possessed enough cows to produce sufficient milk. They therefore agreed to take turns exchanging milk and strippings so each would have enough. Lucinda honored her part of the agreement, but when it was Elizabeth's turn to give Lucinda her milk, she kept part of the strippings. The matter went before home teachers, the bishop, the high council, and eventually the First Presidency, all deciding in favor of Lucinda. But Elizabeth would not admit to her wrongdoing, and Thomas "declared that he would sustain the character of his wife, even if he had to go to hell for it."[1]

It was about this time, according to Heber C. Kimball, that Thomas received a revelation, which he wrote down. "There were from three to five pages of it," observed Elder Kimball, "and when he came out [of the printing office], he read it to brother Brigham and me. In it God told him what to do, and that was to sustain brother Joseph and to believe that what brother Joseph had said was true. But no; he took a course to sustain his wife and oppose the Prophet of God, and she led him away."[2]

Becoming bitter toward the Church and its officials, Elder Marsh drafted and signed an affidavit claiming the existence of a Church organization called the "Danites," whose main purpose was to carry out retribution against the enemies of the Church, and stating that Joseph planned to take over the land by blood and sword, if necessary. This affidavit increased persecutions against the Saints and eventually lead to Governor Boggs's infamous extermination orders.

Consequently, Thomas was excommunicated. Regarding his treachery, Joseph Smith remarked that Thomas B. Marsh "had been lifted up in pride by his exaltation to office and the revelations of heaven concerning him, until he was ready to be overthrown by the first adverse wind that should cross his track, and now he has fallen, lied and sworn falsely, and is ready to take the lives of his best friends. Let all men take warning by him, and learn that he who exalteth himself, God will abase."[3]

During the ensuing eighteen years, Thomas became a vagabond, without a resting-place and without peace. According to John Taylor, Thomas was "a poor, decrepit, broken down, old man. He has had a paralytic stroke—one of his arms hangs down. He is . . . an object of charity, destitute, without wife, child, or anything else. . . . He has been all the time . . . afraid for his life—afraid the Mormons would kill him; and he durst not let them know where he was." Elder Taylor went on to say that Marsh, meeting with some apostates, said to them, "You don't know what you are about; if you want to see the fruits of apostasy, look on me."[4]

It became Thomas's desire to reunite with the Saints in Utah, but with all his efforts he only managed to raise $5.10. Looking upon his small sum, he said, "Lord, if you will help me, I will go."[5] Before leaving Missouri, he had managed to obtain $55.05. He concluded that the Lord was with him and started west. In July 1857, he was rebaptized at Winter Quarters, Nebraska.

Arriving in Salt Lake City in early September of 1857, Marsh spoke before the Saints gathered in the Bowery. "Many have said to me, 'how is it that a man like you, who understood so much of the revelations of God as recorded in the Book of Doctrine and Covenants, should fall away?' I told them not to feel too secure, but to take heed lest they also should fall." Regarding his own apostasy, he explained,

> I became jealous of the Prophet, and then I saw double and overlooked everything that was right, and spent all my time in looking for the evil. . . .
> I saw a beam in Brother Joseph's eye, but it was nothing but a mote, and my own eye was filled with the beam. . . . I talked to Brother Brigham and Brother Heber, and I wanted them to be mad

like myself; and I saw they were not mad, and I got madder still because they were not. Brother Brigham, with a cautious look, said, "Are you the leader of the Church, Brother Thomas?" I answered, "No!" "Well then," said he, "why do you not let that alone?" Well, this was about the amount of my hypocrisy—I meddled with that which was not my business.[6]

Following his remarks, Church members unanimously voted to receive him into full fellowship in the Church.

His physical health broken and his mental faculties impaired, Thomas lived in obscurity and died in Ogden in January 1866, at the age of sixty-six.

*David W. Patten*

Born: November 14, 1799, Theresa, New York
Ordained Apostle: February 15, 1835
Killed: October 25, 1838, Battle of Crooked River, Missouri, at age 38

**B**orn November 14, 1799, David left home when but a boy and traveled to Michigan, where he built a small log home. When he was twenty-one years of age, he was moved upon by the Holy Ghost to repent of his sins. During the following three years, he lived close to the Lord, receiving dreams and visions. On one such occasion it was made known to him that the Church of Christ would be established upon the earth during his lifetime. From that time on, he anxiously looked forward to that day.

In 1830, he first saw a copy of the Book of Mormon but only had the opportunity to read its preface and the testimonies of the witnesses. Then, in 1832, his brother John wrote to him that the gospel of Jesus Christ had been restored to the earth. David got on his horse and rode the 300 miles to Fairplay, Indiana, where he was taught and baptized by his brother. Two days later he was ordained an elder and sent to preach the gospel in Michigan. This would be the first of many missions.

While serving on his missions, he discovered that he had the gift of healing. His style of healing the sick was unique to him. He would teach the sick the principles of the gospel, testify of its truth, and promise them they would be healed if they would accept baptism. Abraham O. Smoot stated that he never knew of an instance where David's petition in the behalf of the sick was not answered. Throughout his missions, his reputation for healing spread to where people would come from afar to have him administer to them. Almost daily he healed the sick, many who had been infirm for years, and even those near death's door. On many occasions, they were healed instantly. On one occasion, he healed a young woman, May Ann Stearns, who had suffered chronic heart disease for many years, promising her that she would be completely restored to perfect health. She later became the wife of Parley P. Pratt and lived until eighty-two years of age without any further heart problems. David would later record: "The Lord did work with me wonderfully, in signs and wonders following them that believed in the fullness of the Gospel of Jesus Christ, insomuch that the deaf were made to hear, the blind to see, and the lame were made whole. Fevers, palsies, crooked and withered limbs, and in fact all manner of diseases, common to the country, were healed by the power of God, that was manifested through his servants."[1]

When David was a missionary, the Lord sustained him in other ways. Once when he was preaching to a group, a man who had disrupted many meetings began to heckle David. When asked to be quiet, he refused and defied any man to put him out of the house. David, moved upon by the Spirit, told the man to be quiet or he would remove him. "You can't do it," said the man. David replied, "In the name of the Lord I will do it." David then grabbed the man with both arms, carried him to the door, and threw him ten feet into a wood pile. The saying soon went out that Patten had "cast out one devil, soul and body."[2] On another occasion, an armed mob had gathered outside the building where David was preaching. After the meeting, David went out and faced the mob, telling them to shoot him if they wished. Although David had only a walking stick, the mob fled. In Tennessee, a mob took him and his companions before a judge for a mock trial that found them guilty of charges. David stood and rebuked the mob and the proceedings. One companion, Warren Parrish, later said, "My hair stood up straight on my head, for I expected to be killed."[3] They were released, but that night as they slept, David was warned in a dream that they were to leave, for the mob would soon arrive at the house.

Through his missions David brought many into the Church, establishing branches along the way. Happily, among those he baptized were his mother, two brothers, and two sisters. His preaching had the ability of leaving deep and lasting impressions upon those who heard him. By chance, he happened to ride horseback for 25 miles with a young man who was on his way to Oberlin College. The young man's name was Lorenzo Snow. According to Lorenzo's sister, Eliza Snow, their conversation opened her brother's mind to a new way of thinking and had a lasting impression upon him that was never erased. It would prove influential in his later joining the Church.

David also had the gift of prophecy. Threatened by a mob while preaching in Paris, Tennessee, he boldly denounced them and prophesied that many of them would live to see the streets of Paris run with the blood of its own citizens. This was literally fulfilled approximately twenty-six years later during the Civil War, when General Morgan conducted his famous raid through Kentucky and Tennessee.

In Ohio, the Spirit of the Lord said to him, "Depart from your field of labor and go unto Kirtland, for behold I will send thee up to the land of Zion and thou shalt [serve] thy brethren there."[4] Arriving in Kirtland, he was sent by the Prophet Joseph to Missouri, to deliver dispatches to the brethren. Arriving in Clay County on March 4, 1834, he remained there until the arrival of Zion's Camp. In February 1835, he was ordained one of the Twelve Apostles. Following other missions, he returned to Kirtland at a time of great apostasy in the Church, only to be disheartened when his good friend and brother-in-law, Warren Parrish, tried to turn him against the Prophet. Again he was sent to Missouri, where, with Thomas B. Marsh, he presided over the Saints until Joseph Smith arrived. In Missouri, his courageous defense of the Saints against mobs earned him the title of "Captain Fear Not."

David's faith was such that he once expressed to the Prophet Joseph the desire to die a martyr's death. The Prophet was deeply moved and expressed extreme sorrow, saying to David, "When a man of your faith asks the Lord for anything, he generally gets it."[5] This prophetic utterance came to fulfillment when, on October 24, 1838, word came that a Missouri mob had taken three Church members captive near Crooked River. Elder Patten led seventy-five men to intercept the mob and rescue the brethren. During a confrontation with the mob the next morning, a battle ensued in which the prisoners were freed, but Patten was mortally wounded, receiving a large ball in his bowels. In severe pain, he was carried to the home of Stephen Winchester, where he died that night. On the day of Elder Patten's funeral, Joseph went to the Patten home where friends had gathered. Pointing to Patten's lifeless body, Joseph testified, "There lies a man who has done just as he said he would: he has laid down his life for his friends."[6] Joseph later recorded, "[David W. Patten] died as he lived, a man of God, and strong in the faith of a glorious resurrection, in a world where mobs will have no power or place."[7]

*Brigham Young*

Born: June 1, 1801, Whitingham, Vermont
Ordained Apostle: February 14, 1835
Sustained President of the Quorum of the Twelve: April 14, 1840
Sustained President of the Church: December 27, 1847
Died: August 29, 1877, Salt Lake City, at age 76

**B**righam's father was a poor yet hardworking itinerant farmer who frequently moved his family in search of better opportunities that continually eluded him. Brigham, the ninth of eleven children born to John and Abigail Howe Young, grew up knowing a lack of food and clothing. Instead of attending school, Brigham attended hard frontier farm work. By his own calculations, he had only eleven days of formal schooling. When he was sixteen, his father told him it was time he was on his own and provided for himself. Becoming apprenticed to a cabinet maker, painter, and chair manufacturer, he eventually became known for being a skilled artisan as well as for being honest and reliable. When his wife, Miriam, contracted tuberculosis, he also assumed much of her housework and the caring of their children, leading him to teasingly boast in later years that in housekeeping he could beat most women in the community.

In 1830, Brigham first saw a copy of the Book of Mormon that his brother Phineas had obtained from Samuel Smith. "I examined the matter studiously for two years before I made up my mind to receive that book," he recorded. "I wished time sufficient to prove all things for myself."[1] He was baptized in April of 1832.

The same year of his baptism, his wife, Mirian, died and left him with two small children. Leaving them in the care of Vilate Kimball, the wife of his good friend Heber, he traveled to Kirtland, Ohio, preaching along the way. In Kirtland he found the Prophet Joseph Smith chopping and stacking wood. "Here my joy was full at the privilege of shaking the hand of the Prophet of God, and receiving the sure testimony, by the spirit of prophecy, that he was all that any man could believe him to be as a true Prophet."[2]

Brigham and his brother Joseph soon went to Canada to preach the gospel. Later they took part in Zion's Camp. A Church member in Kirtland who had refused to join the camp met Brigham on his return from Missouri and said to him: "Well, what did you gain on this useless journey to Missouri with Joseph Smith?" "All I went for," promptly replied Brigham. "I would not exchange the experience I gained in that expedition for all the wealth of Geauga County."[3] The value of this experience would later prove itself in the Saints' expulsion from Missouri and in their trek to the Rocky Mountains.

In February of 1835, Brigham was ordained an Apostle. He soon earned a reputation as a valiant defender of the Prophet Joseph. In 1836, a time of crisis in Kirtland, when "the knees of many of the strongest men in the church faltered," Brigham attended a meeting in the upper room of the temple where some were discussing deposing Joseph and installing David Whitmer at the head of the Church. Brigham recalled:

> I rose up, and in a plain and forcible manner told them that Joseph was a Prophet, and I knew it, and that they might rail and slander him as much as they pleased. They could not destroy the appointment of the Prophet of God, they could only destroy their own author-ity, cut the thread that bound them to the Prophet of God, and sink

themselves to hell. . . . This meeting was broken up without the apostates being able to unite on any decided measures of opposition. . . . During this siege of darkness I stood close by Joseph, and with all the wisdom and power God bestowed upon me, put forth my utmost energies to . . . unite the quorums of the church.[4]

His defense of Joseph led to his having to flee Kirtland to save his own life from threatening apostates.

June of 1844 found Brigham in the eastern states promoting the political platform of Joseph Smith. In Boston on June 27, 1844, he "felt a heavy depression of spirit" for which he could find no reason. It was nearly two weeks later that he received word of the death of Joseph and Hyrum. Returning to Nauvoo, he defended the authority of the Quorum of the Twelve to lead the Church. It was while addressing the Saints that the mantle of the Prophet fell upon him and many would testify that his appearance and voice were that of Joseph Smith. Through the westward trek to the Great Salt Lake Valley, Brigham led the Church as President of the Quorum of the Twelve. Then in December of 1847, upon his return to Winter Quarters, Brigham called a meeting of the Twelve where he announced the need to reorganize the First Presidency. Orson Hyde recorded that in that meeting the voice of the Lord was heard from on high saying, "Let my servant Brigham step forth and receive the full power of the presiding Priesthood in my Church and kingdom." Neighbors, having felt the ground tremble and their homes shake, came running, thinking it was an earthquake, to which one of the Twelve responded, "The Lord was only whispering to us a little. The voice of God has reached the earth. He is probably not very far off."[5]

Brigham's leadership abilities have been described as follows:

Frank, kind, and concerned, he was as a father among [the Saints]. Working alongside them, he chopped wood, cut timber, made bridges, cleared land, and built roads. During the exodus he was the first up in the morning and the last to retire at night, always making the rounds to see that all were as comfortable as possible. But above all, he was the prophet of God. He could rebuke, yet love and inspire; demand, yet give; lead always, yet follow. And the courage and humor with which he faced trials served as an anchor and a model for the persecution-weary Saints.[6]

But Brigham could also receive counsel. The story is told that Jedediah M. Grant sought out Brigham one day on public business. Finding Brigham shingling a roof, he was told to come back that evening when Brigham was not so busy. At this, Jedediah chided Brigham, telling him that the valley was filled with carpenters who could do the shingling, but that the Saints had only one Church President and one governor. According to the story, this was a turning point for Brigham. From that time forward, he gave little time to manual labor but rather focused on traveling throughout the settlements looking after the welfare of the Saints and administering in his office as president and as governor.

Of all his accomplishments, he is best remembered to the world as a great colonizer, having overseen the establishment of several hundred settlements throughout the Great Basin area and the West. Yet to Brigham, how people remembered him was insignificant compared to what he saw as the greater matter of life. "I care nothing about my character in this world," he said. "I do not care what men say about me. I want my character to stand fair in the eyes of my Heavenly Father."[7]

Brigham Young died on of August 29, 1877, in Salt Lake City. His last words, as he fixed his gaze upward, were, "Joseph, Joseph, Joseph," as if communicating with his beloved prophet.

*Heber C. Kimball*

Born: June 14, 1801, Sheldon, Vermont
Ordained Apostle: February 14, 1835
Sustained First Counselor to President Brigham Young: December 27, 1847
Died: June 22, 1868, Salt Lake City, Utah, at age 67

A**t the age** of nineteen, Heber apprenticed with his brother Charles in the potter's trade. After two years as an apprentice, he worked for his brother as a journeyman, helping establish a pottery shop in Mendon, New York. Here, he married Vilate Murray, a niece of Brigham Young. He then purchased the pottery establishment from his brother and went into business for himself, which trade he was engaged in for about ten years. When Mormon missionaries began preaching in the town of Victor, Heber and many of the Young family attended their meetings. On June 15, 1832, Heber told the missionaries he was ready to be baptized. That summer, Heber was ordained an elder and, with the Youngs, began preaching the gospel. They succeeded in raising up several small branches of the Church in the surrounding area. In September of that same year, in company with Brigham and Joseph Young, he traveled to Kirtland to meet the Prophet Joseph for the first time. Later, with his wife, he moved to Kirtland.

Heber took part in Zion's Camp and from that experience became a leader in two later exoduses: the removal of twelve thousand Saints from Missouri to Illinois, and the westward trek to the Rocky Mountains. In February of 1835, he was ordained to the Quorum of the Twelve Apostles. It was on Sunday, June 4, 1837, as Heber sat in the Kirtland Temple, that the Prophet Joseph came up to him and said, "Brother Heber, the Spirit of the Lord has whispered to me: 'Let my servant Heber go to England and proclaim my Gospel, and open the door of salvation to that nation.'"[1] Heber felt overwhelmed by such a burden but determined that, with the Lord's help, he would go and do his best. Accompanied by Orson Hyde, Willard Richards, and Joseph Fielding, he traveled to New York harbor and sailed for England, arriving at Liverpool on the July 20, 1837. Here they were impressed to travel on to Preston, where they found a congregation of people who advocated "the rise of a Latter-day Church in fulfillment of the Prophets." Many recognized Heber as the man seen in their dreams, the man God would send to them with the restored Church. In consequence of the opening of the Lord's work in England, the missionaries were attacked by evil spirits whom they beheld in vision for an hour. Heber was knocked senseless to the floor, and Orson Hyde stood between him and the devils, contending with them face to face until they diminished in number. Some years later, when talking of the incident, the Prophet Joseph said to Heber, "When I heard of it, it gave me great joy, for I then knew that the work of God had taken root in that land. It was this that caused the devil to make a struggle to kill you."[2]

Heber, along with Joseph Fielding, later traveled to Chatburn, a factory town where he was warned previously that he would not find anyone to baptize. The first night of preaching, they baptized twenty-five persons. After five days, they had baptized 110 new members. One day, as Heber walked the streets of Chatburn, he was overcome by a feeling of awe and reverence. "I pulled off my hat, and felt that I wanted to pull off my shoes, and I did not know what to think of it." When later recounting the incident to Joseph Smith, Joseph said to him that "some of the old Prophets traveled and dedicated that land, and their blessing fell upon you."[3] Heber returned to Kirtland May 22, 1838, after an absence of eleven months. He and his associates had baptized nearly fifteen hundred people, organized branches in several cities, and established what would be the European Mission.

Following the Prophet and other Church leaders, Heber took his family and moved to Far West, Missouri, where he was confronted with the persecutions against the Saints. When Joseph was imprisoned, Heber, along with Brigham Young, visited Joseph frequently and worked hard trying to secure his release. In April 1839, he was among those who met secretly at the Far West temple site as prelude to the Twelve's departure for England. Heber then moved to Nauvoo, where he built a residence for his family before departing for England in September. Under the direction of the Twelve, the Church in England was strengthened by hundreds of new converts.

Returning home, Heber was called on a mission to the eastern states. It was on this mission that he learned of the death of Joseph and Hyrum Smith. In 1847, he was part of the Pioneer Company that entered the Salt Lake Valley. In December 1847, when Brigham Young was sustained as President of the Church, Elder Kimball was sustained as his First Counselor and later became lieutenant-governor of the Provisional State of Deseret, serving in both positions until the time of his death.

Elder Kimball became known for his prophetic voice, leading President Young to say, "Brother Heber—he is my Prophet, he loves to prophesy, and I love to hear him."[4] Elder Wilford Woodruff said of Heber many years later, "He would at times give utterance to things when preaching under the influence of the Holy Spirit that would frighten himself, and has many times been known to say after he had finished preaching, 'What have I said?'"[5] One such occasion occurred when the Saints were suffering, hungry, and destitute, with a thousand miles separating them from commercial locations. Filled with the spirit of prophecy, Elder Kimball stood in a public meeting and said that within six months, the Saints would be able to purchase clothing and other goods in Salt Lake City cheaper than they could be bought in New York. Those present were astonished at his words. After the meeting, one of his brethren told him he did not believe it. "Neither did I," replied Kimball, "but I said it. It will have to go."[6] His words were literally fulfilled when, within six months, large companies of emigrants, anxious to reach the gold fields of California, unloaded their merchandise in the streets of Salt Lake City, selling it for less than New York prices.

In May of 1868, Elder Kimball was thrown from his carriage, sustaining injuries that led to partial paralysis. Slipping into a coma, he died peacefully in his home June 22, 1868. At his funeral, President Young eulogized Heber, saying, "He was a man of as much integrity I presume as any man who ever lived on earth, . . . a man of truth, a man of benevolence, a man that was to be trusted. Now he has gone and left us, . . . to be prepared for a glorious resurrection."[7]

*Orson Hyde*

Born: January 8, 1805, Oxford, Connecticut
Ordained Apostle: February 15, 1835
Dropped from the Quorum of the Twelve: May 4, 1839
Restored to Quorum: June 27, 1839
Sustained as President of Quorum of the Twelve: December 27, 1847
Moved from original position in the Quorum: April 10, 1875
Died: November 28, 1878, Spring City, Utah, at age 73

When Orson was only seven years of age, his mother died. Consequently, Orson, his eight brothers, and his three sisters were placed under the care of various families, Orson living with Nathan Wheeler. When Orson was fourteen years of age, Wheeler moved to Kirtland, Ohio. It was there that Orson, at the age of eighteen, set off on his own, working in several occupations, including part-time clerk in the Gilbert & Whitney store, and eventually joined the Campbellites through the preaching of Sidney Rigdon. Orson then set out preaching, becoming a pastor over several Campbellite branches. When Mormon missionaries visited the area with their "golden Bible," he preached against it but did not feel right about doing so. He decided to investigate Mormonism and traveled back to Kirtland, where Mormons had now settled. To his surprise, Sidney Rigdon and other former associates had joined the Church. In the fall of 1831, Orson was baptized by Sidney. Shortly afterward, Orson was ordained a high priest, and in company with Hyrum Smith, he performed a mission among the Campbellites, organizing several branches. Other missions followed.

In the spring of 1834, Orson was sent east to collect money to finance Zion's Camp. Having little success and little food, he was visited one evening by a glorious personage who fed him a fruit he had never before seen, but it was delicious beyond description and very nourishing. The personage also told Orson of his future duties and privileges. He seldom spoke of this visitation, considering it a personal revelation for him alone. In 1835, Orson was ordained an Apostle, and in 1837, at his request, he accompanied Elder Heber C. Kimball to open missionary work in England.

In the summer of 1838, having returned from England, Elder Hyde moved his family to Far West. While struck with a bilious fever that plagued him until the following spring, he constantly heard rumors and complaints from those who visited him, foremost among them being Thomas Marsh. Consequently, he signed an affidavit written by Marsh that slandered the Prophet and led to increased persecutions against the Saints, resulting in Thomas being dropped from the Quorum of the Twelve. Joseph Smith proposed that Lyman Sherman take Hyde's place in the Twelve, but Lyman unexpectedly died, leaving Heber C. Kimball to later observe that "it was not the will of God for a man to take Brother Hyde's place."[1] By summer of 1839, Elder Hyde's deep sorrow and repentance led to his reinstatement in the Twelve. John Taylor said of this incident, "Thomas B. Marsh was unquestionably instigated by the devil. . . . It would be here proper to state, however, that Orson Hyde had been sick with a violent fever for some time, and had not fully recovered. . . . When he subsequently returned, and made all the satisfaction that was within his power, he was forgiven . . . and was again re-instated in the quorum."[2]

When the Twelve left for their mission to England in 1839, Elder Hyde was too sick with malaria to join them. In the April

1840 conference of the Church, Orson reported a recent vision he had had in which he was commanded to take the gospel to the Jews and was shown the cities he would visit. Consequently he was called on a mission to dedicate the Holy Land for the return of the Jews. John E. Page was called to accompany him. In the East, as they lingered to gather funds, Page dropped out, leaving Hyde to continue on his own. It was during this time that a stranger gave Orson a purse of gold, asking only that Orson remember him in his prayer when he stood upon the Mount of Olives. Orson then continued on his journey, preaching in several cities and arriving in Jerusalem October 21, 1841. On October 24, he climbed the Mount of Olives, where he offered a prayer dedicating the land for the gathering of the Jews. True to his word, he remembered the stranger who had given him the purse of gold, asking the Lord that "he never lack for the necessities of life." It was not until 1924 that the stranger's identity was discovered. He was Joseph Ellison Beck, a humble farmer who eventually settled in Spanish Fork and enjoyed good health until his death at the age of ninety-three. During his lifetime, though never rich, he always had sufficient for his family.

On June 27, 1844, while on assignment in Washington, DC, Orson felt saddened in spirit but could not determine why. Days later he learned that the cause of his depression was the martyrdom of Joseph and Hyrum. Speaking of their death, he said prophetically to a crowd in Boston, "I will prophesy that instead of the work dying, it will be like the mustard stock that was ripe, that a man undertook to throw out of his garden, and scattered seed all over it, and next year it was nothing but mustard. It will be so by shedding the blood of the Prophets—it will make ten Saints where there is one now."[3] As a member of the Twelve, Orson remained in Nauvoo to supervise the completion and dedication of the temple. He then presided over the Saints at Winter Quarters 1848–1851, moving his family to the Salt Lake Valley in 1852. In 1855, he led settlements in Carson Valley, Nevada, and in 1860 he was called to the Sanpete area of Utah, where he presided until the time of his death. His contributions to the settling of the West were many and varied, including supervisor of Utah immigration, irrigation specialist, regent of the University of Deseret, lawyer, judge, and legislator.

Prior to the April 1875 Church conference, the Brethren discussed seniority in the Quorum and decided that Orson Hyde and Orson Pratt should assume the places they would have held when reinstated in the Quorum rather than their original positions (see Orson Pratt). Elder Hyde was relieved, for with his age and living so far from Salt Lake City, he had found it difficult to function as President of the Twelve. Elder Hyde died November 28, 1879. Speaking at his funeral, Wilford Woodruff observed: "The vision of my mind is open" as he saw the rejoicing of "the prophets of every age and generation, at the birth of brother Hyde into the spirit world."[4]

*William E. McLellin*

Born: January 18, 1806, Smith County, Tennessee
Ordained Apostle: February 15, 1835
Excommunicated: May 11, 1838
Died: April 24, 1883, Independence, Missouri, at age 77

The exact date of William's birth is not known. He was born about the year 1806 in Tennessee. While residing in Paris, Illinois, where he taught school, he first heard the gospel preached by David Whitmer and Harvy Whitlock, who were traveling through the area on their way to Missouri. William recorded in his journal that Whitlock "expounded the Gospel the plainest I thot [*sic*] that I ever heard in my life, which astonished me." So impressed was William that he closed up his school and traveled with the missionaries, attending their meetings. Following a nearly three-hour discourse by Whitlock, William recorded: "I never heard such preaching in all my life. The glory of God seemed to encircle the man and the wisdom of God to be displayed in his discourse."[1] William followed the brethren to Jackson County, where he was taught and baptized by Hyrum Smith on August 20, 1831.

William journeyed to Hiram, Ohio, where he stayed with the Prophet for three weeks. About this time, Joseph received a revelation at the request of William (D&C 66). Concerning this revelation, William recorded: "I went before the Lord in secret, and on my knees asked him to reveal the answer to five questions through his Prophet, and that too without his having any knowledge of my having made such request. I now testify in the fear of God, that every question which I had thus lodged in the ears of the Lord of Sabbaoth, were answered to my full and entire satisfaction. I desire it for a testimony of Joseph's inspiration. And I to this day consider it to be an evidence which I cannot refute."[2]

It has been said of William McLellin that he was a man of superficial education but had a good command of the language. At a special conference held in Hiram, Ohio, on November 1, 1831, Joseph Smith received a revelation that would become the preface to the Doctrine and Covenants. Joseph recorded that, after receiving this revelation, conversation arose among some of the brethren concerning the language in the revelations. Consequently, Joseph Smith received a revelation (D&C 67) in which the Lord challenged anyone to imitate the language found in even the least of the revelations given by him. Joseph later recorded: "After the foregoing was received, William E. M'Lellin, as the wisest man, in his own estimation, having more learning than sense, endeavored to write a commandment like unto one of the least of the Lord's, but failed; it was an awful responsibility to write in the name of the Lord."[3] Joseph further stated that those who observed McLellin's struggling failure had a renewal of faith in the truthfulness of the gospel and in the revelations.

William went on to serve a mission with Hyrum Smith in Tennessee, and then with Parley P. Pratt through Missouri and Illinois, where they preached with much success. He was one of a committee selected to confer with the Jackson County committee in trying to settle the problems in Missouri. In 1834, William was called to the high council in Clay County. During the winter of 1834–35, he taught in the Kirtland School of the Elders, and on February 15, 1835, he was called to the Quorum of the Twelve Apostles. However, his faithfulness soon began to waver. In 1835, while serving a mission in the East, he wrote a letter censuring the First Presidency, for which he was suspended from fellowship with the Twelve. Upon his return to Kirtland, he confessed the error of his letter and was restored to fellowship. The following winter he officiated as clerk for the Quorum of the Twelve, but his problems continued. In May of 1838, William was called before a bishop's court in Far West wherein he explained that he had no confidence in the Presidency of the Church and that he had consequently quit praying and keeping the commandments for a time, and that he had indulged in sinful lusts. He stated it was from what he had heard and not anything he had seen, that caused him to believe that the Presidency was out of the way. He was excommunicated for unbelief and apostasy.

Unfortunately, William's loss of faith led to his becoming an enemy to the Church and to the Prophet Joseph. While leading brethren were imprisoned at Richmond, William sought to do violence to the Prophet. "McLellin, who was a large and active man, went to the sheriff and asked for the privilege of flogging the Prophet. Permission was granted on condition that Joseph would fight. The sheriff made known to Joseph, McLellin's earnest request, to which Joseph consented, if his irons were taken off. McLellin then refused to fight unless he could have a club, to which Joseph was perfectly willing; but the sheriff would not allow them to fight on such unequal terms."[4] Under the pretense of law, he and others plundered and robbed the houses of Sidney Rigdon and others while they were imprisoned in Liberty Jail. Many witnesses signed an affidavit testifying they had seen McLellin plunder the house and stables of Joseph Smith. When Joseph pled with Emma to send more blankets to him at Liberty Jail, she replied that she had none to send, William McLellin having stolen them.

Following the Prophet's death, McLellin went on to become involved with various break-off factions of the Church, including the Strangites, in which he tried to oust James Strang from leadership. After attempting to found his own Church, he became affiliated with the Church of Christ (Temple Lot) for a time but died in 1883, unaffiliated with any Church. Yet, his testimony in the Book of Mormon seems not to have wavered. Three years before his death, he wrote in a letter to T. J. Cobb:

I have set to my seal that the Book of Mormon is a true, divine record and it will require more evidence than I have ever seen to ever shake me relative to its purity. . . . When a man goes at the Book of M. he touches the apple of my eye. He fights against truth—against purity—against light—against the purist, or one of the truest, purist books on earth. . . . Fight the wrongs of L.D.S.ism as much as you please, but let that unique, that inimitable book alone. . . . For you might just as well fight against the rocky mountains as the Book!⁵

William went on to adopt medicine as his profession and died in obscurity in Independence, Missouri, April 24, 1883.

*Parley P. Pratt*

Born: April 12, 1807, Burlington, New York
Ordained Apostle: February 21, 1835
Assassinated: May 13, 1857, Van Buren, Arkansas, at age 50

While preaching the Campbellite faith in western New York, Parley visited an old Baptist deacon named Hamlin, who told him of a new and strange book. "I felt a strange interest in the book," he records, and the next day he returned to Hamlin's home "where, for the first time, my eyes beheld the 'BOOK OF MORMON—that book of books. . . . I opened it with eagerness and read its title page. I then read the testimony of several witnesses. . . . After this I commenced its contents. . . . I read all day; eating was a burden, I had no desire for food; sleep was a burden when the night came, for I preferred reading to sleep. As I read the spirit of the Lord was upon me, and I knew and comprehended that the book was true."[1] Traveling to Palmyra, he met Hyrum Smith, who related to him the story of the coming forth of the Book of Mormon and the Restoration of the gospel. Parley immediately accepted the truthfulness of what he heard and was later baptized by Oliver Cowdery and ordained an elder. Parley was soon off on the beginning of his missionary endeavors and was successful in bringing his brother, Orson Pratt, into the Church.

In October 1830, Parley, along with Oliver Cowdery, Peter Whitmer, and Zeba Peterson, was called on a mission among the Lamanites. En route westward, they traveled through Kirtland, Ohio, and stopped at the home of Sidney Rigdon, a Campbellite minister acquainted with Parley. As a result, Sidney came into the Church with many of his congregation, thus laying the groundwork for the Church's later move to Kirtland. They then continued their journey to the western regions of Missouri where they preached to the Indian nations and helped lay the groundwork for the Church's settling in that region. In the autumn of 1833, Parley and his family were among the twelve hundred Saints who were driven by mobs from Jackson County. He recorded, "All my provisions for the winter were destroyed or stolen, and my grain left growing on the ground for my enemies to harvest. My house was afterwards burned, and my fruit trees and improvements destroyed and plundered."[2]

In 1834, during the Zion's Camp expedition, Parley was engaged in traveling to various branches of the Church, recruiting men, arms, and money, catching up with the camp from time-to-time with his cache. On one occasion, Parley had lain down on the prairie grass to rest when he heard a loud voice declare, "Parley, it is time to be up and on your journey."[3] He immediately mounted his horse and went on his way. He and Orson Hyde were later sent to Governor Dunklin of Missouri to plead the cause of the Saints. The governor replied that while their demands were just, he dared do nothing for fear of starting a civil war in his state. On February 21, 1835, Parley was ordained an Apostle, after which he served several successive missions to the eastern states and Canada.

In 1838, he returned again with his family to Missouri, settling in Caldwell County. Again they suffered at the hands of mobs and were driven from their homes. This time Parley was imprisoned for eight months without a trial. His wife visited him several times at first, but under the governor's exterminating orders, she was eventually forced to flee the state with their children, leaving Parley abandoned. Under these circumstances, and finding himself descending into despair, he fasted and prayed for several days to know if he would ever regain his freedom and be with his wife and children again. One evening, as he lay in silence, a spirit of calm came over him and he beheld his departed first wife, Thankful, who had died two years earlier. She assured him he would yet be free and then withdrew. Parley later escaped and fled to Illinois to join the Saints in the building of Nauvoo.

In 1840, Parley, along with most of the Quorum of the Twelve, departed for England. In Manchester, his ministry focused mainly on the publication of the *Millennial Star,* which provided the Saints in England with the first published material on Joseph Smith's revelations and his history. It contained general news from the Church in the United States as well, thus linking the English Saints with the Saints in America. When the Twelve left England, Parley stayed behind to preside over the missionary work. He returned to Nauvoo in the winter of 1842.

While serving a later mission in the eastern United States, he was "constrained by the spirit to start prematurely for home." While traveling on a canal boat, "a strange and solemn awe came over me, as if the powers of hell were let lose. I was so overwhelmed with sorrow I could hardly speak."[4] Soon afterward he learned of the deaths of Joseph and Hyrum Smith. As he wondered what he should say to the Saints upon his return to Nauvoo, the Spirit of the Lord said to him, "Lift up your head and rejoice; for behold! it is well with my servants Joseph and Hyrum. . . . Go and say unto my people in Nauvoo, that they shall . . . make no movement in Church government to reorganize or alter anything until the return of the remainder of the Quorum of the Twelve."[5]

In 1846, Parley again left for England and the European Mission. Returning to the States, he joined the Saints at Winter Quarters and was part of the first emigration that followed the Pioneer Company to the Salt Lake Valley. In Utah, he assisted in forming a constitution for the Provisional Government of Deseret, was elected a member of the Senate and General Assembly, and was later elected to the Legislative Council when Utah became a United States territory. Parley would go on to serve other missions, including a mission to the Pacific that would take him to the islands and to South America. Years later, Elder Orson F. Whitney would write of him, "Up to the period of his untimely death, Parley P. Pratt had probably traveled more miles, preached more sermons and published more original literature in behalf of Mormonism than any other of its numerous missionaries. . . . As a preacher he perhaps had no equal in the Church."[6] Two of his major writings, *Voice of Warning* and *Key to Theology*, still stand as classics in LDS literature today.

His final mission came in the fall of 1856, when Brigham Young asked him to help direct Church activities in the eastern United States. While in the east, he was hunted down and viciously murdered by Hector McLean, who held Pratt responsible for his estrangement from his former wife, who had converted to the Church and moved to Salt Lake City. Pratt was killed near Buren, Arkansas, at the age of fifty.

*Luke S. Johnson*

Born: November 3, 1807, Pomfret, Vermont
Ordained Apostle: February 15, 1835
Excommunicated: April 13, 1838
Rebaptized: 1846 in Nauvoo, Illinois
Died: December 9, 1861, Salt Lake City, Utah, at age 53

L uke and Lyman Johnson, both later to become Apostles, were the sons of John and Elsa Johnson. It was at the Johnson home in Hiram, Ohio, that the Prophet resided while he and Sidney Rigdon worked on the translation of the Bible. It was also here that section 76, the vision of the three degrees of glory, was received. In the winter of 1830–31, John and Elsa traveled to Kirtland to investigate the Church. While there, the Prophet Joseph healed Elsa of chronic rheumatism in her arm that had plagued her for the past two years. This miracle was partly instrumental in their conversion, as well as in the conversion of other family members. Luke was baptized by Joseph Smith May 10, 1831. Shortly after his baptism, Luke traveled through southern Ohio, baptizing many and establishing a branch of the Church. Following this mission, he traveled with Sidney Rigdon to New Portage, where they baptized over fifty persons and established a branch. They then journeyed to Pittsburg, where Luke baptized Sidney's mother and oldest brother, along with other converts. In 1831, Luke was ordained a high priest. In 1832–1833, he served a mission to Ohio, Virginia, and Kentucky, where he baptized over one hundred people and organized two branches in Ohio and Virginia. In February of 1834, he and his father, John, were called as members of the first Church high council.

In May of 1834, Luke became a member of Zion's Camp. Near Jacksonville, Illinois, Luke reported that a Baptist minister wanted the camp stopped, afraid because the camp consisted of "Mormons." Luke accompanied him to see the magistrate, who declared that the Mormons were minding their own business and the minister should mind his. Later the minister took Luke to his home where he fed him, washed his clothes, and warned him of 400 Missourians who were planning to destroy the camp. Upon his return to Kirtland, Luke testified at the trial of Sylvester Smith, that during the camp's journey, he saw nothing in the conduct of Joseph Smith to lessen his esteem of Joseph as a man of God. It was in February 1835 that Luke was called to the Quorum of the Twelve.

During the following months, Luke spent much of his time on missions. But the spirit of apostasy, fostered in large part by a spirit of monetary speculation, was growing in Kirtland, and almost all the Johnson family was affected by it. Luke became critical of the Prophet and eventually joined with a group of dissidents who attempted to take control of the Church, claiming that Joseph was a fallen prophet and that they represented the "old standard" of the Church. Describing those dark days, Luke wrote: "Having partaken of the spirit of speculation, which at that time was possessed by many of the saints and Elders, my mind became darkened, and I was left to pursue my own course. I lost the spirit of God, and neglected my duty."[1] In September 1837, he was disfellowshipped. However, the following Sunday he made full confession of his faults and was reinstated. But in April of 1838, he was excommunicated from the Church. Notwithstanding his excommunication, Luke remained friendly toward the Church and the Smith family. When set apart as a member of the

Twelve, he was promised that if he were cast into prison, he would be a comfort to the hearts of his comrades. This came to be true not as a fellow prisoner but as a constable of the law. He enabled the Prophet Joseph to legally escape efforts by others to bring fraudulent lawsuits against him, for which the Prophet expressed his gratitude. He also enabled Joseph Smith Sr. to escape imprisonment on charges instigated through malice. Bringing Father Smith to court for trial, Luke put him in an adjoining room to await the trial. He then removed a nail that fastened the window closed and went outside into the court room where he engaged the men in stories, the men's laughter covering up the sounds of escape. He then went back into the now empty room, replaced the nail, and called out that the prisoners had escaped. The men, not being able to determine any way the prisoner could have escaped, declared that it must be another Mormon miracle. Luke said that Joseph Sr. would bless him all the days of his life for aiding him. Upon hearing this statement, Joseph Sr. affirmed that he would.

Luke went on to teach school in Cabell County, Virginia, and then turned to the study of medicine. For eight years he had a medical practice in Kirtland. In 1846 Luke and his family returned to the Church. He told the Saints that "he had stopped by the wayside and he had stood aloof from the work of the Lord, but his heart was with this people and he wanted to be associated with the Saints and go with them into the wilderness and continue with them to the end."[2] He was rebaptized by his brother-in-law, Orson Hyde, on March 8, 1846.

Yet his faith was not left untried. On his way to join the Saints at Council Bluffs, his wife, Susan Poteet, died. After burying her at St. Joseph, Missouri, he was left to continue his westward journey with six motherless children. The Brethren worried whether this might prove too much for his newly found faith, but in Council Bluffs he was remarried to America Clark, by whom he would have eight children.

Luke became a member of the original Pioneer Company that forged the way to Salt Lake Valley, being appointed as one of the captains of tens. He settled in Tooele County and later became bishop, probate judge, and doctor. He was known for his acts of kindness toward those in need. The wife of George Burridge recalled that one winter she came to his home seeking milk, "my feet wrapped in gunny-sacks, to keep them warm. Luke looked at my feet and laughed [a kindly laugh] and said, 'Hannah, is that the best you can do for shoes?' I told him they were all I had. The next morning when I called for the milk, Luke presented me with a good substantial pair of shoes."[3]

He died December 9, 1861, at the home of his brother-in-law, Orson Hyde, at the age of fifty-four. Brigham Young eulogized, "Since his return to the Church he lived to the truth to the best of his ability and died in the faith."[4]

*William Smith*

Born: March 13, 1811, Royalton, Vermont
Ordained Apostle: February 15, 1835
Dropped from the Quorum of the Twelve: May 4, 1839
Restored to Quorum: May 25, 1839
Dropped from Quorum: October 6, 1845
Excommunicated: October 19, 1845
Died: November 13, 1893, Osterdock, Iowa, at age 82

**W**illiam's character seems to have been a conflict of emotions. When thinking of him, there comes to mind the old adage, "the spirit is willing but the flesh is weak." He appears to have accepted the visions of his older brother Joseph from the beginning. At the age of eighty-two, about two weeks before his death, William was asked in an interview, "Did not you doubt Joseph's testimony [about the Book of Mormon] sometimes?" He replied: "No; we all had the most implicit confidence in what he said. He was a truthful boy. Father and mother believed him, why should not the children? I suppose if he had told crooked stories about other things we might have doubted his word about the plates, but Joseph was a truthful boy. That father and mother believed his report and suffered persecution for that belief shows that he was truthful. No, sir, we never doubted his word for one minute."[1] And while William's name is not affixed as one of the eight witnesses of the Book of Mormon, he testified that he "was permitted to lift them [the plates] as they laid in a pillow case; but not to see them, as it was contrary to the commandments he [Joseph Smith] had received. They weighed about sixty pounds according to the best of my judgment."[2]

William could also be a man of action and courage in defense of his brother Joseph. On one occasion, learning of a plot to waylay the Prophet on his return to Kirtland, Brigham Young and William took a horse and buggy to intercept Joseph's stagecoach. William then traded places with Joseph, allowing Joseph to continue on safely by a different route. Fortunately, when William was recognized, he was left unharmed.

William was baptized in June of 1830. He labored as a missionary in the eastern states and was later ordained a high priest by Sidney Rigdon in June of 1833. A hard worker, he spent the following winter chopping cord wood near Kirtland to support himself and his wife, Caroline Grant. In 1834, he was a member of Zion's Camp, and on February 15, 1835, he was ordained a member of the Quorum of the Twelve.

Despite his spiritual endeavors, William was a person often governed by hot temperament, pride, and materialism, given to the dictates of the natural man rather than the promptings of the Spirit. His flaring temper can be seen in an incident that occurred in the fall of 1830, when unscrupulous creditors had besieged his mother in their Palmyra home, laying claim to the Smiths' belongings. Entering the house and seeing what was happening, "William seized a large handspike, sprang up the stairs, and in one instant, cleared the scoundrels out of the chamber. They scampered down stairs; he flew at them, and bounding into the very midst of the crowd, he brandished his handspike in every direction, exclaiming, 'Away from here, you cutthroats, instantly, or I will be the death of every one of you!'"[3] On occasions, his anger was directed toward Joseph. While serving in the Quorum of the Twelve, he once lost his temper in a discussion to the extent that he violently attacked Joseph and inflicted such injuries upon him that Joseph occasionally felt their effects until the time of his death. In a letter of apology, William asked to withdraw from the Twelve, stating, "You know my passions and the danger of falling from so high a station; . . . I feel afraid, if I don't do this [withdraw from the Twelve], it will be worse for me some other day." Joseph wrote to William, readily granting him the requested forgiveness. He then instructed: "You desire to remain in the Church, but forsake your Apostleship. This is the stratagem of the evil one; when he has gained one advantage, he lays a plan for another. But by maintaining your Apostleship, in rising up and making one tremendous effort, you may overcome your passions and please God. . . . When a man falls one step, he must regain that step again, or fall another; he has still more to gain, or eventually all is lost."[4]

In 1838 William moved his family to Far West, Missouri. After Joseph was sent to jail and the mobs began to drive out the Saints, William expressed himself against Joseph in such a vindictive manner that he was disfellowshipped. Later, through the intercession of Joseph and Hyrum, he was restored. But when the Twelve were sent to England, William refused to go, claiming poverty as his excuse. His explanation did not sit well with the other Apostles, for he was probably better situated to leave his family than any other members of the Twelve. Yet, in the winter of 1842–43, he was elected to the State House of Representatives, where his service, especially in defending the Nauvoo Charter, gained him high praise from the people. In his last conversations with Joseph, he asked Joseph for a city lot near the temple for settling his family. Joseph agreed to give him a lot if he promised to build upon it and not sell it. William agreed. But within a few hours, word came to Joseph that William was attempting to sell the lot for $500 (it was worth approximately $1,000.) When Joseph then refused the transfer of property to William, he became so threatening that Joseph felt it best to stay out of his way until William left for the east with his family.

Following Joseph's martyrdom, William gave support to the leadership of the Twelve and was ordained as patriarch to the Church. In announcing his calling, the *Times and Seasons* reported that he had been ordained as "patriarch over the church." Some felt that being patriarch "over" the church made him "president of the church." When correction was made in the newspaper, William was offended. Eventually his aspirations to lead the Church, along with increased reports on his misconduct in the East, which concerned his misappropriation of collected temple funds for his own personal use and his questionable conduct toward females, led to his excommunication from the Church. Following his association with the apostate James Strang, and failed efforts to start his own church, William identified himself with the Reorganized Church of which his nephew was president. William died in 1893 at the age of eighty-two.

*Orson Pratt*

Born: September 9, 1811, Hartford, New York
Ordained Apostle: April 26, 1835
Excommunicated: August 20, 1842
Rebaptized and restored to former office in the Quorum of the Twelve:
    January 20, 1843
Died: October 3, 1881, Salt Lake City, Utah, at age 70

Although Orson's parents were Christian, they were not affiliated with any denomination. Consequently, Orson grew up a person of moral values, being a prayerful student of the Bible, yet unassociated with organized religion. He recorded that "in the nineteenth year of my age, I began to consider on the evil of my ways and the danger I was in of being cast off forever. . . . Wherefore I began to mend my ways, and cry unto the Lord for mercy."[1] It was at this time that his brother Parley, who had embraced the gospel, came preaching in the area where Orson lived. Orson believed and was baptized in September of 1830. The following month he traveled to Fayette, New York, to meet the Prophet.

There he was ordained an elder by Joseph Smith and sent off on the first of what would be many missions. In February of 1832, he was ordained a high priest by Sidney Rigdon, then proceeded on a mission throughout the northeast that continued through the year. Traveling without purse or script, he traveled over four thousand miles, baptized 104 people, and established several new branches of the Church. Returning to Kirtland, he attended the School of the Prophets and worked on the construction of the temple prior to joining Zion's Camp. Following his Zion's Camp experience, he served a mission in Ohio. It was at this time he recorded in his journal: "April 20. . . . We inquired of a man who I felt impressed to speak to, who was standing in the streets, . . . and found that he was a brother. Therefore we tarried with him all night, at which place I saw a late number of the *Messenger and Advocate*; found I had been chosen one of the Twelve Apostles, and was requested to be in Kirtland on the 26th of April."[2] He arrived in Kirtland within two days, and he was subsequently ordained to the Quorum of the Twelve.

In 1840 the Quorum of the Twelve arrived in England on a joint mission. Orson was assigned to take the gospel to Scotland. In the later part of May he dedicated Scotland for the preaching of the gospel and, in so doing, asked the Lord for two hundred converts. His prayers were answered. By the time he left in March 1841, the membership of the Church in the Edinburgh conference was 226.

On the return of the Twelve from England, the Prophet Joseph began to teach them the doctrine of plural marriage. Orson Pratt, returning after most of his Quorum, was deceived concerning the doctrine by John C. Bennett, which caused Orson to become mentally agitated and estranged from the Prophet, leading to his eventual excommunication. Elder John Taylor defended Orson by stating that he had been deceived by those who had disaffected from the Church, but when he learned the truth he was satisfied. Orson was consequently rebaptized and restored to the Twelve.

Orson was a studious person from his early boyhood. Although his family was poor and the boys were hired out at a young age as farm laborers, he nonetheless attended school during every opportunity and came to pay special attention to mathematics, grammar, geography, surveying, and so forth. In later years, he delved into the mysteries of astronomy, theology, and languages and became one of the most profound thinkers and logical speakers and writers of the early days of the Church. These studies and his natural intellect would serve him and the Church well in the coming years.

In the Church's western trek, Orson kept a careful log of the miles traveled, took astronomical and other scientific observations, and determined latitudes, longitudes, and elevations in anticipation of a roadway for the Saints to follow. In the Green River area, Orson was directed to take an advance company and endeavor to find a route across the mountains. Consequently, Orson and Erastus Snow were the first two of the company to enter the Salt Lake Valley, where they could not restrain themselves from giving a shout of joy. Concerning Orson Pratt's leadership of this vanguard company B. H. Roberts wrote: "Orson Pratt was appointed to this leadership because in the things now required—engineering skill and science—he had been leading all along. His place was always in the van, and even leading that van, and this from the very nature of the duties required of him, as being placed in charge of and using the splendid set of scientific instruments carried in the camp—and which he alone, perhaps, could use."[3]

He would go on to serve several missions to the eastern United States, England, and Europe. In the territory, he was elected to the legislative assembly and chosen as Speaker of the House seven times. His writings became known throughout the Church. And herein was the basis of his difficulties with President Brigham Young.

President Young referred to Elder Orson Pratt as "our philosopher brother," for Orson's philosophical writings often led to disagreement between the two, resulting in President Young censuring Orson over the pulpit. "With all the knowledge and wisdom that are combined in the person of brother Orson Pratt," President Young once observed, "still he does not yet know enough to keep his foot out of it, but drowns himself in his own philosophy, every time that he undertakes to treat upon principles that he does not understand."[4] On another occasion, President Young instructed that Orson was to clear his new ideas on doctrine through him before teaching them.

Yet there was no doubt in Brigham's mind concerning the testimony and devotion of Orson. Said he, "If Brother Orson were chopped up in inch pieces, each piece would cry out Mormonism was true."[5]

When Elder Pratt was reinstated into the Quorum of the Twelve, he was placed in the seniority he held before his excommunication. But in June of 1875, President Young announced that seniority was a matter of "continuous service" in the Quorum. Thus, Orson Pratt, along with Orson Hyde, was placed in the position he would have held as a new member at the time of his reinstatement, changing him from second to fifth in seniority. To this change, Orson apparently gave his support.

Orson died October 3, 1881, the last surviving member of the original Quorum of the Twelve Apostles.

*John F. Boynton*

Born: September 20, 1811, Bradford, Massachusetts
Ordained Apostle: February 15, 1835
Dismissed from the Quorum of the Twelve: September 3, 1837;
    reinstated one week later
Dismissed again: December 1837
Excommunicated: April 12, 1838
Died: October 20, 1890, Syracuse, New York, at age 79

A s a young man of keen intellect, John Boynton attended Columbia University in his teenage years and at the age of twenty entered medical school in St. Louis, Missouri. Notwithstanding his intellectual abilities, he humbled himself upon hearing the message of the restored gospel and, in September of 1832, was baptized by the Prophet Joseph Smith in Kirtland, Ohio, and ordained an elder by Sidney Rigdon. He then set out to proclaim the gospel, proving himself to be an effective missionary. Writing from Maine in 1834, he stated that he had baptized about forty persons in that area. He went on to say that he and his companion, from January 1833 until the time of his writing, had baptized 130 persons. He was called to the Quorum of the Twelve and ordained an Apostle in February 1835.

Following his ordination, he continued in his missionary labors in the eastern states. However, in 1837 he was caught up in the spirit of financial speculation and became involved in a get-rich scheme that failed. Borrowing considerable money to enter a mercantile venture, he was negligent in paying off his debts, although he was apparently capable of doing so. Boynton explained that his subsequent financial difficulties resulted from the failure of the Kirtland Safety Society Bank, which he had understood was established through revelation from the Lord and subsequently would never fail. When it did fail, he lost faith in Joseph Smith as a prophet of God. When Heber C. Kimball began his mission to England in June, Boynton told him he was a fool for leaving his home at the call of a "fallen prophet."

On September 3, 1837, a conference was held in which Boynton, along with Luke and Lyman Johnson, was disfellowshipped and dismissed from the Quorum of the Twelve. Each was given an opportunity "of making their confession if they had any to make." Boynton "partly confessed his sins and partly justified his conduct," which was not satisfactory to Brigham Young, and the disfellowshipment carried. A week later, however, satisfactory confessions were made and the brethren were restored.

But in November, strife returned when Boynton and others united together in an attempt to overthrow Joseph Smith and the Church. On a Sabbath morning, the dissidents entered the temple armed with knives, swords, and pistols and sat in the Aaronic Priesthood pulpits. During the meeting, they drew their arms and rushed the congregation, attempting to take control of the building. Local officials were summoned and, with the help of the congregation, the dissidents were expelled from the temple and order was restored. It was apparently at this meeting that Joseph Smith Sr., in speaking to the congregation, made insinuations toward Warren Parrish regarding a recent fraudulent withdrawal of funds from the Kirtland Bank. Enraged, Parrish attempted to drag Father Smith from the pulpit. William Smith, seeing the abuse his father was receiving, stepped forward, caught Parrish in his arms, and began to carry him out of the building. At that point, Boynton drew a sword from his cane and, placing it at William's breast, said, "If you advance one step further, I will run you through."[1] Before William could react, others surrounded him and added to Boynton's threat. Such increased violent behavior and threats against the Prophet led to Joseph fleeing from Kirtland to join the Saints in Missouri. In 1838 Boynton and others were excommunicated from the Church.

Given Boynton's violent behavior in the temple, his false accusations against the Prophet Joseph, and his eventual excommunication, it is interesting that after his departure from the Church, he never spoke against it but appears to have maintained friendly feelings toward it and the Brethren during the remainder of his life. Andrew Jenson, a Church historian who was baptized by Boynton, wrote of him years later:

> He has always been considerate to his former friends and co-laborers in the ministry, and never said or done anything against the Church. When he visited Utah in 1872, he called on President Brigham Young twice, in my company. The President was then a prisoner in his own house, guarded by US marshals, and Boynton denounced in strong terms the persecutions then being carried on against the Saints. He also met Erastus Snow, who, when only sixteen years of age, was ordained a Teacher by Bro. Boynton. Elder Snow told him that he had been preaching the same gospel ever since. Bro. Boynton remarked, "Stick to it, for it is good." He also called on Orson Pratt and others, with whom he was very friendly, and they all called him Brother John. Since leaving the Church Mr. Boynton has never joined himself to any other denomination and does not believe in any religion whatever. He says, however, that if anything is right, "Mormonism" is.[2]

Unlike some apostates, Boynton did not drop into oblivion after being separated from the Church. Rather, he became well-known as a scientist and an inventor. He was a noted lecturer and natural historian, and led a government-appointed contingent on a geological-surveying expedition to California. During the Civil War, he became an internationally known inventor and was employed in the invention of torpedoes and other destructive implements of war. So inventive was he that, by the year 1886, he was credited with thirty-six different patents in the US Patent Office.

Following a brief illness, Boynton died at his home in Syracuse, New York, at the age of seventy-nine. He was recognized as one of the community's most outstanding citizens.

*Lyman E. Johnson*

Born: October 24, 1811, Pomfret, Vermont
Ordained Apostle: February 14, 1835
Excommunicated: April 13, 1838
Died: December 1856, Prairie du Chien, Wisconsin, at age 45

Lyman was the younger brother of Luke Johnson, who was also a member of the Quorum of the Twelve Apostles. Traveling to Kirtland to investigate the Church, he was baptized in February 1831, at the age of nineteen, by Sidney Rigdon. He then answered the call to missionary labors. On October 25, 1831, he was ordained an elder by Joseph Smith and a week later ordained a high priest by Sidney Rigdon. In a revelation to Joseph Smith, given in January of 1832, the Lord said, "I say unto my servant Lyman Johnson, and unto my servant Orson Pratt, they shall also take their journey into the eastern countries" (D&C 75:14). One of the major consequences of this mission was the teaching and baptizing of Amasa Lyman, later to become a member of the Quorum of the Twelve. Upon Lyman's return to Ohio, he was called upon to recruit volunteers for Zion's Camp in Vermont. It was recorded that as a member of Zion's Camp, Lyman spoke to the brethren at a meeting concerning the need for them to live uprightly and to honor the Sabbath day and keep it holy. On February 14, 1835, Lyman became the first man called to the Quorum of the Twelve Apostles in this dispensation. However, because Joseph Smith established the seniority of that first quorum based on age rather than by order of selection, Lyman became the twelfth member, being the youngest in the quorum. He was twenty-three years old.

Unfortunately, Lyman's faith did not remain for long. His apostasy began in the trying year of 1837. Concerning this period, Joseph Smith recorded: "At this time the spirit of speculation in lands and property of all kinds, which was so prevalent throughout the whole nation, was taking deep root in the Church. As the fruits of this spirit, evil surmisings, fault-finding, disunion, dissension, and apostasy followed in quick succession, and it seemed as though all the powers of earth and hell were combining their influence in an especial manner to overthrow the Church at once, and make a final end."[1] It was during this period that Lyman entered a merchandizing venture in Kirtland that resulted in his losing a large sum of money. Consequently, he placed blame upon Joseph Smith and the failure of the Kirtland Bank for his financial failures. Questioning Joseph's prophetic calling, he, along with others, filed trumped-up charges against the Prophet.

The extent to which the Spirit of the Lord had left Lyman is seen on an occasion when the sacrament was being passed at a meeting in the Kirtland Temple. Lyman stood and cursed the Prophet, who was sitting on the stand. When the bread was passed to Lyman, " 'he reached out his hand for a piece of bread and flung it into his mouth like a mad dog.' His face turned black 'with rage and with the power of the devil.' "[2] The charges against Joseph were dismissed; however, Lyman was charged with misrepresentation. Consequently, at a conference held in Kirtland, in September of 1837, Lyman, along with his brother Luke and John F. Boynton, was disfellowshipped. But a few days later, upon confession, they were restored to their former standing. They were immediately granted the privilege of exercising their priesthood, for the records of that meeting state that elders

Luke S. and Lyman E. Johnson and John F. Boynton administered the sacrament. However, it would appear that Lyman's repentance was not genuine. Elder Heber C. Kimball recorded that when he was called to go to England on a mission, Elder Johnson came to him: "He did not want me to go on my mission, but if I was determined to go, he would help me all he could; he took his cloak from off his back and put it on mine; which was the first cloak I ever had."[3]

Lyman was excommunicated in April 1838. Yet, though no longer a member of the Church, he remained friendly to the Saints and his former associates. He frequently visited Nauvoo and often lamented about his spiritual downfall. Brigham Young recalled Lyman speaking to the Quorum of the Twelve after he had left the Church. On this occasion he said:

> Brethren,—I will call you brethren—I will tell you the truth. If I could believe 'Mormonism'—it is no matter whether it is true or not—but if I could believe 'Mormonism' as I did when I traveled with you and preached, if I possessed the world I would give it. I would give anything. I would suffer my right hand to be cut off, if I could believe it again. Then I was full of joy and gladness. My dreams were pleasant. When I awoke in the morning my spirit was cheerful. I was happy by day and by night, full of peace and joy and thanksgiving. But now it is darkness, pain, sorrow, misery in the extreme. I have never since seen a happy moment.

Following his remarks, President Young commented: "The testimony that he gave of his bitter experience is the testimony that every apostate would give if they would tell the truth. But will they acknowledge it? No, because they do not want to tell the truth."[4]

When the Saints moved west, Lyman stayed in Davenport, Iowa. There he engaged in merchandising but later entered into the practice of law. After a few years, he moved to Keokuk, Iowa, located just a few miles downriver from Nauvoo. On December 20, 1856, he died in a drowning accident in the Mississippi River near Prairie du Chien, Wisconsin.

The tragedy of Lyman's life can be seen in the comparison of two statements. Upon being ordained an Apostle, Lyman received a marvelous blessing in which he was told that his faith would be like unto Enoch's and that he would "be called great among all the living, and Satan shall tremble before him."[5] And yet, following news of his death, Wilford Woodruff said: "He did not go and hang himself [like Judas] but he did go and drown himself, and the river went over his body while his spirit was cast into the pit, where he ceased to have the power to curse either God or his Prophet in time or in eternity."[6] While Elder Woodruff's statement may appear somewhat harsh, it serves to illustrate the tragedy of those who lose the faith and fall from their high and holy callings in the Church.

*John E. Page*

Born: February 25, 1799, Trenton Township, New York
Ordained Apostle: December 19, 1838
Disfellowshipped: February 19, 1846
Excommunicated: June 27, 1846
Died: October 14, 1867, Sycamore, Illinois, at age 68

John Page was baptized into the Church in August 1833 in Brownhelm, Ohio, by Emer Harris, the brother of Martin Harris, and ordained an elder the following September. In the fall of 1835, he moved to Kirtland, Ohio, to be with the Saints who were gathering there. The following spring of 1836, he was called to go on a mission, but he informed the Prophet that he could not go because of his lack of clothing, that he did not even have a coat to wear. Joseph then removed the coat he was wearing and gave it to Page, telling him to take it and the Lord would bless him abundantly. Page then left for Canada, returning after seven months and twenty days absent from his family. In February 1837, he set off on a second mission to Canada, this time taking with him "my family, a wife and two small children, taking with me all the earthly goods I possessed, which consisted of one bed and our wearing apparel of the plainest kind, to continue my mission in the same region of country as before."[1] In June 1837, he presided over a conference of the Church held in upper Canada, which was attended by 305 members, whom Page had brought into the Church during his previous thirteen months of preaching. Called "Son of Thunder" by his associates because of the power of his preaching, he baptized nearly six hundred people and traveled more than five thousand miles during his two years in Canada.

In May of 1838, he traveled with a body of Saints to Missouri. Arriving at DeWitt, "we were attacked by an armed mob, and by them barbarously treated for near two weeks." From there they managed to travel on to Far West, where they joined the general body of the Church, only to suffer further violence at the hands of a furious mob, "by which means I buried one wife and two children as martyrs to our holy religion, since they died through extreme suffering for the want of the common comforts of life—which I was not allowed to provide even with my money."[2] Shortly thereafter, in December of 1838, Page, along with John Taylor, was ordained an Apostle under the hands of Brigham Young and Heber C. Kimball.

In April of 1839, as the remaining Saints were leaving Far West, Brigham Young held a meeting in Quincy, Illinois, at which it was decided that the Twelve would secretly return to Far West to fulfill a commission given them of the Lord (see D&C 115:11; 118:5). On their journey to Far West, Brigham Young's group met Elder Page, who was hurrying his family to Quincy. His wagon had overturned, and he was elbow deep in soft soap, scooping it up with his hands and returning it to the barrel as best he could. Brigham Young requested that Page return with the Twelve to Far West. Page replied that he needed to get his family to Quincy. Brigham said, "Never mind, your family will get along. I want you to go with us." Page asked how much time he had to get ready. "Five minutes," replied Brigham. The brethren helped him reload his wagon. He then drove down the hill, made camp for his family, and returned to Far West with his brethren.[3]

Unfortunately, when the Twelve left for England as commanded by the Lord, Page neglected to accompany them. Perhaps as an opportunity to demonstrate his faithfulness, he was then called in the April 1840 conference of the Church to accompany Orson Hyde on a mission to Palestine, but arriving in the East, he aborted his mission, leaving Hyde to continue alone. In 1843 Elder Page traveled to Pittsburg, where he organized a branch of the Church. However, when Elders Heber C. Kimball and Orson Pratt came to Pittsburg, they, along with Page, reorganized the branch. After Kimball and Pratt left, Page annulled the reorganization and reestablished the old one. Later, when Brigham Young, Wilford Woodruff and George A. Smith came east, they disapproved of Page's action, saying that it was not right for one Apostle to undo what three had done. Page was further admonished by Brigham for disobeying the counsel of Joseph Smith in preaching against other religious denominations. "He hammered the sectarian churches unmercifully."[4] Brigham therefore "exhorted him to be mild and gentle in his teachings and not fight the sects, but endeavor to win the affections of the people." Soon after the martyrdom of Joseph and Hyrum, an advertisement appeared in the Beaver (Pennsylvania) *Argus* newspaper saying that Elder John E. Page was out of employment and would preach for anybody that would sustain his family.

Returning to Nauvoo, Elder Page gave his support to the Twelve. However, in February of 1846, he was disfellowshipped from the Quorum of the Twelve "in consequence of his murmuring disposition, and choosing to absent himself from our councils."[5] In consequence of this action, Page became bitter against his former associates and became a supporter of James Strang's claims as successor to the presidency of the Church. While traveling to Strang's gathering place in Voree, Wisconsin, Page intercepted a company of Saints on their way from Canada to Nauvoo and tried to persuade them that it was God's will that they go to Voree. He succeeded in misleading a few, but for the most part, he failed in his deception. His continual support of Strang led to his eventual excommunication. In a letter to Brigham Young, Orson Hyde told of the rebaptized Luke Johnson stopping to visit John Page, who did not know him. Not knowing of Page's apostasy, Johnson said, "You are my successor in office and I am come to call you to an account for your stewardship." Hyde reported that Page "colored up and hung his head. This was an innocent joke converted into the most cutting truth by unknown circumstances."[6]

Page served for a time as president of the Strang's Twelve Apostles. He then went on to affiliate with other apostate groups, the last being the Hedrickites. He died on October 14, 1867, at his rural home in Sycamore at the age of sixty-eight.

*John Taylor*

Born: November 1, 1808, Milnthorpe, England
Ordained Apostle: December 19, 1838
Sustained President of the Quorum of the Twelve: October 6, 1877
Sustained President of the Church: October 10, 1880
Died: July 25, 1887, Kaysville, Utah, at age 78

One of ten children, John Taylor was raised in a close-knit, religious family where he was taught the value of hard work. Baptized as an infant, John grew up with little interest in the creeds of his parents but received instruction through dreams and visions. "When but a small boy he saw, in vision, an angel in the heavens, holding a trumpet to his mouth, sounding a message to the nations. The import of this vision he did not understand until later in life."[1] In his mid-teens, John joined the Methodist Church, where his enthusiasm and ability in speaking so impressed Church leaders that he was appointed a lay preacher at the young age of seventeen. One day, while walking to an appointment, he turned to his companion and said that he had a strong impression that he should go to America and preach the gospel.

In 1832, he immigrated to Toronto, Canada, where he resumed preaching the Methodist faith. Soon he and some close friends he met with to study the scriptures found that the doctrines taught by Jesus and the Apostles were not found in the various religious sects, and therefore if the Bible was truly the word of God, then the doctrines of modern Christendom must be wrong. They began to pray that if there were authorized ministers of Christ's gospel upon the earth, God would send one to them. About this time in May of 1836, Parley P. Pratt called upon John Taylor with a letter of introduction from a mutual acquaintance. As a result of Parley's teaching, John and a number of others were baptized on May 9, 1836.

In March of 1837, Taylor traveled to Kirtland and met the Prophet Joseph for the first time. He also found that some members were faltering in their faith and becoming highly critical of the Prophet. Among them was Parley P. Pratt. Taylor said to him, "I am surprised to hear you speak so, Brother Parley. Before you left Canada you bore a strong testimony to Joseph Smith being a Prophet of God. . . . You gave me a strict charge to the effect that though you or an angel from heaven was to declare anything else I was not to believe it. . . . If the work was true six months ago, it is true today; if Joseph Smith was then a prophet, he is now a prophet."[2] John Taylor soon gained a reputation as a defender of the faith and in the fall of 1837 was called to the apostleship.

In 1839, in response to an earlier revelation, the Twelve were to leave for England. In the midst of poverty and sickness, Elder Taylor housed his family in an old log barracks in Montrose, Iowa, and, dedicating them to the care of the Lord, left on his mission. So ill was he that when he reached Germantown, Indiana, he was forced to stay in an inn where he was kindly attended to by the proprietor and his wife. While recuperating, he preached in the nearby courthouse but never mentioned his personal circumstances. Impressed by this and being aware of his illness, some strangers gave him sufficient money to settle his bills and continue on his journey. Upon reaching England, he was assigned to introduce the gospel to Ireland and later took the gospel to the Isle of Man, successfully bringing hundreds into the Church. He also assisted in the emigration of eight hundred converts to Zion.

Returning to Nauvoo, Elder Taylor became a close and trusted friend to Joseph Smith. Concerning that friendship, Elder Franklin D. Richards of the Twelve said, "There were but few men who attained the warm, personal relation that he attained to and maintained most successfully with the Prophet Joseph Smith till he died, and the story of that personal affection was consummated by the bullets he received in Carthage Jail with the Prophet when he was slain."[3] Concerning the martyrdom, Taylor said, "I felt a dull, lonely, sickening sensation at the news [that the Prophet was dead]. . . . Oh, how lonely was that feeling! How cold, barren and desolate!"[4]

As a member of the Twelve and a gifted writer, Elder Taylor spent his time defending the gospel in writing. He served as editor of the *Times and Seasons,* the *Wasp,* and the *Nauvoo Neighbor,* all Nauvoo periodicals. He wrote two books that are still classics today, *The Government of God* and *Mediation and Atonement.* His writings led Brigham Young to say of him, "I will say that he has one of the strongest intellects of any man that can be found; he is a powerful man, he is a mighty man, . . . he is one of the strongest editors that ever wrote."[5]

In addition to proclaiming the gospel through his writings, Elder Taylor served four full-time missions: two to England, one to France and Germany, and one to New York, totaling seven years away from his loved ones. Yet, in spite of his absences, Elder Taylor was a loving and devout husband and father who cherished his time with his family. They, in turn, deeply loved him. This family bond made the closing years of his life especially difficult.

Following the death of President Brigham Young, Elder Taylor led the Church for three years as President of the Quorum of the Twelve. He was sustained as President of the Church in October of 1880. His administration was marked by increased persecution against the Church over the doctrine of plural marriage. Learning of federal marshals' plans for their arrest, and fearing that their imprisonment might cause some Church members to respond in such a way as to bring added persecution and increased government pressure against the Church, the First Presidency went into a self-imposed exile. It was while in hiding that President Taylor's wife, Sophia, died after suffering the effects of a paralytic stroke. Sadly, President Taylor could not be with her in her suffering or attend her funeral services. Yet, from his exile, he wrote the Saints, "However grievous the persecutions for which we suffer today, there is much yet to be thankful for. . . . [God] has made promises concerning Zion; be assured he will not forget those promises."[6]

Under the continual stress of his separation from loved ones and of trying to carry on with his responsibilities while moving from place to place in hiding, President Taylor's health finally failed, and he died July 25, 1887, in Kaysville, Utah, at the age of seventy-eight.

*Wilford Woodruff*

Born: March 1, 1807, Farmington, Connecticut
Ordained Apostle: April 26, 1839
Sustained President of the Quorum of the Twelve: October 10, 1880
Sustained President of the Church: April 7, 1889
Died: September 2, 1898, San Francisco, California, at age 91

In his youth, Wilford gave much time to reading and pondering the scriptures. Robert Mason, an elderly friend of the Woodruff family and a godly man considered to have the gift of prophecy, told Wilford that he would live to be a participant in the restoration of the Church of Jesus Christ, but that he, Roger Mason, would not live to partake of its blessings. Later, when Wilford heard the testimonies of two Mormon missionaries, he recognized the truth and was baptized two days later on December 31, 1833. Years later, when the principle of baptism for the dead was revealed, Wilford's thoughts immediately turned to Roger Mason, and he was baptized in Mason's behalf.

Wilford's early years, prior to his receiving the gospel, were marked with many life-threatening mishaps in which, according to his own record, he was spared only through the mercy of the Lord. At the age of three, he fell into a cauldron of scalding water. At age five, he slipped from a beam in his father's barn, landing on his face on the bare floor. At about the age of six, he avoided being gored by a bull only because he fell as he ran and the bull leaped over him and gored a rolling pumpkin Wilford dropped as he fell. When he was eight, he was in a wagon that overturned due to a runaway horse. He once fell fifteen feet from a tree, landing flat on his back. When he was twelve, he nearly drowned in the river, sinking in thirty feet of water before being rescued. At age thirteen, he crawled into the hollow of a tree to get out of the cold and would have frozen to death had he not been seen by a man who aroused him and carried him to his house. At fifteen, he was bitten by a mad dog in the last stages of rabies. At seventeen, he was nearly killed when thrown from a runaway horse. And the list goes on. Years later he would observe:

> The devil has sought to take away my life from the day I was born until now, more so even than the lives of other men. I seem to be a marked victim of the adversary. I can find but one reason for this: the devil knew if I got into the Church of Jesus Christ of Latter-day Saints, I would write the history of that Church and leave on record the works and teachings of the prophets, of the Apostles and elders. I have recorded nearly all the sermons and teachings that I ever heard from the Prophet Joseph. I have in my journal many of the sermons of President Brigham Young, and such men as Orson Hyde, Parley P. Pratt and others. Another reason I was moved upon to write in the early days was that nearly all the historians appointed in those times apostatized and took the journals away with them.[1]

Wilford began keeping a personal journal in 1835 and continued to do so until the time of his death in 1889. One of the great values in his journals can be seen in his recounting that whenever he heard the Prophet Joseph preach, "I felt as uneasy as a fish out of water until I had written it. Then I felt right. I could write a sermon of Joseph's a week after it was delivered almost word for word, and after it was written, it was taken from me or from my mind. This was a gift of God unto me."[2]

Shortly after his baptism, Wilford turned to missionary work. In 1834 he was called on a mission to the southeastern United States. Returning from his mission, he joined the Zion's Camp expedition to Missouri. Following his Zion's Camp experience, he responded to the Spirit's call to preach the gospel in the Fox Islands, where he baptized over a hundred people. It was while laboring there that he received a letter from Thomas B. Marsh informing him that he had been called to the Quorum of the Twelve. In 1840, he traveled to England with the Twelve. There he was directed by the Spirit to the farm of William Benbow, where his now famous labors resulted in nearly two thousand souls coming into the Church in eight months. In later years, Heber J. Grant said of Elder Woodruff, "Perhaps he was the greatest converter of men we have ever had in the Church."[3]

After this mission, his life followed the path of the Saints, the building the Nauvoo Temple, the trek westward, and the settling of the Salt Lake Valley. In 1856, he was officially called as Church historian, although he had unofficially recorded history throughout his years in the Church, his journals forming the basis of much of early Church history. In 1877, he was called to preside over the St. George Temple. And at the April 1889 general conference, he was sustained as President of the Church. This was a time of severe persecution against the Church due to the doctrine of plural marriage. After struggling with the issue through much prayer and fasting, President Woodruff issued the Manifesto in September of 1890, ending the practice of plural marriage.

As Elder Woodruff's early years had been marked by accidents, so his apostolic years were marked by visions and revelations. His January 26, 1880, journal entry reads,

> I fell asleep and remained in slumber until about midnight, when I awoke. The Lord then poured out His spirit upon me and opened the vision of my mind so that I could comprehend in a great measure the mind and will of God concerning the nation and concerning the inhabitants of Zion. I saw the wickedness of the nation, its abominations and corruptions and the judgments of God and the destruction that awaited it. Then I also comprehended the great responsibility which rested upon the Quorum of the Apostles.[4]

The vision was submitted to the Quorum of the Twelve and accepted as the word of the Lord. In the Church archives are some seven thousand pages of President Woodruff's journals containing many such visions, adding great significance to President Woodruff's statement: "I will here say that God has inspired me to keep a journal and write the history of this church, and I warn the future historians to give credence to my history; for my testimony is true."[5] Many years later he would state: "I will say to the Latter-day Saints, as an Elder in Israel and as an Apostle of the Lord Jesus Christ, we are approaching some of the most tremendous judgments God ever poured out upon the world. You watch the signs of the times, the signs of the coming of the Son of Man."[6]

Traveling to the west coast for health reasons, President Woodruff died in San Francisco on September 2, 1898, at the age of ninety-one.

*George A. Smith*

Born: June 26, 1817, Potsdam, New York
Ordained Apostle: April 26, 1839
Sustained First Counselor to President Brigham Young: October 7, 1868
Died: September 1, 1875, Salt Lake City, Utah, at age 58

O f necessity, young George A. worked to help support his family. Thus, his opportunities for education were greatly limited, but he valued knowledge and made every effort to obtain it. He showed a superior intellect, and as he grew older, his memory became phenomenal. His father, John Smith, was brother to Joseph Smith Sr., thus making George A. a first cousin to the Prophet Joseph. When Joseph Smith Sr. and his son Don Carlos brought the Book of Mormon to John's family, young George A. studied it carefully and accepted it as inspired. A wealthy and influential Presbyterian in his neighborhood offered to send him to college to prepare for the ministry if he would not join the Mormons, but he declined the offer and was baptized at the age of fifteen in September of 1832.

In May 1833, he moved with his family to Kirtland, where he met the Prophet Joseph for the first time. He spent that summer working in the quarry and hauling rock for the construction of the Kirtland Temple. In 1834, at the age of sixteen, George A. joined Zion's Camp, being the youngest member of the expedition. Sleeping in the same tent with Joseph and Hyrum, he was present during most of their council meetings and learned much about the Prophet's method of governing men and handling difficulties. These lessons would prove valuable to George A. in the coming years.

Upon his return to Kirtland, his missionary service began. Before departing on his mission in 1835, George A. was given the following advice by the Prophet Joseph: "Preach short sermons, make short prayers, and deliver your sermons with a prayerful heart."[1] Between 1835 and 1839, he served four missions, traveling approximately seventy-two hundred miles, much of it on foot. At one point, when becoming somewhat discouraged, George A. reported, "He [the Prophet] told me I should never get discouraged, whatever difficulties might surround me. If I were sunk into the lowest pit of Nova Scotia and all the Rocky Mountains piled on top of me, I ought not to be discouraged, but to hang on, exercise faith, and keep up good courage, and I should come out on top of the heap."[2]

In April of 1839, George A. accompanied several of the Quorum of the Twelve from Illinois back to Far West, Missouri, from whence they were to depart on a mission to England, as commanded in an earlier revelation (D&C 118:4–5). At this time, George A. was ordained an Apostle. When the Twelve eventually left Nauvoo for England in 1840, George A., the youngest Apostle, was so sick he had to be carried to a wagon. One man, seeing him, asked the driver if they had been robbing the graveyard. In England he was prominent in establishing a branch of the Church in London. While there he injured a lung, which bothered him the remainder of his life and eventually contributed to his death. Returning to Nauvoo, he was elected to the city council, and in the summer and fall of 1843, he served a mission to the eastern United States, during which he traveled about six thousand miles. His tireless efforts and devotion to the cause of truth earned him great affection from the Prophet. George A. later recalled: "At the close of the conversation, Joseph wrapped his arms around me, and squeezed me to his bosom and said, 'George A., I love you as I do my own life.' I felt so affected, I could hardly speak."[3]

Following the Prophet's death, George A. became active in the Saints' migration west. At a council where the exodus was being discussed, many discouraging views were expressed. George A., after listening to the pessimistic statements, arose and said: "Well, brethren, if there's no God in Israel, we're a sucked in set of fellows; I'm going to cross the river."[4] Laughter followed and the spirit of gloom was dispelled. His speeches were short but always pithy and to the point. At Winter Quarters, when one of his wives and four of his children died from scurvy, he began promoting the growing of potatoes as a cure for the dreaded disease, thus becoming known as "the potato Saint." In 1851, he led a mission into southern Utah to establish iron works for the Church. While the iron works did not prove successful, the venture did result in the establishment of Parowan and Cedar City. For many years, he was in charge of settlements in southern Utah, St. George being named after him. Possessed of a legal and statesmanlike mind, he turned to the study of law. He practiced law out of a pure love for justice and the legal system, giving his legal services free of charge. In 1854, following the death of Willard Richards, George A. was called as Church historian, and, working with Wilford Woodruff, completed *The History of the Church* up to the time of Joseph Smith's death.

In the winter of 1860–61, tragedy came to George A. Smith. His son George A. Smith Jr. was killed by Navajos in a missionary expedition into the area of northern Arizona. In the effort of the others to escape, his body was left behind. In response to a request by Brigham Young, Jacob Hamblin led a group of men to recover the body of the young man. Upon reaching the location where he was left, they were only able to find the head and a few scattered large bones. These were gathered and sent back to Salt Lake City for burial.

In 1868, George A. was called to replace Heber C. Kimball as first counselor in the First Presidency. George A. Smith died on September 1, 1875, at the age of fifty-eight, resulting from a severe cold that had settled in his lungs. His character and his value to the Church were reflected in a letter written by Brigham Young. "By his removal to a higher sphere," he wrote, "I lose a devoted friend, a wise counselor, and a lifelong companion. He leaves behind him, so far as my knowledge extends, and that is very extensive, a record as pure and as worthy of imitation as that of any servant of the Most High, who ever lived upon His footstool. He gave his heart, his mind, his energy, his love, in fact his all, to the furtherance of the great purposes of our God. In youth and in manhood, in sunshine or in storm, in peace or in persecution, he was true to his religion, his brethren and his God. And more than this, what can we say of anyone?"[5]

*Willard Richards*

Born: June 24, 1804, Hopkinton, Massachusetts
Ordained Apostle: April 14, 1840
Sustained Second Counselor to President Brigham Young:
    December 27, 1847
Died: March 11, 1854, Salt Lake City, Utah, at age 49

Ever studious, Willard had earned a teacher's certificate and was teaching school by the age of sixteen. His interests then turned to science and mechanics, resulting in his lecturing on those subjects. He then turned to the study of medicine and established a medical practice. Being a person of religious feelings, and having witnessed several religious revivals, he applied to join the Congregational Church at the age of seventeen, but his application was denied. Their rejection to his admission led him to a deeper study of religions, resulting in a conviction that all religious sects were wrong, that God had no Church upon the earth. Then, in the summer of 1835, he came in contact with a copy of the Book of Mormon. Opening the book at random and reading but half a page, he exclaimed, "God or the devil has had a hand in that book, for man never wrote it."[1] Within ten days, he had read the book twice. Believing that the book and its doctrines were true and that God had something greater for him to do than peddle pills, he moved to Kirtland, where he stayed with his cousin, Brigham Young. After further investigating the Church, he was baptized by Brigham on December 31, 1836.

Shortly afterward, he was ordained an elder and accompanied Brigham on a business trip to the East. Upon returning to Kirtland, he was called to accompany Heber C. Kimball, Orson Hyde, Joseph Fielding, and others to open up the missionary work in England. When Apostles Kimball and Hyde returned to the States, Joseph Fielding was left in charge of the mission with Willard as his first counselor. It was during this time that he married a recent convert, Jennetta Richards (her maiden name). She had been baptized by Heber C. Kimball, who meeting Willard afterward, and before Willard had ever met her, said, "Willard, I baptized your wife today." Sometime later, after making acquaintance with Jennetta, Willard said to her, "Richards is a good name; I never want to change it, do you, Jennetta!" "No, I do not," she replied, "and I think I never will."[2] They were married a few months later. In 1840, when the Quorum of the Twelve came to England to further the work, Willard was ordained an Apostle. He continued to labor in England, editing the *Millennial Star* during the temporary absence of Parley P. Pratt, who had returned to America for his family.

Returning to America after four years in England, he settled temporarily in Warsaw, Illinois, where he looked after immigrants. Moving to Nauvoo, he was elected to the city council, became editor for the *Times and Seasons,* and was a general Church clerk and private secretary to Joseph Smith. As the Prophet's secretary, he kept Joseph's private journal and was with him almost continuously up to the time of his death. On one occasion, Joseph wrote in his journal, "I have been searching all my life to find a man after my own heart whom I could trust with my business in all things, and I have found him. Dr. Willard Richards is the man."[3] To Willard's wife, Joseph wrote, "He is a great prop to me in my labors."[4] One of his major responsibilities was organizing Joseph's papers and historical events into a history of the Church, which project he worked on until the time of his death. Following his death, George A. Smith and Wilford Woodruff completed the history, which was later edited by B. H. Roberts and published as *The History of the Church.*

When threats against the Prophet's life became such that he crossed the Mississippi River in starting for the Rocky Mountains, Willard was one of those who went with him. When Joseph returned to Nauvoo and surrendered himself to be taken to Carthage, Willard was again by his side. When the Carthage jailor suggested that the imprisoned men would be safer in the jail cell rather than in the room they occupied, Joseph turned to Willard and asked, "'If we go into the cell, will you go with us?' Doctor Richards replied, 'Brother Joseph you did not ask me to cross the river with you—you did not ask me to come to Carthage—you did not ask me to come to jail with you—and do you think I will forsake you now? But I will tell you what I will do. If you are condemned to be hung for treason, I will be hung in your stead, and you shall go free.' Joseph said, 'You cannot!' The Doctor replied, 'I will!' "[5] Willard was not under arrest and could have left at any time. But he chose to remain and was consequently caught up in the events of the Martyrdom, though he, himself, miraculously escaped injury amid the shower of bullets. His escape from physical injury literally fulfilled an earlier prophecy by Joseph Smith, who told Elder Richards that the time would come when the balls would fly around him like hail, and he would see his friends fall upon the right and upon the left, but there should not be a hole in his garments.

At the time of the Martyrdom, the Twelve were gone on missions. Only Willard and John Taylor were in Nauvoo. It was Willard who mainly prevented things from getting out of hand and helped to maintain a spirit of calm among the Saints. From Carthage he sent a note to the Saints in Nauvoo that read: "Joseph and Hyrum are dead. Taylor wounded, not badly. I am well. . . . The citizens here are afraid of the 'Mormons' attacking them. I promise them no."[6] The next day as the Saints gathered about the Mansion House, Willard addressed them and admonished them "to keep the peace, stating that he had pledged his honor and his life for their good conduct."[7] On July 1, under the signature of Willard Richards, John Taylor, and

W. W. Phelps, a communication appeared in the *Times and Seasons*, "'beseeching the saints everywhere to hold fast to the faith' and to be 'quiet, peaceful citizens, doing the works of righteousness.'"[8] Through such efforts, retaliation and further violence were prevented.

Leaving Nauvoo with his family in February of 1846, he spent the year at Winter Quarters. Willard was a member of the Pioneer Company that opened the way to the Salt Lake Valley. He then returned to Winter Quarters for his family. When the First Presidency was reorganized in the fall of 1847, he was called as second counselor to Brigham Young. With the organization of the provisional government of the State of Deseret, Richards was appointed territorial secretary. In 1850, he was appointed the founding editor of the *Deseret News*. He was postmaster of Salt Lake City, as well as general historian of the Church, until the time of his death. He died of palsy, a disease that plagued him most of his life, in March 1854, at the relatively young age of forty-nine.

*Lyman Wight*

Born: May 9, 1796, Fairfield, New York
Ordained Apostle: April 8, 1841
Excommunicated: December 3, 1848
Died: March 31, 1858, Mountain Valley, Texas, at age 63

Born in 1796, Lyman Wight served the young republic in the War of 1812 against Great Britain. He later became a member of Sidney Rigdon's Campbellite congregation in Kirtland, Ohio, joining with Isaac Morley and others in forming a society based upon common stock principles, referred to as the "Family." When missionaries came to Kirtland preaching the restored gospel, Lyman and his wife believed and were baptized on November 14, 1830. Six days later, Lyman and Oliver Cowdery went into the woods where Oliver intended to ordain Lyman a priest. However, after solemn prayer, Oliver ordained him an elder, claiming afterward that he had done it in conformity to a vocal voice. At the June 1831 conference of the Church, held in Kirtland, he was ordained a high priest by Joseph Smith. It was during this conference that he testified he had seen the Savior in a vision.

Following a revelation to Joseph Smith, Lyman moved his family to Missouri as directed. Soon after, in 1832, he was sent on a mission to Cincinnati. On this mission, he established himself as a powerful preacher of the gospel. Arriving in the city, he engaged his board for several weeks at a hotel. When the landlord asked his profession, he said he was a preacher of the gospel. Asked what order he belonged to, he answered that he belonged to the order of Melchizedek. This created much curiosity, and the courthouse was opened for him to preach a series of lectures, resulting in his building up a branch and baptizing upward of one hundred people.

Many of those he baptized followed him back to Missouri where persecution was intensifying. He commanded the brethren in Jackson County in their defenses against the mobs and became a dread to the enemies of the Church. Consequently, his life was often sought after. On one occasion, he had to flee an armed group of men, riding a horse without saddle or bridle. He managed to escape by leaping a wide ditch that his pursuers dared not follow.

Following the Saints' expulsion from Jackson County into Clay County, volunteers were called for to go to Kirtland, a thousand miles distant, to see the Prophet Joseph for counsel to know what to do. Parley P. Pratt, who with his family was now destitute of all earthly means of support, and Lyman Wight, with his wife lying beside a log in the woods with a babe three days old and without raiment or shelter and only a few days' supply of food, volunteered and made the trip. When Zion's Camp was organized, Lyman went to Pennsylvania, New York, Michigan, Indiana, and Illinois recruiting volunteers. Joining up with the camp, he was made second in command. He walked the entire distance without stockings for his feet. Under appointment by Joseph Smith, he gave a written discharge to each member of the camp as he was dismissed.

In June 1838, he was appointed second counselor to John Smith, president of the Adam-ondi-Ahman Stake. He was also commissioned a colonel in the Caldwell County militia. Upon learning that Far West was surrounded by a mob, he gathered fifty-three volunteers to march to their support. It was here that Joseph and Hyrum, along with Lyman and other leaders, were betrayed and turned over to the mob, Joseph being sentenced to be shot for treason the next morning. That evening General Moses Wilson took Lyman aside and tried to persuade him to betray Joseph Smith by swearing false accusations against the Prophet. At this time the following conversation took place.

> General Wilson said, "Colonel Wight, we have nothing against you, only that you are associated with Joe Smith. He is our enemy and a damned rascal, and would take any plan he could to kill us. You are a damned fine fellow; and if you will come out and swear against him, we will spare your life, and give you any office you want; and if you don't do it, you will be shot tomorrow at 8 o'clock." Colonel Wight replied, "General Wilson, you are entirely mistaken in your man, both in regard to myself and Joseph Smith. Joseph Smith is not an enemy to mankind, he is not your enemy, and is as good a friend as you have got. Had it not been for him, you would have been in hell long ago, for I should have sent you there, by cutting your throat, and no other man but Joseph Smith could have prevented me, and you may thank him for your life. And, now, if you will give me the boys I brought from Diahman yesterday, I will whip your whole army." Wilson said, "Wight, you are a strange man; but if you will not accept my proposal, you will be shot tomorrow morning at 8." Colonel Wight replied, "Shoot and be damned." This was the true character of Lyman Wight; he was true as the sun to Joseph Smith, and would die for his friends.[1]

Lyman's life was spared, but he accompanied the Prophet in the ill treatment and suffering of the Richmond and Liberty Jails. In April 1841, he was ordained an Apostle. In 1842, Lyman stopped by Kirtland, where he rebaptized some two hundred wayward Saints who had remained in Kirtland in defiance of the Prophet's order to move west and led them to Nauvoo to rejoin the main body of the Saints. From Nauvoo, he traveled up the Mississippi River to Black River, Wisconsin, in February of 1844, to help supervise the cutting of timber in the pineries for the temple and the Nauvoo House.

Following the Martyrdom, Lyman returned to Nauvoo. But upon the Saints sustaining the Twelve, he said, "I would not turn my hand over to be one of the Twelve; the day was when there was somebody to control me [referring to Joseph Smith], but that day is past."[2] This proved to be true. He led a company of Saints to Texas, settling near the site of Austin, although this was not a permanent settlement. His insubordination to the authority to the Twelve eventually led to his excommunication in 1848. Upon his death, the *Galveston News* reported: "Mr. Wight first came to Texas in November, 1845, and has been with his colony on our extreme frontier ever since, moving still farther west as settlements formed around him, thus always being the pioneer of advancing civilization, affording protection against the Indians. He has been the first to settle five new counties, and prepare the way for others."[3] Following his death, his followers scattered, some finding their way back into the Church.

*Amasa Lyman*

Born: March 39, 1813, Lyman, New Hampshire
Ordained Apostle: August 20, 1842
Replaced in the Quorum of the Twelve: January 20, 1843
Appointed Counselor to First Presidency: February 4, 1843
Retired from First Presidency: June 27, 1844
Returned to the Quorum of the Twelve: August 12, 1844
Deprived of apostleship: October 6, 1867
Excommunicated: May 12, 1870
Died: February 4, 1877, Fillmore, Utah, at age 63
Blessings restored: January 12, 1909

Young Amasa had to endure an unstable childhood. When he was only two years old, his father abandoned the family. When his mother remarried, he went to live with his grandfather until he was eleven years old. Upon his grandfather's death, he lived with an uncle for seven more years. At the age of seventeen, Amasa began to think seriously about religion. It was at this time that Elders Lyman E. Johnson and Orson Pratt came into the neighborhood preaching the gospel. Lyman was consequently baptized April

27, 1832. Due to ill feelings of his uncle's family, Amasa set out for Kirtland, having only $11.35 in his pocket.

Arriving in Hiram, Ohio, he worked for the Johnson family until called on a mission. It was on this early mission that he demonstrated the spiritual gift of healing.

Returning from his mission, Amasa joined Zion's Camp in 1834. Following this journey, he went on several missions before moving with his family to Far West, Missouri, in the fall of 1837. Along with Joseph Smith and others, he was imprisoned in Richmond. Upon his release, he returned to Far West, where he aided the brethren in disposing of their properties before removing his family to Illinois. Settling in Nauvoo, he served several missions. In August 1842, he was ordained an Apostle to fill the vacancy left by Orson Pratt's being dropped from the Twelve. But upon repenting, Pratt was soon restored to his former position, leaving Amasa outside the Quorum. Joseph Smith then took Amasa into the First Presidency, although he was never formally sustained by the Church membership. Nonetheless, he was always honored by the Twelve both before and after the Martyrdom of Joseph as one of the leaders of the Church. On August 12, 1844, he was formally sustained into the Quorum of the Twelve.

Following the Prophet's martyrdom, Amasa sustained the leadership of the Twelve, declaring to the Saints, "I am gratified with the open, frank and plain exposition of President Young. . . . I do not make exception to anything he has said. I believe there is no power, or officer, or means wanted to carry on the work, but what is in the Twelve."[1] In 1847, he was a member of the Pioneer Company to the Salt Lake Valley; in 1851, he and Elder Charles C. Rich led a company of Saints to settle the San Bernardino area of California; in the early 1860s, he presided over the European Mission. It was here an incident occurred that would tragically lead to his eventual excommunication from the Church.

In March of 1862, he delivered a sermon in Dundee, Scotland, in which he virtually denied the necessity of, and the fact of, the Atonement of Jesus Christ. For some unknown reason, this matter was allowed to pass apparently unnoticed until January 21, 1867, at which time Lyman was brought before the Council of the Twelve for his heresy. "'The quorum of the Twelve' says the account of the meeting, 'were horrified at the idea that one of the Twelve Apostles should teach such a doctrine.'" The seriousness of Lyman's position, as well as the sacred responsibility of an Apostle, was expressed by Wilford Woodruff, who said that he "felt shocked at the idea that one of the Twelve Apostles should get so far into the dark as to deny the blood of Christ, and say that it was not necessary for the salvation of man and teach this as a true doctrine, while it was in opposition to all the doctrine taught by every prophet and Apostle, and saint from the days of Adam until today. . . . And I can tell Brother Lyman that his doctrine will send him to perdition if he continues in it, . . . it is the worst heresy man can preach."[2] Being greatly humbled, Amasa asked forgiveness and published a confession to the Church, and thus he retained his apostolic calling. Unfortunately, he returned to his doctrine within a few months and was consequently deprived of his apostleship October 6, 1867.

Yet he appeared to retain his testimony of the gospel. Speaking at a Church meeting a year later, he said: "The value of the gospel is increasing every day. I have proved that it is true, and I am pleased and satisfied with it. My chief desire is to keep my connection with it unbroken. I have no other hope but this work. I never have had. The gospel provides me all the blessings I enjoy. I love it because it is pure and holy."[3]

Inexplicably and in spite of his apparent testimony, he could not let go of his conclusions concerning the Atonement of Christ. Consequently, he was excommunicated on May 12, 1870. It is hard to contemplate Amasa's fall from grace. It may be that it was symptomatic of something else going on with him mentally or physically. Referring to his changed condition upon his returning from his mission to Europe in the early 1860s, Amasa's wife, Elisa, said that he "seemed to feel uncomfortable in his mind and I thought many times did not enjoy that portion of the Spirit of the Lord that a man in his position should. I did not know what was wrong with him but I could see that he was very unhappy. He left his family mostly to their fate, or to get along as best they could, although he was with them."[4] His condition worsened until his excommunication. Following several years of serious illness and physical pain, Amasa died on February 4, 1877, at Fillmore, Utah, at the age of sixty-three.

Upon becoming a member of the Quorum of the Twelve, Francis Lyman, Amasa's eldest son, sought for many years to have his father's blessings restored. After much deliberation by the Twelve, Amasa Lyman's blessings were restored January 12, 1909. Writing to his son Richard, Francis expressed his heartfelt feelings on that day: "My son, this is one of the most important and happiest days of my life. In the temple today, President Joseph F. Smith placed his hands on my head, and by proxy restored my father to all his former blessings, authority and power."[5]

*Ezra T. Benson*

Born: February 22, 1811, Mendon, Massachusetts
Ordained Apostle: July 16, 1846
Died: September 3, 1869, Ogden, Utah, at age 58

Ezra grew up working on his family's farm until the age of sixteen, and then his grandmother's farm following the sudden death of his grandfather. The year after his marriage, he bought out his brother-in-law's hotel business in Uxbridge, Massachusetts, which he operated for two years, making considerable money. He then moved to Holland, Massachusetts, where he went into the cotton mill business with his brother. But it was unprofitable, so he returned to the hotel business, again making a considerable income. Despite his prosperity, he was not content and had an unexplainable urge to move west.

Taking his wife and family, he migrated west, engaging in various business enterprises as he moved. In the winter of 1839, he moved to Quincy, Illinois, where he first became acquainted with the Latter-day Saints, who were being driven from their homes in Missouri.

He had heard that they were a peculiar people but found them to be agreeable. As he and his wife, Pamelia, listened to their preaching and debates with other ministers, they became convinced of the truth of the gospel. It was at a public debate that Ezra first saw the Prophet Joseph Smith. Despite efforts of their sectarian neighbors to dissuade them, Ezra and Pamelia were baptized on Sunday, July 19, 1840, in the Mississippi River.

In the fall of that year, Ezra was ordained an elder at the Church conference in Nauvoo. Shortly thereafter, Hyrum Smith organized the Quincy Stake, calling Ezra as second counselor in the stake presidency and ordaining him a high priest. Ezra took delight in his calling but felt his weaknesses and his need for the guidance of the Spirit. He often sought the Lord in secret prayer. He recorded,

> One evening as the moon shone bright, I retired near a grove to pray. There was about one foot of snow upon the ground with a crust which was about half an inch thick. I knelt down on my hay stack and commenced calling on the Lord, and heard a sound as though some one was walking on the frozen snow. I got upon my feet and looked in the direction of the sound, but saw no one, nor yet any signs of any one. The noise was repeated three times, yet I saw no one; I became satisfied it was an opposing power to keep me from praying, and I said, "Mr. Devil, you may break snow crust, but I will pray," and when I had so determined, I heard nothing more.[1]

In March of 1841, he moved to Nauvoo where he built a log cabin upon the city plot he had purchased. He supported his family through various jobs he obtained. He also worked on the construction of the temple. In 1842, he was called on his first mission to the eastern United States. He narrowly escaped being thrown overboard from a river boat and later being tarred and feathered, being saved by strangers who stepped up to his defense. He was disheartened that family members and friends of his past did not respond to the gospel message. Ezra was again in the East when word came of Joseph's death. Asked by a Church member, "Who will lead the Church now?" Ezra replied: "I do not know who will lead the church, but I know who will lead me. It will be the Twelve Apostles, and I will follow them."[2]

Returning to Nauvoo, he helped work on the temple until Brigham Young urged him to leave with the first company heading west. Ezra evacuated from Nauvoo, leaving a good brick house he could not sell and borrowing a wagon and horses to accompany Brigham Young in the first company west. He traded his wife's shawl for about two hundred pounds of flour, a few bushels of Indian corn-meal, twelve pounds of sugar, and some bedding and clothing. Both of his two wives were pregnant as they left Nauvoo in February 1846. One baby was born with only a tent to cover the mother and child, and the other—President Ezra Taft Benson's grandfather, George Taft Benson—was born on the trail in a wagon box at Garden Grove, Iowa.

While at the Mount Pisgah encampment, he received correspondence from Brigham Young, informing him that he was to be a member of the Quorum of the Twelve. After traveling to the main camp at Council Bluffs, he was ordained by Brigham Young. Shortly thereafter, he was called on a mission to the eastern United States. Upon completion of his mission, he returned to the encamped Saints to be a part of the Pioneer Company in its journey to the Salt Lake Valley. He continued to assist with the migration of the Saints, and in one trip to the valley, he became so sick he was not expected to live. The camp fasted and prayed for him and he recovered. There were other missions to the eastern United States, to England where he presided over the British Mission, and to the Sandwich (Hawaiian) Islands. He, along with Joseph F. Smith, Lorenzo Snow, and others, was sent to Hawaii to set the Church in order, which had been put in disarray by the operations of the imposter Walter M. Gibson, who had set himself up among the native Saints as a kingly and priestly ruler. This would prove to be the last time Elder Benson would be called upon to leave Utah.

Besides serving these missions, Elder Benson filled many important assignments at home. He was a member of the provisional government of the State of Deseret, previous to the organization of the territory; he was a member of the Territorial House of Representatives for several sessions, and during the last ten years of his life, he was elected to the Territorial Council every term. In 1869, he associated himself with two other brethren in taking a large grading contract on the Central Pacific Railway. The fact that he was not able to obtain a settlement with the railway company caused him considerable anxiety. But he is probably best remembered for his important role in the settlement and establishment of Cache Valley. Called by Brigham Young to move to Cache Valley, he was the presiding authority over that area for nearly a decade until the time of his death. Such a calling well suited his personality, for it has been said of him that while he was an earnest and faithful disciple, his zeal found expression in physical pioneering activities rather than in works of scholarship and doctrinal exposition.

On Friday, September 3, 1869, Elder Benson had just arrived in Ogden from his home and was caring for a sick horse, when he suddenly fell dead, stricken with apoplexy. His funeral and burial took place in his hometown of Logan.

## Charles C. Rich

Born: August 21, 1809, Campbell County, Kentucky
Ordained Apostle: February 12, 1849
Died: November 17, 1883, Paris, Idaho, at age 74

Charles worked on his father's farm until the age of twenty, at which time he learned the cooper trade, though he never followed it. His parents, who were well-to-do for their time, did not want him to leave home, so he continued on the farm and, having obtained a good education while growing up, taught a local country school. Religiously inclined from childhood and having a studious disposition, he began to investigate Mormonism when he first heard of it in 1831. "I studied carefully, anxiously, and prayerfully, that I might know if it were the Church of Jesus Christ. I did not want to run any risk in the matter, and remain in uncertainty. . . . The spirit would then whisper, you have not been baptized, you have not obeyed the Gospel; but when I had complied with the law, then I . . . obtained a perfect knowledge of the truth, and could then bear a testimony of it to all the world."[1] He was baptized in April 1, 1832.

The following month, he traveled to Kirtland, where he met the Prophet for the first time. Having been ordained an elder, he spent the next few years as a missionary throughout Kentucky, Ohio, Indiana, and Illinois. He also made two trips with Lyman Wight to Missouri to purchase lands for the Church. In 1834, he joined Zion's Camp, serving as captain of one of the branches and remaining with the camp until its disbandment. Following the march, he returned to Kirtland, where he was ordained a high priest. He then moved to Far West, Missouri, where he married Sarah D. Pea, who was his faithful companion for fifty-five years and who bore him nine children. During the persecutions in Caldwell and Davies Counties, he was a captain of fifty. Known for his courage, he was second in command at the battle of Crooked River, and when David W. Patten fell mortally wounded, while bullets were flying about him thick and fast, he laid down his sword and administered the ordinance of laying on of hands for the healing of the sick to his dying comrade; then Charles arose and led the charge upon the enemy, forcing the mob to flee. Because of his role at Crooked River, he was charged with murder and was subsequently forced to flee Missouri for his life, leaving his wife to join him later in Illinois.

In Illinois, Charles was active in ecclesiastical and civic affairs. He served on the high council, the stake presidency, the Nauvoo City Council, and as captain and then brigadier general in the first regiment of the Nauvoo Legion (many called him General Rich up until the time he died), and as regent of the University of Nauvoo. When Joseph was kidnapped and taken to Missouri in 1843, Rich led a group of twenty-five men from Nauvoo in an attempt to render the Prophet assistance, returning to Nauvoo after having traveled 500 miles in seven days. In 1846, he left Nauvoo in the exodus west. In the Mount Pisgah encampment, he was the presiding elder and spent much of his time visiting the sick. He, himself, was so seriously ill that he was bedridden for two months. On one occasion, a woman came to him and tearfully told him that her husband was away with the Mormon Battalion and she and her children had no food. Elder Rich told his wife to give the woman what little food they had left and to trust in the Lord for their own welfare. Later that day, wagons stopped in front of the Rich's home and a stranger gave them fifty dollars, saying that the Spirit told him the family was in need of money. He also told them that a wagon full of flour was coming to Mt. Pisgah and they would be able to buy what they needed. Both Elder and Sister Rich burst into the tears at the news and the Lord's watchful care over them. Leading a company of pioneers to the Salt Lake Valley in 1847, Charles then served in the Salt Lake Stake presidency until he was called to the Quorum of the Twelve Apostles in February of 1849. It was during this time that he was among a small number of men appointed to draft a constitution for the proposed State of Deseret.

While presiding over the California Mission in 1850–51, Elder Rich sent a group of ten men to open up the mission in the Hawaiian Islands, which eventually resulted in thousands of its native population coming into the Church. In September of 1851, Elder Rich and Elder Amasa Lyman purchased the San Bernardino Ranch, where they began a settlement. However, when word of the approaching Utah War reached the settlement, the land was sold and they returned to Utah to help in the defense of their people.

In 1860, Elder Rich was assigned to preside with Elder Amasa Lyman over the European Mission. Upon his return, in the autumn of 1863, he explored the Bear Lake Valley and moved there with his family the following spring, along with other settlers. There he made new homes for his family, constructed a grist-mill, and took the lead in building up a prosperous line of settlements. During the early years of the Bear Lake settlements, the only way residents could receive mail when the winter snows were deep was by crossing the mountains on snowshoes. When violent storms prevailed and others would shrink from the hazardous journey, Elder Rich would set out. His great strength and endurance, which often seemed limitless, along with his knowledge of the country, enabled him to always get through, though the fatigue he bore would probably have killed an ordinary man. This became his mode of transportation on many occasions when traveling to Salt Lake City to attend sessions of legislature and Church conferences. Rich was the leader of the original settlers of the Bear Lake area, and the settlers showed their esteem for him by naming their new county "Rich" and the settlement "St. Charles." Indeed, he was less noted for his brilliant talents than for his genuine goodness, being a man of generosity who seemed to live more for the happiness of others than for his own.

In October of 1880, Elder Rich suffered a paralytic stroke that rendered him helpless. His physician ordered him to Salt Lake City, where he improved somewhat over the winter months but did not regain the use of his legs. He returned to his home in Paris, Bear Lake County, Idaho, where he died November 17, 1883, at the age of seventy-two. During his three years of paralysis, he was never heard to complain but manifested a spirit of contentment and resignation.

*Lorenzo Snow*

Born: April 3, 1814, Mantua, Ohio
Ordained Apostle: February 12, 1849
Sustained Counselor to President Brigham Young: April 8, 1873
Sustained Assistant Counselor to President Brigham Young: May 9, 1874
Sustained President of Quorum of the Twelve: April 7, 1889
Ordained President of the Church: September 13, 1889
Died: October 10, 1901, Salt Lake City, Utah, at age 87

Lorenzo was born the fifth of seven children. Being the eldest son, he assumed a great deal of responsibility for running the family farm and shipping produce downriver to New Orleans. The Snow family was prosperous and influential within their community and encouraged their children in the pursuit of intellectual and social accomplishments. As a young man, Lorenzo became interested in pursuing a military career and, at age twenty-one, won a lieutenant's commission by appointment from the governor of Ohio. Feeling that a college education would further his career, he attended Oberlin College. He did well in his studies but became dissatisfied with the religious teachings. In the spring of 1836, at the invitation of his sister Eliza, who had been baptized into the Church, he went to Kirtland to study Hebrew. One day after he was introduced to Joseph Smith Sr., the patriarch said to him: "You will soon be convinced of the truth of the latter-day work, and be baptized. And you will become as great as you can possibly wish— EVEN AS GREAT AS GOD, and you cannot wish to be greater."[1] True to Father Smith's words, he was baptized June of 1836, but the statement "even as great as God" troubled him. Four years later, his mind would be opened by the Spirit of the Lord and he "saw as clear as the sun at noon day, with wonder and astonishment, the pathway of God and man." He later tried to express what he saw in a couplet:

*As man now is, God once was.*

*As God now is, man may be.*[2]

Because of the reported experiences of others, he had expected some significant witness to follow his baptism, but it did not come, and he was left disappointed. Some weeks later, he wandered the fields feeling a gloomy, oppressive spirit over him. He knelt down determined to pray, and as he opened his lips, the Spirit of God descended upon him. Of what followed, he recorded: "I then received a perfect knowledge that God lives, that Jesus Christ is the Son of God, . . . dispelling forever, so long as reason and memory last, all possibility of doubt."[3]

Soon after, Lorenzo was ordained an elder and started off on a lifetime of missionary work that would result in thousands coming into the Church. He would go on to serve missions to many of the states, England, Italy, Hawaii, and the Holy Land, and to the Nez Perce and Shoshone Indian nations. On an apostolic mission to Hawaii with Joseph F. Smith and others, their boat capsized. Elder Snow, who was presumably drowned, was pulled to the beach where it was twenty minutes before he showed any signs of life. Lorenzo was instrumental in leading Saints across the plains. Soon after his arrival in the Salt Lake Valley, he was called to the Quorum of the Twelve. It was shortly thereafter that he was called to open up the missionary work in Italy.

Like so many others, Lorenzo served in both ecclesiastical and civic positions. Because Snow was known as an organizer, Brigham

Young sent him to preside over and strengthen the settlements north of Salt Lake City. Under Lorenzo's direction, the community he named Brigham City became one of the most prosperous and progressive settlements in the territory. Lorenzo also served a prison term for the practice of plural marriage. He was promised amnesty if he would renounce the principle of plural marriage. He replied, "Thank you, but having adopted sacred and holy principles for which we have already sacrificed property, home and life on several occasions in their defense, we do not propose, at this late hour, to abandon them because of threatened danger."[4] During his imprisonment, he was a model prisoner and an inspiration to his fellow prisoners. He developed a school to teach reading, writing, math, and bookkeeping; organized activities; led gospel studies; and held Church meetings. In February of 1887, the Supreme Court reversed the Snow decision and he was released the following day. A cheering crowd of General Authorities, family, and friends welcomed him home.

Lorenzo was in Brigham City when he learned of President Wilford Woodruff's death. He immediately traveled to Salt Lake City and went to the temple. There in prayer, he reminded the Lord of how he had prayed for the life of President Woodruff and had never sought nor desired the responsibility of Church leadership. " 'Nevertheless,' he said, 'Thy will be done. . . . I ask that Thou show me what Thou wouldst have me do.'" The Lord's reply came in a glorious vision. "It was right here," he later told his granddaughter while in the temple, "that the Lord Jesus Christ appeared to me at the time of the death of President Woodruff. He instructed me to go right ahead and reorganize the First Presidency of the Church at once and not wait as had been done after the death of previous presidents, and that I was to succeed President Woodruff."[5]

At the time of Lorenzo's presidency, the Church was facing financial bankruptcy due to persecution, unjust legislation, and expensive litigation. Submitting to the promptings of the Spirit, President Snow traveled to St. George, not understanding why. While speaking at a special conference, he saw in vision how the Saints had neglected the principle of tithing and how this principle would free the Church from its debts. He then traveled to various settlements preaching tithing. Heber J. Grant later observed: "In three years this man, beyond the age of ability in the estimation of the world, this man who had not been engaged in financial affairs, who had been devoting his life for years to laboring in the temple, took hold of the finances of the Church of Christ, under the inspiration of the living God, and in those three years changed everything financially from darkness to light."[6]

President Snow died October 10, 1901, due to complications from a cold in his lungs. The funeral services opened with the hymn "O My Father," written by his sister Eliza.

*Erastus Snow*

Born: November 9, 1818, Saint Johnsbury, Vermont
Ordained Apostle: February 12, 1849
Died: May 27, 1888, Salt Lake City, Utah, at age 69

Elder Orson F. Whitney wrote, "Of all the distinguished characters surrounding Brigham Young, . . . perhaps no other resembled him in so many respects as did this man, whose record as a colonizer and a statesman is second only to that of the pioneer chieftain himself."[1] Erastus was fourteen years of age when Elders Orson Pratt and Luke S. Johnson came to St. Johnsbury preaching the restored gospel. Erastus's two older brothers, William and Zerubbabel, were first to join, followed by all the family. Erastus was baptized by his brother William on February 3, 1833. In June of the next year, he was ordained a teacher and immediately began making short missionary excursions to neighboring villages. In August 1835, he was ordained an elder by Elder Luke S. Johnson and continued in his missionary zeal. In November of that year, he traveled the seven hundred miles to Kirtland, where he met Joseph Smith and lived with him for several weeks.

From Kirtland, Erastus was sent on a mission to Pennsylvania in April of 1836. He was gone for eight months, during which time he traveled 1,600 miles, delivered 220 sermons, baptized 50 persons, and established several branches throughout western Pennsylvania. This was the beginning of a lifetime of missions. Throughout his missions, he became known for his public debates with ministers of others faiths, some lasting late into the night, some being continued over several days, drawing hundreds of spectators, and Erastus always proclaimed the victor. On many occasions, he manifested the gift of healing, but he also knew persecution. On one occasion, while he was preaching in Bridgeport, a mob gathered and drove him from the place, pelting him with rotten eggs.

Returning to Kirtland from one of his missions, Erastus joined with the Saints, who were moving to Missouri due to the increasing apostasy and persecutions in Ohio. When Joseph and others were imprisoned in Liberty Jail, Erastus and other brethren went to visit the prisoners. As a result of a failed attempt by the prisoners to escape, the visitors were also jailed. When Erastus asked Joseph if he should engage a lawyer, Joseph told him, "Go and plead for justice as hard as you can and quote Blackstone and other authors now and then, and they will take it all for law."[2] Following the hearing, in which Erastus was acquitted, lawyers flocked around him asking where he had studied law and saying they had never heard a better plea. Also, in fulfillment of an earlier promise made to him by the Prophet, all of his belongings, which were taken at the time of his arrest, were restored to him, nothing being lost. He then traveled to Jefferson City, the state capital, and through the assistance of the Secretary of State, managed to get an order issued for a change of venue, through which the prisoners were started from Davies to Boone County. During the journey, Joseph and fellow prisoners escaped and joined the Saints in Illinois.

From Nauvoo, Erastus set out again on a mission, having his family with him during the latter part. During this mission, he was instructed by Hyrum Smith to go to Salem, Massachusetts. Joseph had earlier received a revelation in which he was told that the Lord had much treasure there that He would gather in time (D&C 111:2). There in Salem, Erastus baptized many souls and established a branch.

He returned to Nauvoo after being away for two and a half years. There the Prophet Joseph Smith personally taught him the principle of celestial and plural marriage. Again, he left on a mission, only to return after the Martyrdom of Joseph and Hyrum.

Erastus was a member of the original Pioneer Company that forged the way west. He and Orson Pratt were the first to enter the Salt Lake Valley. He recorded, "We simultaneously swung our hats and shouted, Hosannah! for the Spirit told us that here the Saints should find rest."³ When he later returned to Winter Quarters to get his family, he found that one of his children had died. In the valley, he was called as second counselor in the Salt Lake Stake. Then, in February of 1849, he was called to the Quorum of the Twelve Apostles. He became active in government, the militia, and in providing for his family. But in the general conference of October 1849, he was called to go and open the door of the gospel to the Scandinavian people. On June 14, 1850, he arrived in Copenhagen, the capital of Denmark, where he labored for eighteen months. When a conference was held at the end of his mission, there were over six hundred members of the Church in Denmark, and a few in Norway and Sweden. This would prove to be the most successful mission, next to England, in the early days of the Church. During the 1800s and the early 1900s, over twenty-five thousand Scandinavian Saints would emigrate to the Mountain West, giving great strength to the Church.

In October of 1853, he was called, with George A. Smith, to take fifty families to strengthen the settlements in Iron County. In September of 1860, Elder Snow and Elder Orson Pratt left for the eastern states to labor among branches of the Church, which, for several years, had been left mostly to themselves. Through their efforts, many of those who had fallen away were awakened to a sense of their position and were reactivated. One of the factors that reawakened their faith was the impending fulfillment of Joseph Smith's prophecy concerning the Civil War, and great preparations were being made for the Saints to leave for the West. As the war grew more severe, President Young called all the elders in the United States to return home "in consequence of the war now raging throughout the land."⁴ This put an end to all missionary work in the States until sometime after the end of the war.

Following Elder Snow's return home in the fall of 1861, his efforts turned almost exclusively to southern Utah and neighboring locals, exploring new areas, locating settlements, and directing the settlers. He represented that area as a member of the legislature until he was disenfranchised under the Edmunds-Tucker Law. When sent into exile along with other Church leaders to escape harassing US marshals during the anti-polygamy crusade, he visited and counseled the southern settlements. He died in Salt Lake City on May 27, 1888, at the age of sixty-nine. Speaking at his funeral, Elder John W. Taylor said, "When a man of courage was wanted to go to Northern Scandinavia, Brother Snow was called and performed the great labor. . . . When a man who would stand by his post was wanted to go to Southern Utah, Erastus Snow was chosen. When, in more recent years, a man of wisdom and experience was wanted in Mexico, he was elected. He has always been with the outposts."[5]

*Franklin D. Richards*

Born: April 2, 1821, Richmond, Massachusetts
Ordained Apostle: February 12, 1849
Sustained President of Quorum of the Twelve: September 13, 1898
Died: December 9, 1899, Ogden, Utah, at age 78

The conversion of the Richards family began when their cousins, Brigham and Joseph Young, came to their community, bringing the Book of Mormon. After careful study of the book, Franklin joined many of his family who had converted. On June 3, 1838, at the age of seventeen, he was baptized by his father. Franklin's faith would be forged through trials of heartache. In the fall of that same year, he said good-bye to family and started toward Far West, where the Saints were gathering. On his way, he heard tales of persecution and mobocracy against the Saints. He came through Haun's Mill after the massacre of that settlement, not knowing that among those brutally murdered victims, who were hurriedly buried in a well, was his beloved brother, George Spencer Richards. In the spring of 1839, he found his way to Quincy, Illinois, with the other refugee Saints, where he met the Prophet Joseph for the first time. Ordained a Seventy, he was sent on his first mission to Indiana, where he successfully baptized many.

Called on a mission to England, he had arrived at the Atlantic seaboard when he received news of the Martyrdom. He also received a change in his mission call, being sent to Michigan to gather means for the completion of the temple. Later, as the Saints left Nauvoo, Franklin was called on a mission to Europe. Leaving his pregnant wife and young daughter at the Sugar Creek encampment, he headed eastward. On the eve of his sailing for Europe, he received word that his wife had given birth to a baby boy who had died. During his absence, his daughter, and only remaining child, died at Winter Quarters, and his brother Joseph, a member of the Mormon Battalion marching to California, died at Pueblo, Colorado. In February of 1848, he rejoined his wife at Winter Quarters. He captained fifty wagons in the company of Saints being led west by the First Presidency, arriving in the Salt Lake Valley on October 19. The following February of 1849, he was called to the holy apostleship. In October of that same year, he was again called to England, where he replaced Orson Pratt as Mission President. In England, he established the Perpetual Emigration Fund, which he had helped institute earlier in Utah, and in 1852 he sent the first group of European Saints to the States under that program.

It was also during this mission that Franklin saw the need and the anxiousness of the British Saints to have access to the writings and teachings of Joseph Smith. Taking copies of sermons and articles he had in his possession, Elder Richards compiled them into a publication he called *Pearl of Great Price*. While undergoing some changes from the original, this publication would later be canonized as scripture in the Church.

Returning to Utah in 1852, Franklin served in the territorial legislature and helped establish the iron works in Iron County. In 1854, he again went to England, this time to preside over all Church affairs in the British Isles, East Indies, Australia, New Zealand, Africa, and Europe. Prior to his leaving for England, his uncle, President Willard Richards, died, leaving Franklin as head of the Richards family. It was during this mission that Franklin baptized Dr. Karl G. Maeser. That evening, following this baptism, they conversed together with Elder William Budge acting as interpreter, for Richards did not understand German nor did Maeser speak English. But soon, Elder Budge was told that his interpreting was not necessary, that they understood each other perfectly. Maeser felt this incident was an answer to his prayer asking for a spiritual manifestation that he had done the right thing in being baptized. While returning from England in 1856, Elder Richards passed the Willie and Martin Handcart Companies. Having a lightweight conveyance and horses, he continued on rapidly to Salt Lake City, where he reported their plight to President Brigham Young, resulting in their rescue. Back in Utah, he became involved again in civic affairs where he served again in the territorial legislature, was reelected as a regent of the University of Deseret, and was a brigadier general in the militia, while pursuing farming and milling on his own personal account. In the summer of 1866, he was again called to a mission in Europe, where, as before, the work was rejuvenated under his direction.

Upon Elder Richards's return to the United States, Brigham Young recommended that he settle in Ogden. There he served as probate judge from 1869–1883. He tried many civil and criminal cases, and when they were appealed to a higher court, his decisions invariably remained unreversed. Following his retirement from the bench, he was called as assistant Church historian and five years later as Church historian. During the years of 1884–1890, when persecution over plural marriage was at its extreme, he was one of the few Church leaders not compelled to go into hiding. During that time, he presided at the general conferences of the Church and gave counsel and direction to the Church as the visible representative of the First Presidency.

In September of 1898, Elder Richards was sustained as president of the Quorum of the Twelve and pursued his duties with such energy that many friends and family members feared he would break down under the burden. His reply was to the effect that he had never learned to shirk his duty and must continue in that course until the end. He was also known as probably the most studious and wide-read Apostle of the Quorum over which he presided. Believing that "the glory of God is intelligence," he read science, history, and religion, contending for a harmony of all truth regardless of its source.

In August of 1899, Elder Richards's health failed. He traveled to California, where he recovered somewhat, but a few months after his return, he died at the age of seventy-eight. At his funeral services, President Joseph F. Smith remarked that he had seen President Richards placed under such trying ordeals that few men could have endured, but to which Brother Richards had patiently submitted with the faith of Job, when he said, "Though he slay me, yet will I trust in him."[1]

In a tribute to Elder Richards, Elder Orson F. Whitney of the Quorum of the Twelve wrote in part: "The life of Franklin D. Richards affords an example of steadfast devotion to duty and of success in the discharge of many varied and important responsibilities. Beginning his career amid humble surroundings, first as a farm boy, then as a missionary, he rose steadily to prominence both in civil and religious affairs, and died one of the most honored and most conspicuous figures in the community."[2]

*George Q. Cannon*

Born: January 11, 1827, Liverpool, England
Ordained Apostle: August 26, 1860
Sustained Counselor to President Brigham Young: April 8, 1873
Sustained Assistant Counselor to President Young: May 9, 1874
Sustained First Counselor to President John Taylor: October 18, 1880
Sustained First Counselor to President Wilford Woodruff: April 7, 1889
Sustained First Counselor to President Lorenzo Snow: September 13, 1898
Died: April 12, 1901, Monterey, California, at age 74

I know that God lives. I know that Jesus lives; for I have seen him."[1] This was the testimony of a man who served as counselor to four Presidents of the Church. George Q. was born the son of George Cannon and Ann Quayle. In January of 1840, Apostle John Taylor arrived in Liverpool, England, where he visited his brother-in-law George Cannon, bringing the gospel to him and his family. Young George Q. was baptized at the age of thirteen. In later years, he would state that he never got a testimony. "The reason why . . . was because I did not have to get one. It was born with me. Since I first heard the gospel . . . it seemed to be a part of my very nature."[2] In September of 1842, the Cannon family sailed for America. Sadly, George Q.'s mother died and was buried at sea. When the family arrived at Nauvoo, a great crowd met the boat at the river landing. Though George Q. had never seen the Prophet, he recognized him immediately among the people. He later wrote, "There was that about him, which to the author's eyes, distinguished him from all the men he had ever seen."[3] George Q. was seventeen when the Martyrdom occurred. When the Nauvoo Saints gathered to hear Brigham Young speak on who should lead the Church, there was no doubt in George Q.'s mind. "On that occasion," he wrote, "President Brigham Young seemed to be transformed. . . . The tones of his voice, his appearance, everything he said and the spirit which accompanied his words, convinced the people that the leader whom God had selected to guide them stood before them."[4]

In 1844, his father died, after which George Q. lived with his uncle, John Taylor. Elder Taylor was editor of the *Times and Seasons* and the *Nauvoo Neighbor* newspapers, and from him, young George Q. learned the printing trade. Traveling west with the exiled Saints, he arrived in the Salt Lake Valley in October 1849. In 1850, he, along with nine other men, was called on a mission to the Hawaiian Islands. When it was obvious they would have little success among the white population, five of the men returned home, but George Q. and four of his companions decided to stay and teach the native population. During the next three and a half years, George translated the Book of Mormon into the Hawaiian language, and over four thousand Hawaiians were brought into the Church. A few weeks after his return home, George was married. Shortly thereafter, he returned to Hawaii, where he and his wife served a mission together.

In 1859 and 1860, George Q. was placed in charge of the branches of the Church in the East, where he also acted as Church Emigration Agent. It was during this time that he was called to the Quorum of the Twelve, following the assassination of Parley P. Pratt, thus fulfilling a prophecy given a few years earlier by Elder Pratt that George Q. would succeed him as a member of the Twelve. Elder Cannon recorded that the Lord had revealed to him in his youth that he would be called to the Twelve and that he often pled with the

Lord that if he could gain eternal life "without being called to that high and holy responsibility, I would much rather He would choose some other person."[5]

Elder Cannon would go on to a distinguished career in business and government service. In Church service, he presided over the European Mission and later served as Brigham Young's private secretary during the last three years of President Young's life. In 1866, he commenced the publication of the *Juvenile Instructor*; and in 1867, he was appointed General Superintendent of the Sunday School at the time it was organized. He continued in both positions until the end of his life. In 1867, he was also appointed editor of the *Deseret News* and expanded it from a weekly to a daily newspaper. He served professionally as president and vice president to many prominent business enterprises, and he served as an elected delegate from Utah to the United States Congress from 1872 until 1882, when the Church was disenfranchised by the Edmunds-Tucker Act, making him ineligible for the office of delegate.

Yet, even during his years in the First Presidency, his faith was continually growing, as seen in his reactions to the deaths of Presidents Brigham Young and John Taylor. Reflecting upon President Young's death, Elder Cannon said: "On Tuesday night, as I sat at the head of his bed, and thought of his death, if it should occur, I recoiled from the contemplation of the view. It seemed to me that he was indispensable. What could we do without him? He had been the brain, the eye, the ear, the mouth and hand for the entire Church of Jesus Christ of Latter-day Saints. . . . And while I was thus thinking of all this, it seemed as though we could not spare him; he was indispensable to this great work. And while I felt it, it seemed as though a voice said, 'I am God, this is my work; it is I who build up and carry it forward; it is my business to guide my Saints.'"[6]

The lesson was well learned. Ten years later, upon the death of President John Taylor, his counselors, George Q. Cannon and Joseph F. Smith, issued a communication to the *Deseret News* that read in part: "We feel to say to the Latter-day Saints: Be comforted! The same God who took care of the work when Joseph was martyred, who has watched over and guarded and upheld it through the long years that have since elapsed, and who has guided its destinies since the departure of Brigham, still watches over it and makes it the object of His care. John has gone; but God lives."[7]

In March of 1901, Elder Cannon moved from Utah to Monterey, California, for health purposes. However, his illness assumed a fatal form, and he died in the early morning of April 12, at the age of seventy-four. Business, civic, and religious leaders telegraphed their praise of Elder Cannon and their sense of loss at his passing. At the close of 1901, the show windows of the celebrated commercial emporium of the most noted avenue in Berlin, Germany, the magnificent Unter den Linden, displayed his portrait, along with six others, as the principal world personalities whom death had taken during the previous twelve months.

*Joseph F. Smith*

Born: November 13, 1838, Far West, Missouri
Ordained Apostle, named counselor to First Presidency: July 1, 1866
Set apart as a member of the Quorum of the Twelve: October 8, 1867
Sustained Second Counselor to President John Taylor: October 10, 1880
Sustained Second Counselor to President Wilford Woodruff: April 7, 1889
Sustained Second Counselor to President Lorenzo Snow:
    September 13, 1898
Sustained First Counselor to President Lorenzo Snow: October 6, 1901
Sustained President of the Church: October 17, 1901
Died: November 19, 1918, Salt Lake City, Utah, at age 80

Joseph's younger years were unusually strenuous, but the experiences matured him beyond his years. At age six, he lost his father, Hyrum Smith; when only eight, he drove an ox team over two hundred miles from Nauvoo to Winter Quarters; and when nine, he became a responsible herd boy. It was during that same time that he saved the pioneers' cattle from an Indian attack. Helping his family prepare for the trek west, he again drove a team of oxen, this time over one thousand miles to the Salt Lake Valley. In the valley, at the age of ten, he again took care of the family herd, adding to his responsibilities of plowing, canyon work, farming, and harvesting. He would later say, "I cannot recall the loss of a single hoof by death, straying away, or otherwise, from neglect or carelessness on my part during that period."[1] When he was fourteen, his mother died, leaving him an orphan. At fifteen, he was ordained an elder and began a three-year mission in Hawaii. On his way home after his mission, he demonstrated his courage and the depth of his testimony. Several anti-Mormon toughs entered Joseph's camp, threatening him and his companions with what they would do to Mormons. One thug, with his pistol in hand, asked Joseph, "Are you a Mormon?" Joseph answered, "Yes, siree; dyed in the wool; true blue, through and through." The ruffian grasped Joseph by the hand and replied, "Well, you are the —— pleasantest man I ever met! Shake, young fellow, I am glad to see a man that stands up for his convictions."[2] Joseph would later reflect that he fully expected to be killed by admitting he was a Mormon. Following his marriage at age twenty-one, he was called on a mission to England, followed by a second mission to Hawaii. Home again, he was employed in the Church Historian's Office.

On July 1, 1866, Joseph F. Smith met with President Brigham Young and a number of the Apostles in a council meeting for which he served as secretary. After the closing prayer, President Young said to the Brethren, "Hold on, shall I do as I feel led? I always feel well to do as the Spirit constrains me. It is my mind to ordain Brother Joseph F. Smith to the apostleship, and to be one of my counselors."[3] He then called upon the Brethren to express their feelings. All heartily approved. They then laid their hands on Joseph's head and ordained him. He would go on to also serve as counselor to the next three Presidents of the Church. His complete dedication to his calling can be seen in the following incident. In 1873, President Young called him to preside over the European Mission. At that time, Elder Smith had served four years on a homestead, requiring only one more year for the land to be his. He reflected years later, "And I went. I lost the homestead, and yet I never complained about it; I never charged Brother Brigham with having robbed me because of this. I felt that I was engaged in a bigger work than securing 160 acres of land. I was sent to declare the message of salvation to the nations of the earth. I was called by the authority of God on the earth, and I did not stop to consider myself and my little personal rights and privileges."[4]

Sustained as President of the Church in October 1901, he continued the emphasis on tithing begun by President Snow and saw the Church completely free of financial debt. During his presidency, he sought to improve the image of the Church to the world. He established a visitors' center on Temple Square in order to provide accurate information to tourists. He also authorized the purchase of Church historical sites. His many days of testifying before the US Senate in the "Senator Reed Smoot" case won respect and admiration among the nation's leaders, the press, and the people. During his years as President, the Church nearly doubled in membership. President Charles W. Nibley said of him, "As a preacher of righteousness, who could compare with him? He was the greatest that I ever heard—strong, powerful, clear, appealing. It was marvelous how the words of living light and fire flowed from him."[5] He was also a man of peace. In spite of hateful words and false accusations spoken against him, he silently endured it all without ever speaking in his defense or in retaliation toward others.

President Smith was well acquainted with death during the course of his lifetime. Beside losing his father and mother in the early years of his life, he lived to bury thirteen of his children. The death of his oldest son, Apostle Hyrum Mac Smith, in January of 1918, was especially grievous for him. President Smith himself suffered from the effects of his advanced age during the last six months of his life. It should not be surprising these last months were a time of deep contemplation and numerous spiritual manifestations. At the opening session of general conference, October 4, 1918, he said, "I have not lived alone these five months. I have dwelt in the spirit of prayer, of supplication, of faith and of determination; and I have had my communication with the Spirit of the Lord continuously."[6] In February 1918, he delivered at a temple fast meeting an address on "The Status of Children in the Resurrection," and shortly thereafter he received the vision of the redemption of the dead, now section 138 of the Doctrine and Covenants, a fitting capstone to his life and ministry. He died November 19, 1918, at the age of eighty.

It is fitting to note that on one occasion President Smith incidentally stated, in his general, unassuming way, that when he passed away, unlike many of his brethren, he would leave no written work by which he might be remembered. Hearing this remark, Dr. John A. Widtsoe determined that would not be the case. With the aid of others, extracts from President Smith's sermons and writings were gathered, edited, and published in what has become the widely read volume *Gospel Doctrine.* He is remembered.

*Brigham Young Jr.*

Born: December 18, 1836, Kirtland, Ohio
Ordained Apostle: February 4, 1864
Sustained to Quorum of the Twelve: October 9, 1868
Sustained Counselor to President Brigham Young: April 8, 1873
Sustained Assistant Counselor to President Brigham Young: May 9, 1874
Sustained President of the Quorum of the Twelve: October 17, 1901
Died: April 11, 1903, Salt Lake City, Utah, at age 66

**B**righam was born in Kirtland, Ohio, December 18, 1836, the son of Brigham Young and Mary Ann Angell. His twin sister, Mary, died at the age of seven from the effects of head injuries she suffered in a wagon accident at the age of two. Nauvoo was the home of his early childhood. When the Saints were driven from Nauvoo, President Young led the crowd of stricken Saints across the river to a place of safety. The rest of the family followed across on ferry. During the time of evacuation, young Brigham became separated from his family. Running down to the river front, he leaped upon the last boat to cross the river that night. He hunted vainly for his family, living off the meat of an ox that had drowned in the cross-ing. After three days of searching, he found his family at the Sugar Creek encampment.

The following year, while President Young led the pioneer com-pany across the plains, young Brigham stayed at Winter Quarters with his mother. The following spring in April 1848, President Young, having returned to Winter Quarters for his family, led a com-pany to the Salt Lake Valley. Brigham Jr., a boy of twelve, was made driver of two yoke of oxen and was equal to the task. His early years in the valley were spent herding stock and performing considerable hard manual labor. He participated in many dangerous expeditions against hostile Indians and during the Utah War went on recon-naissance missions in the mountains where he often suffered untold hardships. He was also part of the relief party sent back to meet a handcart company of emigrants, on which trip he was attacked by inflammatory rheumatism, which came near to killing him, and the effects of which he suffered for many years afterward.

Deprived of an education and social contacts during his early years, Brigham was hesitant to take on leadership responsibilities. He felt that he lacked the oratory skills and social graces expected of a son of the Church President and consequently shied away from public assignments. On one occasion at a meeting held in Farming-ton, when he was invited to stand, he arose and ran out the door. A mission to England, where everyone was anxious to hear the son of Brigham Young speak, provided him the opportunity to overcome his shyness. Writing to his father, he reported, "I have been afraid that more is expected of me than I can do. They consider that such a father had ought to have a smart son. I can't help it if they are disappointed in their expectations but I will do my best to answer the prayers of my friends. But I can do nothing without the help of God."[1] Later he wrote, "Give my love to Lott Smith and tell him that I am not so afraid to stand up before a congregation as I once was in Farmington. . . . I'me [sic] getting broke a little."[2]

In April of 1861 he was called as a member of the Salt Lake Stake High Council. The following year, he accompanied Delegate Bernhisel to the eastern United States. It was while there that he received a letter from his father, who wished him to go again on a mission to England. He arrived in Liverpool July 26, 1862 and served in England, Scandinavia, and other parts of Europe, returning home in 1863. On February 4, 1864, he was ordained an Apostle but did not become a member of the Quorum of the Twelve until October 1868, when filling the vacancy left by George A. Smith's being called to the First Presidency. Years later, upon the death of President Lorenzo Snow in 1901, a discussion concerning succession would arise among the Twelve. Brigham Young Jr. was ordained an Apostle (1864) two years before Joseph F. Smith (1866), but Joseph F. was sustained a member of the Quorum of the Twelve (1867) a year before Brigham Jr. (1868). It was decided that seniority was based upon date of sustaining to the Quorum of the Twelve rather than date of ordination to the apostleship. Thus, Joseph F. Smith became President of the Church and Brigham Young Jr. the President of the Quorum of the Twelve. This precedent remains in effect today.

In 1864, Brigham Jr. was called again on a mission to Europe, this time taking his wife, Catherine, with him. There he presided over the European Mission, traveling extensively throughout the British Isles and the Continent, visiting numerous European countries. Upon request from his father, he returned home, leaving Catherine in England. While crossing the Atlantic, the ship encountered a severe storm that blew away part of the ship's rigging. A big, burly Irishman who was a religious crank declared that the storm was due to a Jonah onboard in the shape of a "Mormon" elder and demanded that Brigham be tossed overboard. He raised such a terrible fuss that the captain finally had to intervene. They arrived safely. After his visit in Salt Lake City, Brigham Jr. returned to England and resumed his presidency over the mission. He returned home with his family in the summer of 1867. He would again serve as president of the British Isles Mission from 1890 to 1893. After the death of Ezra T. Benson, he was called by his father to take charge of the affairs of the Church in Cache Valley. He presided there from 1869 until 1877. In 1873, he was called as one of the five assistant counselors to President Brigham Young, acting in that capacity until President Young's death. He served several terms in the Utah Legislature, making several trips east in behalf of the Church. He also traveled extensively throughout the stakes in the Southwest.

For two years following President Brigham Young's death, there was serious and bitter litigation over his estate. Suits and fraudulent claims resulted in the three executors, including Brigham Young Jr., being imprisoned for contempt of court. Sentences were later reversed. Through it all, Brigham Young Jr. gained a reputation for his honesty and proficiency in the way he handled the management of the estate. He would become known as a labor boss, a business manager, a legislator, and a diplomat.

Writing of her brother, Susa Young Gates described Brigham Young Jr. as "a noble representative of his father's family. His gentle wisdom, his merry heart, and his integrity and truth are known to all the Saints. . . . He has naught but contempt for all forms of hypocrisy or deceit. His own life and soul is a clear open book, and he would not gain the whole world were it to be secured through policy or subterfuge."[3] He died in Salt Lake City at the age of sixty-six.

*Albert Carrington*

Born: January 8, 1813, Royalton, Vermont
Ordained Apostle: July 3, 1870
Sustained Counselor to President Brigham Young: April 8, 1873
Sustained Assistant Counselor to President Young: May 9, 1874
Excommunicated: November 7, 1885
Rebaptized: November 1, 1887
Died: September 19, 1889, Salt Lake City, Utah, at age 75

Albert Carrington was born January 8, 1813, in Royalton, Vermont. Studious by nature, he went on to graduate from Dartmouth College in the class of 1833. The following three years, he was employed as a school teacher and studied law in Pennsylvania. From there he moved to Hamilton, Wisconsin, where he engaged in the lead mining industry until he married Rhoda Maria Woods. In July 1841, he joined the Church and, leaving his business behind, gathered to Nauvoo, where he soon became recognized as an intellectual leader in the community. His arrival in Nauvoo marked the time of great crisis, for it was just prior to the Martyrdom of Joseph and Hyrum Smith. In February of 1846, he was among the first of the Saints to cross the Mississippi River in their exodus to the West. Sadly, during his family's travels from Nauvoo to Council Bluffs, three of his four children died. From the encampment at Council Bluffs, he was a member of the Pioneer Company that forged the way to the Great Salt Lake Valley.

Shortly after settling his family in the Salt Lake Valley, he was employed as a member of Captain Stansbury's party of US Topographical Engineers in a circumnavigational expedition to survey the Great Salt Lake. At one point, their craft was stranded on a mud flat in the Bear River when a sudden snowstorm nearly took their lives. Upon completion of the survey, Albert continued in his government employ and was trusted to carry the expedition's records and artifacts to Washington, DC, where he spent the winter of 1850–51 helping to prepare the maps and records for publication. Albert's character is shown in Captain Stansbury's official report, in which he wrote the following:

> Before leaving the Salt Lake City for Fort Hall, I had engaged the service of Albert Carrington, Esq., a member of the Mormon community, who was to act as an assistant on the survey. He was without experience in the use of the instruments; but being a gentleman of liberal education, he soon acquired, under instruction, the requisite skill and, by his zeal, industry, and practical good sense, materially aided us in our subsequent operations. He continued with the party until the termination of the survey, accompanied it to this city, and has since returned to his mountain home, carrying with him the respect and kind wishes of all with whom he was associated.[1]

It should be noted that in honor of his contributions to the Stansbury expedition, one of the major islands in the Great Salt Lake is named after him—Carrington Island.

Albert went on to serve a distinguished career, both in the Church and in the community. Upon the organization of wards in Salt Lake City, he was called as second counselor in the 17th ward bishopric, which position he held for about six years. He also served as clerk of the Salt Lake Stake High Council. When the provisional State of Deseret was organized, he was elected as assessor, tax collector, and treasurer. With the organization of the Utah Territory, he was repeatedly elected a member of the legislative council and served as Territorial Attorney General. He was editor of the *Deseret News* for nine years and was later regent and chancellor of the University of Deseret (now the University of Utah).

In 1868, Albert was sent to England to preside over the European Mission. Albert would preside over this mission three more times in the coming years of his life. Upon his return in 1870, he was ordained an Apostle to fill the vacancy in the Quorum of the Twelve caused by the death of Ezra T. Benson. In 1873, President Young sent a special delegation to Palestine, including George A. Smith of the First Presidency and Lorenzo Snow and Albert Carrington of the Quorum of the Twelve, for the purpose of rededicating and blessing the land for the gathering of the Jews. For more than twenty years, he was President Brigham Young's secretary, and from 1873 until the time of President Young's death, he was assistant counselor to the President of the Church. With the death of Brigham Young, Elder Carrington was appointed one of the administrators of President Young's estate, in which capacity he labored until the estate and the many difficulties connected with it were settled. During this legal process, the executors of the estate (Albert Carrington, Brigham Young Jr., and George Q. Cannon) were imprisoned for contempt of court when refusing to comply with the unjust demands of Judge Jacob Boreman, a very bitter anti-Mormon. However, they were released three-and-a-half weeks later when the verdict was overturned by the Territorial Supreme Court.

In 1875, Elder Carrington came under attack from the anti-Mormon *Salt Lake Tribune,* charging him with adultery and immoral conduct. He was apparently cleared of these charges. However, in 1884, the newspaper again pursued their attack. A thorough investigation of the charges by the Quorum of the Twelve resulted in Elder Carrington's being excommunicated for "crimes of lewd and lascivious conduct and adultery"[2] on November 7, 1885. A few months after his being severed from the Church, he suffered two paralytic strokes, resulting in his being bedridden during the remaining four years of his life. Giving heed to his pleas for clemency, the Quorum of the Twelve allowed him to be rebaptized into the Church on November 1, 1887. He died nearly two years later on September 19, 1889, in Salt Lake City.

*Moses Thatcher*

Born: February 2, 1842, Sangamon County, Illinois
Ordained Apostle: April 9, 1879
Dropped from the Quorum of the Twelve: April 6, 1896
Died: August 21, 1909, Logan, Utah, at age 67

Born in Illinois in 1842, Moses's earliest memories were of the Saints' persecutions and expulsion from Nauvoo and the subsequent trek to the Salt Lake Valley. In 1849, Moses went with his family to California, near Sacramento City, where his father established an eating house that catered to travelers and miners. His father being a man of few words, Moses often listened with rapt attention as his mother discussed religion with ministers traveling through the area. When missionaries came through in December 1856, he listened to them teach and was baptized at the age of fourteen. In March, he was ordained an elder and was called on a mission the following month at the age of fifteen. His feelings of inadequacy made him ill, and in his first attempt to speak, he could not utter a word. It was several weeks later, when hearing a minister slander the character of Joseph Smith and Brigham Young, that voice and inspiration came to him as he rose to defend their names. After that he preached fearlessly and effectively. "Wrapt in the spirit he sometimes spoke for an hour, often correctly quoting Scripture he had never read, the words and sentences, as he declared, appearing before his spiritual eyes, were read, as from an open book."[1] The mission ended when he was called home pending the approach of the US Army to Utah.

Moses first attended school when he was eleven years old. Although embarrassed over his older age, he made rapid advancement. In Utah, not yet sixteen, he again attended school, and during the winter of 1860–61, he attended the University of Deseret. Shortly after marriage he located in Cache Valley. As one of the "minute men," he helped protect the settlements against marauding Indians. When the Cache military district was established, he raised to the rank of captain and then staff member to General Hyde. Living in Logan, he entered into the mercantile business with his father. The business thrived and later became a branch of ZCMI with Moses becoming the superintendent. His later business interests would be varied, extensive, and valuable to the business development of northern Utah and southern Idaho.

His work at ZCMI was interrupted by a call from Brigham Young to serve a mission in England. Upon his return, he served as superintendent of the Cache Valley Sunday Schools, and then as president of the newly organized Cache Valley Stake in May 1877. Two years later, in April 1879, he was ordained an Apostle to fill the vacancy in the Quorum of the Twelve left by the death of Orson Hyde. A few months later, he was appointed to travel to Mexico to open the door of salvation to that nation. This would be the first of several trips to Mexico, and not without dangers. On one occasion, he learned of an attempt to poison him, which failed when the person who was to administer the poison to his drink grew fainthearted. On another occasion, he and his companions had to change their travel route, learning shortly thereafter of fifteen Mexican citizens killed in an Apache raid at the place and time they would have been had they not changed their travel plans. In sailing from Mexico to Florida, a young companion died of typhoid pneumonia. Because of the lack of ice aboard the ship and the oppressive heat, the young man had to be buried at sea. The stress of this incident greatly affected Elder Thatcher, both physically and emotionally. In the seventeen years following his dedication of the Mexican Mission, Elder Thatcher made twenty-three trips to Mexico, traveling a quarter of a million miles on behalf of the Church. In 1886, he helped negotiate the purchase of the seventy-five-thousand-acre "Corrales Basin," where he dedicated the town site of Juarez. Elder Thatcher also served missions among the Crow and Shoshone Indians. For a number of years, he acted as President Woodruff's assistant in the superintendency of the Young Men's Mutual Improvement Association.

Having an interest in politics, Elder Thatcher served in the Territorial Legislative Council, was a member of the State Constitutional Convention in 1872, and was one of the delegates authorized to present the State Constitution to Congress. He was also called on at least two occasions to travel to Washington, DC, on behalf of the Church. Unfortunately, his political interest would lead to his being dropped from the Quorum of the Twelve.

When statehood for Utah was apparent, Elder Thatcher and Elder B. H. Roberts of the Seventy ran in the 1895 election for US Senate and House of Representatives respectively. At a special priesthood meeting held in Salt Lake City, Joseph F. Smith of the First Presidency publicly reproved both brethren for accepting nominations, which, if elected, would take them away from their ecclesiastical duties, without having consulted with the Brethren or having made arrangements for their absence. Many felt this was an attempt by the Church to control the political process. Consequently, President Wilford Woodruff released a public statement saying, in effect, that when a man accepted a position in the governing councils of the Church, it became a grave responsibility and that no man should engage in other activities that would take him from those duties without counseling with the Presidency and getting permission. This was not to dictate a man's position in a political party and certainly a man was free to withdraw from his quorum if he preferred to give himself entirely over to the politics or some other calling. This statement, which became known as the "Political Manifesto" was signed by the Quorum of the Twelve and sustained by the Church membership in

April 6, 1896, during general conference. Elder Thatcher, however, refused to sign, feeling that such a manifesto would lead to ecclesiastical interference in political affairs. After various futile attempts to get him to accept the document, he was deprived of his apostleship for being out of harmony with the First Presidency and Quorum of the Twelve.

Moses Thatcher did, however, retain his Church membership and frequently bore a strong testimony of the truthfulness of the gospel and the divinity of the great Latter-day work. He testified in the Reed Smoot investigation held before the Senate Committee on Privileges and Elections, and was supportive of the Church and its positions and true to his friends and former associates. Upon his death, Logan businesses closed in his honor and special trains brought many leading Church authorities to Logan, with thousands attending the funeral services. Newspapers printed tributes from business and government leaders alike attesting to his goodness and his accomplishments.

*Francis M. Lyman*

Born: January 12, 1840, Good Hope, Illinois
Ordained Apostle: October 27, 1880
Sustained President of the Quorum of the Twelve: October 6, 1903
Died: November 18, 1916, Salt Lake City, Utah, at age 76

orn January 12, 1840, Francis was the eldest son of Amasa Lyman, who, two and a half years later, would be called to the apostleship. His father left Nauvoo with the early companies of Saints. It was not until June 1846 that Francis, with his mother and three other children, all under the care of his maternal grandfather, left Nauvoo and rendezvoused with the Saints at Winter Quarters. In the summer of 1848, though he was only eight years of age, he drove a yoke of cattle and a wagon to the Salt Lake Valley. In 1851, at the age of eleven, he drove livestock to California, where his father and Elder Charles C. Rich had purchased a ranch in San Bernardino. Here, Francis attended school during the winter months and in the summer months was employed in handling livestock and freighting goods between southern California and Utah, making sixteen trips over the desert area during the years he lived in California.

It was on the docks of San Francisco that he first saw Rhoda Taylor, who had arrived from Australia with her widowed mother and other converts. He was taken with her immediately but felt unworthy to approach the stately looking girl. Over time he won her heart, and they secretly agreed to marry at a future time. However, when Rhoda's mother heard of their intentions, she was opposed to the marriage, mainly because of Francis's use of tobacco. Eventually the mother consented and the two were married in the mother's home November 1857, both being seventeen years of age. It was said that "the circumstances made the marriage about as gloomy as a funeral."[1] Through prayer and fasting, he overcame his smoking habit, and in his later years as an Apostle, Francis would be remembered for his strict ideas on temperance and the keeping of the Word of Wisdom.

Prior to the marriage, Francis was called on a mission to England. However, when he and others reached Salt Lake City, word came of the approaching Johnston's Army. His mission was subsequently cancelled and he was sent back to San Bernardino to help move California Saints to Utah. It was during this time that the Mountain Meadows Massacre occurred on September 11, 1857. Two days later, Francis came through the meadows with the Tanner Matthews wagon company on his way to San Bernardino. Near the road they saw dead bodies lying on the ground without clothes on. Either the burial party had missed them or animals had already pulled them from their graves. Seventeen year old Francis wrote that a herd of cattle that he assumed belonged to the massacred people "came rushing around our wagons, making the night hideous with their bawling, and that, mingling with the unearthly stench from the decaying bodies of the human beings, made it the most terrific night of my life. I felt great relief as we put distance between us and the fatal spot."[2] So affected was he by the experience that over the ensuing years he would interview people in an attempt to find who was responsible for the massacre. Returning to Salt Lake City with his father's family and his new bride, Francis made Utah his permanent home.

In 1860, Francis was ordained a Seventy and called to fulfill his earlier missionary assignment to England. Before leaving, he built a log room in Beaver, Utah, for his wife and child. In England he was a vigorous missionary, returning to his family after being away two and a half years. The following year he was asked by President Brigham Young to move to Fillmore. Here he lived for fourteen years, becoming a leader in political, Church, business, and manufacturing enterprises in that county. Among his many titles, he was assistant assessor of the US revenue service, lieutenant-colonel of the local militia, member of the House of the General Assembly of the State of Deseret, superintendent of schools, and prosecuting attorney. With his father, he built, owned, and operated flour mills and was secretary and treasurer of the county cooperative companies. Called on a second mission to England in 1873, he traveled through many European countries. In 1877, he was called to move to Tooele and preside over the Tooele Stake. In his new home, he was elected as county recorder and representative to the legislature. He also gained a reputation for his fight against existing political corruption. Three years later he was called to the Quorum of the Twelve Apostles.

In 1883, he was called on a mission to the Ute tribe. Feeling overwhelmed by this assignment, he climbed to the top of a mountain to pray. As he began to pour out his heart unto the Lord, raging winds descended upon him, nearly driving him from the mountain top. No sooner did his prayer end than the winds stopped. On another day, as his group neared the Indian encampments, he was struck down with unbearable pain in his left side. So severe was the pain that he thought he was going to die. He later recorded that during his agony, every good act of his life passed before him and strange to say, not an evil thing that he had done came to his mind—nothing but good. For two hours the pain lasted, until it was finally alleviated through the administrations of the priesthood. Reaching their destination, they were welcomed by both the Indians and the government agents. Among the Indians, many received the Book of Mormon and were baptized.

During the anti-polygamy crusades, Elder Lyman went into hiding while visiting settlements. Eventually, in 1889, he surrendered himself to the US marshals and was sentenced to eighty-five days in prison. Lyman had a talent with youth and served on the Sunday School Union Boards and on the general board of the Young

Men's Mutual Improvement Association. In 1901, he was called as president of the European Mission. With the death of Brigham Young Jr., he was sustained as President of the Quorum of the Twelve on October 6, 1903.

Lyman died in his home of pneumonia on November 18, 1916, at the age of seventy-six. So many turned out for the funeral that services had to be moved from the Assembly Hall to the Tabernacle. It was reported that President Joseph F. Smith leaned over the open casket of his long-time companion and co-laborer and wept, "O, Marion! How can I get along without you?"[3]

*John Henry Smith*

Born: September 18, 1848, Carbunca (now Council Bluffs), Iowa
Ordained Apostle: October 27, 1880
Sustained Second Counselor to President Joseph F. Smith: April 7, 1910
Died: October 13, 1911, Salt Lake City, Utah, at age 63

J ohn was born in September 1848 in what is now known as Council Bluffs, Iowa, the son of President George A. Smith and Sarah Ann Libby. In 1847, George A. Smith was part of the Pioneer Company that forged the way to the Salt Lake Valley. He then returned to prepare his family for the trek westward. In the summer of 1849, he started west with his family, arriving in the valley October 27, 1849. John's mother, who had been an invalid for years, died of consumption in the summer of 1851. He was then taken into the care of his mother's sister, Hannah Maria, who was a plural wife of his father. Inasmuch as his father was away from home much of the time fulfilling his duties as an Apostle, it was to her John owed much of his future success in life. The bond of affection between them would be shown many years later when he recorded in his journal, September 21, 1906, "My Mother Hannah Maria Libby Smith died this morning at 2:30."[1] In the summer of 1852, Elder George A. moved his family to Provo. His duties as an Apostle left him little time at home. Schooling at that time was poor, but every effort was made to give the children as good an education as possible. As early as January of 1852, his grandfather, Patriarch John Smith, gave young John a patriarchal blessing, which would be a guide to him in his future years.

While a young boy living in Provo, John had a miraculous escape from death. In the early summer of 1862, he, along with two other boys, was crossing the Provo River. It was a time of high water, and in crossing, their small boat capsized. John became entangled in some driftwood and was kept under water for some time. People who were standing along the shore had given him up for lost, when suddenly an unseen power seemed to lift his body onto the bank. Later he learned that at that time, his father, being forcibly impressed with the feeling that his son was in extreme danger, had dressed himself in his temple clothing and had prayed to the Lord to save his son.

As a young married man, John Henry lived in Provo and worked as a telegraph operator. He later left that position to help build the Central Pacific Railway during its two hundred miles of completion. Afterward he was offered a good situation in Sacramento, California, by the governor of the state, but he declined in order to work with his father and family in Utah. During the ensuing years, he became involved in politics serving as assistant clerk of the House of Representatives and assistant clerk in the Constitutional Convention. He also traveled to various locations throughout the territory with his father, becoming acquainted with many of the people. Through his father, he became intimate with Brigham Young and asked him many questions concerning Church government. Years later when he was an Apostle, he reported to his Brethren of the Twelve that in answer to his question, "In case of your death to whom should I look to lead the Church?" President Young responded that John should look "to any one of the Council of the Apostles in the order of ordination, baring Orson Hyde and Orson Pratt who had forfeited their right."[2] It was John's given understanding that no man who had faltered or turned back could lead the Church.

*John Henry Smith*

In May of 1874, John was called on a mission to Europe, serving in England. In 1875, in company with President Joseph F. Smith and other elders, he visited Denmark, Germany, Switzerland, and France. However, he was called home in July of 1875 due to the severe illness of his father. He was able to spend fifteen days at his father's bedside before his death on September 1, 1875. At home, he was in the employ of the Utah Central Railway Company and was called as bishop of the 17th Ward in Salt Lake City. Politically active, he served three terms as a member of the Salt Lake City council and, in 1881, was elected a member of the Territorial Legislature. He was one of the first and foremost in advocating the principles of the Republican Party in the territory. He was unanimously elected by the 107 delegates to be the Chair of the Utah Constitutional Convention for the proposed State of Utah that was held between March 4 and May 8, 1895. The result of the convention was a draft Constitution, which was accepted by the United States Congress in 1896, when Utah officially became a state.

John Henry was called to the apostleship by President John Taylor in October of 1880. He was then sent in 1882 to preside over the European Mission, taking him away from home for two and a half years before his return to Utah. In the summer of 1885, he was arrested on charges of unlawful cohabitation, but following a brief hearing, charges were dropped against him. Although John Henry's apostolic duties and public service did not allow him the time to be personally involved in business enterprises to any large extent, he was nonetheless associated with a number of leading business institutions in Utah as an officer or director. In 1891, he received a special commission from President Woodruff. Many of the Saints in Arizona had not had the privilege to be married in the temple due to their poverty, which prevented them from making the necessary journey. In a letter to Elder John Smith, President Woodruff directed him to travel through Arizona and "to dedicate rooms which are now used for prayer according to the holy order [of the temple ceremonies], and in those rooms solemnize marriages such as are properly recommended," for the benefit of those who, through no fault of their own, were unable "to go to the temple of the Lord to be sealed for time and eternity."[3] In 1904, he was summoned to Washington, DC, as a witness before the Senate Committee on Privileges and Elections in the case of Senator Reed Smoot. In December 1905, he traveled with President Joseph F. Smith to Vermont for the dedication of the monument at Joseph Smith's birthplace. In April 1910, he was set apart as second counselor in the First Presidency. Unfortunately, his service in this calling was limited, due to what seemed an untimely death on October 13, 1911. His death came without previous warning because he appeared to be robust and strong, active and full of vitality up until the sudden end of his life.

Among his many children, John Henry fathered George Albert Smith, who later served in the Quorum of the Twelve and became the eighth President of the Church. John Henry Smith and George Albert Smith are the only father-son pair to have served in the Quorum of the Twelve at the same time. They served together between 1903 and 1910.

*George Teasdale*

Born: December 8, 1831, London, England
Ordained Apostle: October 16, 1882
Died: June 9, 1907, Salt Lake City, Utah, at age 75

George Teasdale was born December 8, 1831, in London, England. Being of a studious and thoughtful disposition by nature, he obtained the best education that could be had at the public schools and the London University. Following his schooling, he entered the office of an architect and surveyor, but he left when he became disillusioned because of their dishonesty. He then learned the upholstery business. Although his mother was a member of the Church of England, he was not impressed with its doctrines. Yet his mother impressed the importance of religion upon him and consequently he was a student of the scriptures from childhood. In 1851, he was first introduced to the Church through a tract entitled "Mormonism" put out by the Tract Society of the Church of England. Shortly afterward, a member of the Church came to work where he was employed. He was an unassuming man with a powerful testimony of the gospel. Despite ridicule and arguments from fellow workers, he was never overcome. George was deeply impressed and began investigating the principles of the gospel as the man explained them. Undeterred by the opposition that came from friends and acquaintances, George was baptized in August 1852 at the age of twenty.

So impressed was George with the simplicity and beauty of the gospel that he felt anyone who heard it so taught would naturally be converted. He soon learned how wrong he was. Being ordained a priest, and later an elder, George spent much of his time preaching and giving lectures on religious subjects. At first he was not a natural speaker and had little time to study. His early attempts at preaching the gospel met with total failure. But as he learned to rely more upon the Spirit of the Lord and to seek that Spirit through prayer, he began to meet with some success. While thus laboring, he met Emily Emma Brown, whom he married in 1853. She proved to be a great support to him amid trials of poverty and ridicule. His missionary zeal eventually led to his being called as president of the Somerstown branch of the London conference, as well as his involvement in other Church and missionary-related activities. In 1857, he was called to preside over the Cambridge conference. This would require practically all of his time. Accepting the call with the encouragement of his wife, he gave up an excellent position of employment, sold many of his possessions, and saw that his wife was made comfortable. He then entered into his new calling with complete dedication of time and effort. Within a year, he was presiding over three conferences, and the following year found him in charge of the Scottish Mission.

In 1861 he was released from his callings to come to Zion. Two of his four children had died and it was his desire to make the trip as comfortable as possible for his remaining family. However, most of his financial means had been exhausted and so it was necessary for them to sail to the States in the steerage of an emigrant ship. Upon arriving at Florence, Nebraska, he was called upon to keep the records and accounts of the emigration. Consequently, he and his family did not leave until the last company of the season arrived in Florence. The Teasdale family finally arrived in Salt Lake City on September 27,

1861. There George became engaged in teaching school and became associated with the Tabernacle Choir. In 1862, he was engaged to take charge of President Brigham Young's merchandise store, thereby becoming well acquainted with President Young. Five years later, he took charge of the General Tithing Store. The following year, 1868, he was called on a mission to England, where he labored in the *Millennial Star* office. The next year, he was assigned to New York to assist with the emigration of the Saints. Upon his return to Utah in 1869, he became employed with the newly established Zion's Cooperative Mercantile Institution. His position there was briefly interrupted by a mission to the southern states, after which he returned to his former employment. He would later have to forsake an excellent position at ZCMI, by which he could have comfortably provided for his family because he was called as president of the Juab Stake. While living in Nephi, he took contracts for the construction of a portion of the Utah Southern Railroad, was acting president of a cooperative store, and was involved in other enterprises. He also during this time served in two sessions of the Utah Legislature.

In October of 1882, George Teasdale was called to the Quorum of the Twelve. His apostolic calling led to many varied assignments, including a mission to the Indian Territory, visiting settlements in the Southwest, and assisting in forming a colony in Mexico. In the early and mid 1800s, US marshals were zealously executing the Edmunds-Tucker Law against those Saints who were practicing plural marriage in the United States. Rather than renounce family ties that had already been established or go to prison, many had fled to Mexico as a haven from persecution. President John Taylor commissioned Elders George Teasdale and Moses Thatcher of the Quorum of the Twelve, along with others, to go and locate a place of refuge for the Saints. They were finally granted permission by the Mexican government to purchase lands in northwest Chihuahua, about a hundred miles south of the US border. In November of 1886, he sailed for England where he served as president of the European Mission until 1890. Having a love for children, Elder Teasdale had earlier taught Primary and later served in the Sunday School program. In speaking to children, he endeavored to impress upon their minds the necessity of living near the Lord, and he emphasized the importance of keeping the Word of Wisdom.

Elder Teasdale died in Salt Lake City, June 9, 1907, at the age of seventy-five. An article in the *Deseret News* said of him in part, "The great theme of his discourses was the Atonement of our Savior, and the way in which his precious blood cleanses all men who will succeed Him, from their sins. The subtle distinction in point of doctrine, the careful and detailed explanation of some idea in theology, the defense by the cannonade of argument, of an assailed position—these he left to others. He concerned himself mainly with the simple and tender story of the cross. The main thing with him was the work of the Redeemer of the world, and how it can touch the conduct of man. The Lord gave him light to see it."[1]

*Heber J. Grant*

Born: November 22, 1856, Salt Lake City, Utah
Ordained Apostle: October 16, 1882
Sustained President of the Quorum of the Twelve: November 23, 1916
Ordained President of the Church: November 23, 1918
Died: May 14, 1945, Salt Lake City, Utah at age 88

J ust a week and a half after Heber's birth, his father, President
Jedediah M. Grant, first counselor to President Brigham Young,
died, leaving Heber totally in the care of his mother, Rachel
Ridgeway Ivins Grant. Though they struggled to survive financially,
Rachel was determined to be free of charity and supported herself
and Heber as a seamstress. Heber recalled that many times he sat on
the floor until late at night, pumping his mother's sewing machine in
order to give her much needed relief. Rachel's wealthy brothers in the
East told her that they would see she was well provided for once she
denounced Mormonism. But she chose poverty within the Church
over affluence outside of it. This would leave a lasting impression
upon Heber. Rachel did all she could to see that Heber received

a good education. As for Heber's Church activity, Rachel received much help from the 13th Ward, which included in its membership many General Authorities. In spite of his humble beginnings, there were times when his future in the Church was indicated. Heber C. Kimball once lifted him upon a table and prophesied that he would be an Apostle and become a greater man in the Church than his father. But, as with most youths, his younger years were not without their struggles.

When Heber was seventeen years old, President Young talked to him about serving a mission. Heber became excited, because in his patriarchal blessing he was told that he would begin his ministry at a very young age. But when general conference came, his name was not among the newly called missionaries. He was devastated. What he did not know was that President Young's counselors had objected to the call, stating that he was already serving a splendid mission providing for his mother. Unknown to others, the incident haunted Heber for several years. "'I was tempted seriously for several years to renounce my faith in the Gospel because this blessing was not ful-filled,' he later admitted. 'The spirit would come over me . . . that the patriarch had lied to me, and that I should throw the whole business away.'"[1] His faith uncertain, he became interested in the writings of Robert G. Ingersoll, the nineteenth-century atheist, and started associating with friends not of LDS standards. He later reflected, "I stood as it were upon a brink of usefulness or upon the brink of making a failure of my life."[2] He credited the 13th Ward for his salva-tion. With ward and stake callings came a rejuvenation of his faith.

At the age of fifteen, Heber entered a series of office jobs and found his interests in the world of insurance and finances. By the age of nineteen, he had bought out the insurance company for which he worked. His financial success allowed him to marry before the age of twenty-one. However, his success only led to dreams of further accomplishments. His mother reminded him of his Church destiny, but at that time, he had other plans, telling his mother that he was only interested in becoming a successful business man. But the Lord had His own plans, and at the age of twenty-three, Heber was called as president of the Tooele Stake. At the stake conference in which he was sustained, he spoke for seven and a half minutes, during which he "told everything [he] could think of . . . and part of it twice." After the conference, he overheard someone say, "It is a pity that, if we have to have a boy preside over this Stake of Zion, the Authorities . . . could not find one with sense enough to talk ten minutes."[3] In the coming years he would be in great demand as a speaker before member and nonmember groups alike, receiving standing ovations. His subject was always the same—the history of the Church and the people and principles of the Church.

As he grew spiritually in the calling, his financial problems weighed less and less upon his mind. He began to sense a different future from the one of his earlier ambitions. Fourteen months after his call, he attended a reunion of his old friends known as the Wasatch crowd. He reflected afterward: "They are all good hearted . . . but I am sorry to say [that they] have but little faith. . . . I take greater joy in associating with men that love to talk of the principles of the Gospel than I do in dancing with my old friends."[4] Heber's life had taken a different direction.

On October 16, 1882, less than two years after his calling as stake president, Heber was called to the office of President John Taylor, where he heard President Taylor read a revelation calling Heber to the Quorum of the Twelve. Heber was not quite twenty-six years of age, and during the next few months, he experienced a "dark night of the soul," in which he continued to question his ability and preparation to be an Apostle. Traveling to the Navajo Reservation, he separated himself from the party with whom he had traveled. Alone, he seemed to see and hear in his mind his father, Jedediah Grant, and the Prophet Joseph Smith discussing vacancies in the Quorum of the Twelve and choosing Heber to fulfill it. Heber then took from his pocket and read his copy of President Taylor's revelation calling him to the apostleship and wept. He never doubted his calling again.

The next decade saw Elder Grant involved in a flurry of business transactions designed to assist the Church. But in 1893, financial panic struck the country, which caught the Church financially overextended. Heber was assigned to travel east to renew short-term credit. In New York City, he knelt in morning prayer and offered the Lord his life in exchange for a way of saving the Church's finances.

By that afternoon, he had procured a loan that allowed the Church to get through one of its most difficult times.

As Elder Grant's reputation grew, he found himself in situations where he could have run—probably successfully—for governor and senator. Both were tempting to him, but inner reflections saw such actions as satisfying his pride, not the Lord's purposes.

He went on to become President of the Twelve and then President of the Church. During all this time, his abilities led the Church into the beginning of financial prosperity.

One of his greatest legacies as President was the welfare program of the Church, which he instituted in 1936. He said, "Our primary purpose was to set up, in so far as it might be possible, a system under which the curse of idleness would be done away, the evils of a dole abolished, and independence, industry, thrift and self-respect be once more established amongst our people. The aim of the Church is to help people to help themselves."[5] President Grant died in Salt Lake City, Utah, from cardiac failure as a result of arteriosclerosis at the age of eighty-eight.

*John W. Taylor*

Born: May 15, 1858, Provo, Utah
Ordained Apostle: April 9, 1884
Resigned from the Quorum of the Twelve: October 28, 1905
Excommunicated: March 26, 1911
Died: October 10, 1916, Salt Lake City, Utah, at age 58

John W. Taylor was born the son of John Taylor, the third President of the Church, and Sophia Whitaker. He was born in Provo, Utah, May 15, 1858, at the time that the Saints were taking refuge in Provo as Johnston's army approached Salt Lake City. As with most active members of the Church, he grew up serving in various callings. Occupationally, he worked in his father's sawmill, secured a position in the county clerk's office, and later worked in the office of the *Deseret News.*

In the fall of 1880, he was called on a mission to the southern states. During this time, he enjoyed much power in preaching the gospel; the spirit of prophecy rested upon him to a great extent, and many who were sick were healed through his administrations. In writing to his lifelong friend and early missionary companion, Matthias F. Cowley, he made this prediction: "I believe I speak by the spirit of prophecy when I say, if you are faithful you will yet become one of the Twelve Apostles of the Church of Jesus Christ in all the world, and by the power of God and the eternal Priesthood will become great in wisdom and knowledge. Amen!"[1] Neither of them mentioned this prophecy to anyone until after its fulfillment fifteen years later.

In 1884, John was called to the apostleship. As a special witness of Christ, many other missions and assignments followed. He became especially interested in the development of settlements in Canada, was respected by Mormons and non-Mormons alike, and was held in high esteem by many government officials in that country with whom he had many business transactions. The Taylor Stake in Raymond, Canada, was named in his honor. The stake was later renamed the Raymond Stake; however, Taylor Street and the Taylor Street chapel in that same town continued to give honor to his name. In May of 1888, during the dedicatory services of the Manti Temple, it was reported that in some instances, halos of light were seen around the heads of some of the speakers. Elder Taylor was one of those designated speakers.

In September of 1890, when President Wilford Woodruff presented the Manifesto abolishing plural marriage to the Quorum of the Twelve for their response, Elder Taylor had obvious problems with it. His father, President John Taylor, had defied the US government and declared that the Church would be faithful to God and His laws. Now President Woodruff seemed to be making an about-face. Elder Taylor responded,

> I do not yet feel quite right about it. My father when president of the Church, sought to find a way to evade the conflict between the Saints and government on the question of plural marriage but the Lord said it was an eternal and unchangeable law and must stand. President Woodruff lately received an encouraging revelation in regard to this principle, and now I ask myself, "Is the Lord a child that he thus changes?" Yet I feel the Lord giveth and the Lord can also take it away.[2]

President George Q. Cannon had earlier justified the Manifesto based upon two considerations: When the Lord gives a commandment and His people are effectively hindered from keeping it by their enemies, the Lord accepts their offering and no longer requires their keeping that commandment. And the authority that gives a commandment has the power to revoke it. Yet as difference of opinion arose between Elder Taylor, the First Presidency, and members of the Quorum of the Twelve in regard to the Manifesto, Elder Taylor resigned from his position as one of the Apostles in October of 1905. In his letter of resignation he stated:

> I have always believed that the government of the United States had jurisdiction only within its own boundaries, and that the term 'laws of the land,' in the Manifesto, meant merely the laws of the United States. I find now that this opinion is different to that expressed by the church authorities, who have declared that the prohibition against plural marriage extended to every place and to every part of the church. . . . But I have never taken that as binding upon me or the church, because it [such interpretation] was never presented for adoption by 'common consent' as was the Manifesto itself, and I have disputed its authority as a law or a rule of the church.[3]

Elder Taylor's friend and associate, Elder Matthias Cowley, also resigned from the Quorum of the Twelve, handing in a letter of resignation expressing similar views. Nearly six years later, Elder Taylor was excommunicated from the Church because of his private disregard for the Manifesto.

Notwithstanding the breach that existed between him and the leading Brethren, Elder Taylor remained faithful in his testimony of the gospel. He died of stomach cancer in his home in Forest Dale, Utah, October 10, 1916, at the age of fifty-eight. On the day of his death the *Deseret Evening News* paid tribute to him in an obituary that read in part,

> Early in life John W. Taylor developed a marked spirituality and was the recipient of many manifestations of the power of God. His testimonies of the gospel and of the missions of the Savior and the Prophet Joseph Smith were deeply grounded in his soul, and to them he remained firm and unshaken to the end. . . . His inspired discourses will never be forgotten. He will be remembered as one filled with the inspiration of the Holy Ghost. . . . He was filled with the spirit of prophecy, and many of his utterances have realized a striking fulfillment. . . . He got out of harmony with the Church and as a result the Council of the Twelve

excommunicated him from the Church; but he never became bitter toward the Church. . . . His family and friends who stood by his bedside during his last illness will never forget his beautiful teachings and exhortations, upholding the doctrines of the gospel, the authority of the holy priesthood, exhorting all to keep the commandments of God.[4]

John W. Taylor was posthumously rebaptized on May 21, 1965, and had all his blessings restored to him by proxy under the hands of Joseph Fielding Smith, President of the Quorum of the Twelve, with the unanimous approval of the First Presidency—David O. McKay, President—and the Quorum of the Twelve Apostles.

*Marriner W. Merrill*

Born: September 25, 1832, Sackville, New Brunswick
Ordained Apostle: October 7, 1889
Died: February 6, 1906, Logan, Utah, at age 73

To some is given one gift, and to some another. It would appear that Elder Merrill was blessed with the gift of divine intervention. He was born in New Brunswick, one of thirteen children, and his young life was much like that of any other farmer in the area where he grew up. But at the age of nine he received an open vision showing him his future life and that of the people with whom he would live. He saw the Church, Joseph Smith, and Brigham Young. He saw Brigham leading the Saints from Nauvoo to the Sale Lake Valley. Never before had he seen covered wagons or mule teams as he saw in the vision. He saw two friends of his youth as grown men with more than one wife, and had the divinity of plural marriage revealed to him. He saw the development of the Church and the persecutions it would go through. A voice told him that all he saw was true but that he should speak of it to no one. One day he dared to ask his mother why plural marriage was not practiced as it was in the Old Testament. She answered in surprise by asking what he knew of such things. He dared not mention the subject again.

When missionaries came into the area, Marriner responded to their preaching by being baptized in April 1952, at the age of nineteen. About a year before, he had learned that his mother had been a member of the Church for a long time, having been baptized in 1836. His father never joined the Church. He had a sister who also joined but subsequently married a nonmember and turned away from the faith. Though no other members of his family joined the Church, they showed no hostility toward it. In 1853, following the death of his father, he started west to join the Saints. In Kanesville, he joined a company consisting of eleven wagons on its way to Salt Lake City and arrived in the valley September 11, 1853. During their crossing of the plains, Marriner and one other boy decided to cross the Platte River to get some cattle that had been left on the other side by earlier travelers. Marriner soon became exhausted in the swift current and was swept downriver. As he started to sink beneath the waters, he landed mysteriously on a sandbar. Here he was able to regain some of his strength. But when Brother Reese, who had been swimming after Marriner, caught up to him, he was unable to locate the bar upon which Marriner stood. Together they were able to swim to the safety of the shore.

In the valley, Marriner eventually set up his own profitable business of making shingles. During the winter of 1855 he had a remarkable experience. It was an extremely bitter cold day when he went up the canyon to gather a load of logs. He had thought to join with other men up the canyon, but due to the cold they were not there. He felled and trimmed the trees and began to load them. He had loaded the first log on the sled and had turned away when the blocking gave way and the log slipped from the sled, catching him in the hollow of his legs and throwing him forward across the other logs. With the heavy log across the back of his legs, he could not move. Suffering from the cold and the pain which felt as if his legs were being crushed, and thinking that surely he was going to die, he lost consciousness. When he regained consciousness, he found himself sitting upon the load of logs which had been loaded upon the sled, with all his belongings about him. His oxen, which he had left chained to a stump, were hitched to the sled and pulling the load down the canyon. When he arrived home, his wife, Sarah, helped him into the cabin, where he had to remain for several days before he was again able to be up and about.

In 1854, Marriner moved to sparsely populated Bountiful where he set up his shingle-making business. He received a generous grant of one-hundred acres of land from Brigham Young. He gave one-third to his father-in-law and divided what was left with a poor Scandinavian neighbor. Brigham later said that when giving Marriner the grant, he felt satisfied that he would not keep it all to himself. In March of 1860, Marriner moved to Cache Valley under the advice of Elders Benson and Hyde. Traveling north through the valley, he heard a voice say, "Turn around and go south." The words repeated and immediately he turned around and went southward, stopping in the location now known as Richmond. Here he eventually operated a large farm and a grist mill. He was also a contractor in the construction of the Utah Northern Railroad and helped bring much-needed employment to the people of the area.

Being a natural leader, he was called as bishop in Richmond, a position he held for eighteen years. In 1884, he was called as the first president of the Logan Temple, and in 1889, he was ordained an Apostle, holding both of those positions throughout the remainder of his life. It was during this time that Satan appeared to President Merrill in his office and ordered him to close the temple. When President Merrill refused, Satan threatened to send forth his legions throughout the area to dissuade the people from doing their temple work. For some time afterward a spirit of indifference seemed to take possession of the people and few went to the temple. Another spiritual event took place shortly after the death of one of Elder Merrill's sons, which caused him to grieve deeply. While Elder Merrill was returning home from the temple in his carriage, his departed son appeared to him along the roadside and told him, "Father, you are mourning my departure unduly! . . . You should take comfort, for you know there is much work to be done here and it was necessary for me to be called."[1] It brought comfort to Elder Merrill to know that his son's death was in keeping with God's will.

In the early 1880s, President John Taylor asked Marriner for a thousand dollars without explaining why he needed it. President Taylor then invested the money in a mining company in Marriner's name. For years following, the mine paid rich dividends, which Elder Merrill used to finance his children's educational expenses. When his need for the money came toward an end, the mine, by strange coincidence, became exhausted and ceased to pay dividends. Again, the Lord had intervened in his behalf.

In 1899, Elder Merrill was called to serve as president of the Cache Stake in addition to his two other callings. During his years in Cache Valley, he was also active in civil affairs. He served two terms in the state legislature, he was a member of the county court for over ten years, and he was postmaster in Richmond for twenty years. For nearly four years, he was a member of the agricultural college board, and then he served on the Brigham Young College Board. As an Apostle, he continued his labors in the Logan Temple and traveled to various stakes throughout Zion until the time of his death on February 6, 1906. He died peacefully in his home in Logan after suffering a long illness. He was buried in Richmond, Utah.

*Anthon H. Lund*

Born: May 15, 1844, Aalborg, Denmark
Ordained Apostle: October 7, 1889
Sustained Second Counselor to President Joseph F. Smith:
    October 17, 1901
Sustained First Counselor to President Smith: April 7, 1910
Sustained First Counselor to President Heber J. Grant:
    November 23, 1918
Died: March 2, 1921, Salt Lake City, Utah, at age 76

Born May 15, 1844, in Aalborg, Denmark, Anthon was only three years old when his mother became seriously ill and died. In the fall of that same year, his father was drafted into the Danish army. Consequently, young Anthon was reared primarily by his grandmother, with whom he formed a close bond. In school, Anthon showed an aptitude for learning and rapidly advanced from one grade to another. In some cases, this rapid rise aroused the jealously and ire of some of the students, but over time, Anthon demonstrated leadership among the students in general. Having no brothers or sisters, he spent a great deal of time reading and found special delight in reading the Bible.

When Anthon was nine years old, his grandmother and his uncle converted to "Mormonism." Church members at that time did not send their children to public schools due to persecution. Anthon was the only student associated with the Church in his school, but he was able to gain the respect of the other students, as well as the teachers. His school principal said to him on one occasion, "I thought you were persuaded by others, but I see you are thoroughly convinced of the truth of 'Mormonism.' Follow your honest convictions, my boy. I would not hinder you from obeying the dictates of your conscience."[1] Finally, on his twelfth birthday, he was baptized. A year later, he was called to teach emigrating Saints English, to distribute tracts, and to help the elders hold meetings. He also often read the *Millennial Star* to the Saints, translating it from English into Danish.

During the four and a half years Anthon served as a missionary, he constantly made friends, even in areas where elders suffered persecutions. On one occasion, he was run out of a house and chased down the street by an irate woman brandishing her fire-tongs. Years later in Utah, a woman said to him, "You do not know me, but I saw you once." She reminded him of the incident when he was chased and continued, "I was her neighbor, and seeing her running after you, I asked her what you had done. She said that you had invited her to a Mormon meeting. I became curious to learn something about the 'Mormons' and went to the meeting. I heard you speak and was convinced of the truth."[2] On another occasion, when he was scheduled to address a group of villagers, the locals had gotten the blacksmith, a bully of several parishes, drunk in order to get him to assail Anthon and his companions. But when others began to harass the elders, the blacksmith forcibly defended them and ordered all to be quiet. Only after the meeting was over did the blacksmith seem to realize he had defended the "wrong side." Anthon found that his youth often gained sympathy from others who would listen to him when they would not listen to older elders and that the Lord blessed his efforts with many conversions. At sixteen, he was ordained an elder and was appointed president over the Aalborg branch.

In 1862, at the age of eighteen, Anthon immigrated to Utah, arriving in Salt Lake City the September 23, 1862. From the time of his arrival, his life was one of continual activity and usefulness.

In 1864, he was called to go as a Church teamster to the Missouri River to bring immigrating Saints to the valley. That winter he was engaged in teaching school, which would continue to be his favorite occupation. In 1865, he, along with other young men, was called by Brigham Young to learn telegraphy, after which he ran the telegraph office in Mt. Pleasant. In 1870, he moved to Ephraim, where he married Sarah Ann Peterson. According to family tradition, when Anthon knelt and proposed to Sarah Ann, she accepted on the condition that he would never take a plural wife. Years later, when President Woodruff issued his Manifesto, Anthon was the only member of the First Presidency and the Quorum of the Twelve who was a monogamist.

The following year, he was called on his first foreign mission to Scandinavia. However, he was summoned home early due to his wife's serious illness. Upon his return, he worked at the Cooperative store in Ephraim, eventually becoming the manager, which position he held for ten years. At the time he became manager, stock was down to fifty cents on the dollar. In the first year under his leadership, stock dividends paid 12.5 percent; the second year was 15 percent; and for many years thereafter it was 25 percent. Over the ensuing years, he served in many other callings, including president of the Scandinavia Mission. At the October conference of the Church in 1889, he was called as a member of the Twelve Apostles. In 1891, he became president of the Manti Temple. From 1893 to 1896, he was president of the European Mission, and in 1897, he traveled to the Ottoman Empire, where he organized the Turkish Mission. In 1899, upon the death of Franklin D. Richards, he became Church historian. That same year in general conference, he gave a talk emphasizing that it was no longer Church policy to encourage Saints to emigrate to the Western United States. In civil affairs, he was elected as a member of the Territorial Legislature, during which time he introduced legislation for establishing Utah State University. In business, he became director of Zion's Savings Bank and of ZCMI, as well as working with other businesses.

In 1901, Elder Lund was called to be second counselor in the First Presidency, and with the death of President John R. Winder, he was appointed first counselor. President Lund was known for being focused on the simple, traditional doctrines of the gospel, refusing to speculate. He served on the reading committee for Talmage's manuscripts of *Articles of Faith* and *Jesus the Christ*, offering numerous additions, clarifications, and deletions. As Church historian, he supervised B. H. Roberts's work on the *History of the Church*. Unfortunately, Anthon's impact upon the doctrine and history of the Church has gone unappreciated since he, himself, wrote no books. It was during the prolonged illness of President Joseph F. Smith that President Lund carried much of the burden of the president's office. At the death of President Smith, he was called as President Grant's first counselor. He also served as president of the Salt Lake Temple and was President of the Quorum of the Twelve. He died March 2, 1921, from a duodenal ulcer, an ailment that had troubled him for many years.

*Abraham H. Cannon*

Born: March 12, 1859, Salt Lake City, Utah
Sustained one of Presidents of First Quorum of Seventy: October 8, 1882
Ordained Apostle: October 7, 1889
Died: July 19, 1896, Salt Lake City, Utah, at age 37

Abraham was born the son of George Q. Cannon and Elizabeth Hoagland on March 12, 1859, in Salt Lake City, Utah. Being a studious boy, he was given the best opportunities for education that were available in the territory, eventually graduating from Deseret University. With his father being editor of the *Deseret News,* he worked for the newspaper for a time as an errand boy. Some of the skills learned there would be put to future use. He later went on to learn the carpenter's trade at the Church carpenter shop and worked on the Temple Block. He also took up the study of architecture and became an architect.

In 1879, Abraham was called on a mission to Europe. After spending some time in England, he was assigned to the Swiss-German mission, where he came to master the German language. He traveled throughout both Switzerland and Germany and wrote many of the hymns that were sung by the German Saints. Sadly, during his mission his mother died. Returning home in June of 1882, he felt obligated to attend a German-speaking Sunday School. However, his father, who was unable to spend as much time as he desired with his family due to his many Church responsibilities, assigned Abraham to care for the family and teach them in family Sunday School. In the fall of 1882 he was ordained and set apart as one of the seven presidents of the First Council of Seventy, giving him a General Authority status at the young age of twenty-three. He wrote, "I was never more surprised in my life, as I had received no intimation of this appointment."[1] Following this ordination, he proceeded to travel extensively throughout the Church in the interest of the Seventies. In that same year he assumed business control of the *Juvenile Instructor* and associate publications, developing what had been a small printing office into one of the foremost publishing houses in the West. He continued in this management until the time of his death. Having entered into the practice of plural marriage, he was convicted under the Edmunds Act of unlawful cohabitation and was sentenced to six months in prison and fined $300. He served the full sentence and was released in September of 1886.

At the general conference of the Church in October of 1889, he was sustained as a member of the Quorum of the Twelve Apostles and was ordained to the apostleship on October 7 by President Joseph F. Smith. The call came without any suggestion from his father, who was then first counselor in the First Presidency. Although President Cannon had not promoted his son's call, it nonetheless gave him great joy. As a member of the Quorum of the Twelve, Abraham kept careful minutes of the meetings, which proved valuable to historians. Three years later, in connection with his brother, John Q. Cannon, Abraham took charge of the *Deseret News*. In that same year, he became editor and publisher of the *Contributor*. He was also a member of the Deseret Sunday School Union, a duty to which he gave much of his attention.

Although Elder Cannon died at a relatively young age, his tireless energy and his extraordinary qualifications for business management can be seen in his numerous accomplishments. He was the moving spirit in the Salt Lake, Pacific, Utah, and California railways; he was director, vice president, and manager of the Bullion-Beck mining company; he was the director and one of the organizers of the State Bank of Utah; he was director of the Utah Loan and Trust Company at Ogden, the director of ZCMI, the vice president of George Q. Cannon & Sons Company, the first vice president of the Salt Lake Chamber of Commerce, and an active promoter in canal and irrigation enterprises.

Perhaps one of Cannon's greatest contributions to the Church and to the history of his era is his personal journals. Among historians, they are recognized for their extensive details. The first entries were made in 1879 during his mission in Germany, and entries continue until nearly the time of his death in 1896. Concerning these journals, one individual has written: "The Abraham Cannon journals are full of unexpected treasures: descriptions of small towns visited for stake conferences; summaries of talks heard and delivered; activities of the Cannon family; comments on the theater, horse racing, and other entertainments; business and politics; and summaries of statements made by different General Authorities. It is a great human document and a valuable source for a difficult period in the history of the church."[2]

For some time previous to his death, Elder Cannon suffered from severe headaches. In returning from business in California, he became seriously ill and underwent operations for ear troubles. General inflammation set in, resulting in his death on July 19, 1896, at his residence in Salt Lake City. He was only thirty-seven at the time of his premature death. Speaking at the funeral services, President Wilford Woodruff eulogized: "Brother Cannon has been a very peculiar man. He has been a man that never has complained scarcely of anything on earth. He has been willing to take a great load upon him, and to do all that he could for the benefit of the Church and of his brethren wherever has been."[3]

Speaking on a later occasion, President Woodruff referred to the passing of Elder Cannon in giving us added insight into the spirit world. Said he,

We lost one of our Apostles a short time since. He was about the youngest man in the Quorum of the Apostles. He was suddenly called away from us. There is meaning in this . . . for the Lord had called him to fill another important mission in the spirit world, as a pure and holy Apostle from Zion in the Rocky Mountains—a labor which would not only prove a great benefit to his father's household, but to the Church and kingdom of God on the earth. I feel to name this, because it is true. . . . I had a son, who was in the north country, drowned. . . . I asked the Lord why he was taken from me. The answer to me was, "You are doing a great deal for the redemption of your dead; but the law of redemption requires some of your own seed in the spirit world to attend to work connected with this." That was a new principle to me; but it satisfied me why he was taken away. I name this, because there are a great many instances like it among the Latter-day Saints. This was the case with Brother Abraham Cannon. He was taken away to fulfill that mission. And where we have anything of this kind, we should leave it in the hands of God to reconcile.[4]

*Matthias F. Cowley*

Born: August 25, 1858, Salt Lake City, Utah
Ordained Apostle: October 7, 1897
Resigned: October 28, 1905
Priesthood suspended: May 11, 1911
Restored as a member: April 3, 1936
Died: June 16, 1940, Salt Lake City, Utah, at age 81

**P**rior to young Matthias's sixth birthday, his father was drowned in the Jordan River. His mother later married Jesse W. Fox, a well-known civil engineer and surveyor. Matthias assisted his foster father in his labors for the Utah Southern Railway for seven summers. However, instead of reading books on engineering that would have helped him master that profession, he preferred reading the scriptures as well as studying Church history. Being a serious-minded boy, he preferred listening to adults talk about their experiences with the Prophet Joseph rather than join the other boys in games. Later, in his ministries, Matthias would be recognized for his doctrinal sermons.

In a patriarchal blessing given to Matthias in July of 1876, he was told that he would be called into the ministry, and "travel much for the gospel's sake, both by sea and by land, even unto the ends of the earth."[1] In February 1878, Matthias was called on a mission to the southern states. On one particular night, he dreamed twice of coming home before his time was completed. It so upset him that he ever after determined to be content in the missionary field. Six months after his return home, he was again called to the same mission. Prior to actual missionary service, he was appointed to conduct a company of Saints from the southern states to southern Colorado. Among those in the company were fifty-seven souls from Henderson County, Tennessee. These were the converts of the mysterious preacher Robert Edge, who preached the first principles of the gospel, healing, the millennium, and so on, as taught by the Saints, but would not officiate in any of the ordinances. He said that the authority to do so, however, was upon the earth. When missionaries of the Church came among them, they were so impressed with the similarities of the teachings that they were baptized.

Arriving back home in July of 1882, Matthias was then called on a mission to travel throughout the stakes of Zion to speak to the youth and increase the circulation of the *Contributor,* which he successfully did. It was during these travels that he met his wife-to-be, the radiant Abbie Hyde. Having given much thought to choosing a wife, he had a dream one night in which he saw a young woman who, he was impressed to believe, would be his wife. Thus, on a fall day in 1883, he was introduced to a young lady whom he felt that he had seen before. Then it suddenly came to him: "That's the young lady I saw in my dream."[2] They were married by President Daniel H. Wells on the first day that the Logan Temple was opened for endowments and marriages, May 21, 1884. Years later Matthias would record: "During these days the patriarchal order of plural marriage came into our lives. In this, as in all other activities, she sustained me as a servant of the Lord, even telling me before our marriage that she should expect her husband to obey the law of the Gospel. Through the remainder of her life she proved by her faith and works that she meant what she said in the foregoing statement."[3]

Shortly thereafter, Matthias was called to help further the work in the Oneida Stake in Idaho. There he served as superintendent of the YMMIA for four years and later as counselor in the stake presidency for ten years. In October 1897, at the age of thirty-nine, he was called to the apostleship by President Wilford Woodruff. This fulfilled a prophecy given him years earlier while serving a mission in the southern states. At that time, his friend John W. Taylor, who would himself become an Apostle, had written to him: "I believe I speak by the spirit of prophecy when I say, if you are faithful you will yet become one of the Twelve Apostles of the Church of Jesus Christ in all the world"[4] Following his ordination to the apostleship, he traveled by assignment throughout the settlements and was known as a powerful speaker and exhorter, yet he was mild and persuasive in conversation.

When President Wilford Woodruff presented the Manifesto ending plural marriage in accordance to the laws of the land, Elder Cowley had difficulty accepting it and continued to sanction and perform such marriages. He contended that the "laws of the land" referred only to the United States and that the Manifesto did not apply outside this nation's boundaries. When President Joseph F. Smith issued the second Manifesto, stating that President Woodruff's Manifesto applied to all Saints in all lands, Elder Cowley could not accept this interpretation and, finding himself out of harmony with his brethren, he turned in his letter of resignation from the Twelve on October 28, 1905. He was formally dropped from the Twelve at the following April conference of the Church. Remaining out of harmony and continuing to violate the Manifesto, he was disfellowshipped on May 11, 1911.

Matthias's resignation from the Twelve was not due to any lack of faith or change of attitude toward the Church and its leaders. He continued to support his sons on their missions, and twenty-five years after being disfellowshipped, having placed himself in full harmony with the Brethren, he was restored to full membership. In the later 1930s, he wrote articles and summaries of his talks for the *Millennial Star.* At the age of eighty, he bore his testimony to the thirteen countries of the European Mission, thus fulfilling a patriarch's promise pronounced upon him in a public congregation forty years earlier that "his voice shall be heard long, loud, and strong in foreign lands at a good old age in defense of truth." When Matthias grew seriously ill, his son Matthew was serving as mission president in New Zealand. Matthias said, "Don't send for Matthew. He is right where I want him." Matthias died in his home in Salt Lake City at the age of eighty-one. His funeral services were held in Assembly Hall on June 21, 1940, at which time a cablegram was read from his son Matthew: "Father's memory may be properly honored only by deeds of humility, brotherly kindness, respect for priesthood and undying faith."[5]

*Abraham Owen Woodruff*

Born: November 23, 1872, Salt Lake City, Utah
Ordained Apostle: October 7, 1897
Died: June 20, 1904, El Paso, Texas, at age 31

Abraham Owen Woodruff was born November 23, 1872, the son of Wilford Woodruff and Emma Smith Woodruff. He was born and reared in a log house his father had constructed twelve years earlier, just south of Salt Lake City. Being an enterprising young boy, he would go to Liberty Park Springs, where he gathered watercress for the market. At the age of ten, he herded cows, sometimes making as much as fifteen dollars a month. At the age of eighteen, having attended the Latter-day Saints college, he obtained employment in a bank where he worked as a collector and then as an assistant bookkeeper.

While thus employed, Owen (his preferred name) received a mission call to the Swiss-German Mission. However, his father was not in good health, making it emotionally difficult for him to leave the country and be so far from home. Nevertheless, in acquiescing to his father's wishes, he left for Europe in 1893. Shortly after his arrival, he was assigned to open the work in Frankfort without a companion and not knowing the language. Struggling with the German language, he was undeterred from going out and distributing tracts during the days, and holding meetings at night. At first, people laughed at his efforts, but eventually and in an exceedingly short period of time, the language came. It came to him, he said, as a gift. After several months, he was called to the Dresden Branch presidency. From Dresden, he was transferred to Berlin. Here, civil officials undertook to banish Mormon elders from missionary work. Consequently, Elder Woodruff would disguise himself and play the part of a common worker during the day. At night, he would meet with Saints who would bring friends interested in hearing the elders. Before returning home in 1896, he was granted leave to travel and see much of Europe. In Salt Lake City, he returned to banking and on June 30, was married to Helen May Winters.

On October 7, Owen was ordained an Apostle by his father at the young age of twenty-four. Owen was always close to his father and had profound reverence for him, both as a parent and as the prophet of the Lord. He immediately threw himself into the work, becoming tirelessly diligent in his duties. Despite his young age, Elder Woodruff proved most diligent in the performance of his duties and in fulfilling his calling to the apostleship. In November of 1899, President Lorenzo Snow assigned the young Apostle to be the Church's colonization agent. It was in fulfilling this assignment that Elder Wooduff's untimely death occurred, setting the stage for what President Thomas S. Monson referred to as a "love story, a human drama, a miracle in our times."[1]

In May 1904, Elder Woodruff and his wife, Helen, traveled in company with President Anthony W. Ivins to visit the LDS mission in Mexico. While there, Sister Woodruff contracted a virulent case of smallpox. For two weeks, Elder Woodruff nursed his wife, scarcely leaving her side, and poured out his heart in prayer for her recovery. But after days of viewing her agony, he was given to yield her up and pray, "Father not my will, but Thine be done."[2] She died on June 7, 1904. Because of regulations prohibiting transporting bodies of smallpox victims, she was buried in the American cemetery in

Mexico City. After his wife's death, the young Apostle wrote a letter to Church headquarters expressing his heartbreak over the loss of his wife. He then traveled to Ciudad Juarez, Mexico, where he also began to show symptoms of smallpox and was consequently transported to a hospital in El Paso, Texas. Although he appeared to be recovering, he died unexpectedly on June 20, 1904, and was buried in Evergreen Cemetery in El Paso.

Nearly nine decades later, Roger H. Woodruff visited Mexico City and, leaving the tour group, went to see if he could locate his grandmother's grave. When he found it, he discovered that it had been declared abandoned, and her remains were scheduled to be exhumed within two months and buried in a common grave so her plot could be resold. The family sprang into action and through their efforts, the remains of Elder and Sister Woodruff were exhumed and reinterred in the Salt Lake City Cemetery on July 17, 1993. The couple, who once were buried a thousand miles apart in two different countries, were now buried alongside three of their children and other members of the Woodruff family, including President Wilford Woodruff. Speaking at the funeral service held in their honor, President Thomas S. Monson said,

> Husbands and wives should not be separated, even their physical remains. . . . To Elder and Sister Woodruff, the words spoken by John Taylor in the Doctrine and Covenants pertaining to Hyrum and Joseph are fitting: "In life they were not divided, in death they were not separated. . . .
>
> Perhaps they have been hoping that their physical remains might somehow be brought together again someday.
>
> Do you think it was just chance that one of your kinsmen happened to be in Mexico City just before they were going to destroy what remained of Helen Woodruff? Do you think it was just by chance that he was driven to do something?
>
> God bless you who brought together this wonderful couple: A woman of strength, a woman of character, a woman of service, and her noble husband, Abraham Owen Woodruff.
>
> Welcome home, Helen. Welcome home, Owen.[3]

*Rudger Clawson*

Born: March 12, 1857, Salt Lake City, Utah
Ordained Apostle: October 10, 1898
Sustained Second Counselor to President Lorenzo Snow: October 6, 1901
Sustained President of the Quorum of the Twelve: March 17, 1921
Died: June 21, 1943, Salt Lake City, Utah, at age 86

**B**orn March 12, 1857, in Salt Lake City, Rudger Clawson was religiously inclined from his earliest childhood. "Early in life," he said, "I became deeply interested in the Book of Mormon, which I have read and re-read, and drew from its divine pages inspiration and hope. Faith sprang up in my heart. By a careful study of that glorious book, well-defined ideas of right and wrong were firmly fixed in my youthful mind, and I was thus measurably able to withstand the temptations that assailed me and was able to escape many of the sins and follies to which some of the young are addicted."[1] He also recalled how, as a boy, he enjoyed attending Sunday meetings in the Tabernacle, where he listened with interest to Church leaders such as Brigham Young, Heber C. Kimball, and George A. Smith, as well as other priesthood leaders. Because of the profound influence for good those men had on his life, he became convinced that the teachings of Church leaders had a greater effect upon those young children who sat practically unnoticed in the church than many adults supposed.

Shortly after finishing school and at only eighteen years of age, Rudger became private secretary to Hon. John W. Young, president of the Utah Western Railway company. In this capacity, he spent two years in the eastern United States, where he gained a great deal of practical experience from visiting prominent cities, including New York. In 1879, he was called on a mission to the southern states. It was in the state of Georgia that his friend and companion Joseph Standing was shot down in cold blood by an angry and brutal mob. Standing was two and a half years older than Clawson and had served a previous mission in the eastern states. At the time that Clawson was with his companion, Standing presided over the Georgia conference, responsible for overseeing all Church affairs in that state. Standing had great concerns over the anti-Mormon atmosphere in Georgia's backcountry. Methodist and Baptist ministers were zealous in their hatred of the Mormons, and the Ku Klux Klan posted notices and rode out at night to rout out any Mormons that dared live in their community. Most of those who joined the Church there quickly migrated to Utah and Colorado.

On July 21, 1879, Elders Standing and Clawson were traveling from Varnell to Rome, Georgia, when they were accosted by a mob of twelve men. The men commanded the elders to follow them into the woods, where they stopped at a stream and for an hour the men verbally assaulted them. It does not appear that the mob meant to murder them, for one of them said, "Gentlemen, I want you to understand that I am the captain of this party, and after today, if we ever again find you in this part of the country we will hang you by the neck." The spokesman of the mob then commanded the elders to follow them. It was then that Elder Standing jumped up and wrestled a pistol from one of the mob, or possibly grabbed a pistol that had been left carelessly on a tree stump, (another account says he merely jumped up clapping his hands together) and ordered the men to surrender. A shot rang out and he fell, being shot in the forehead.

Another man pointed to Clawson and said, "Shoot that man!" Clawson folded his arms and responded, "Shoot!" The man then ordered, "Don't shoot!"[2] By maintaining a calm disposition, Clawson was able to convince the men that he should go and get help in removing the body of Elder Standing. He walked away slowly, fearing that any sign of fear or haste would bring a volley of bullets down upon him. When he returned with help, the mob had fled and others had gathered around the scene. Standing's body had been riddled with more than twenty bullet wounds in the face and neck. It was believed the mob had done so to prevent one man from being accused of the murder, although the carnage clearly demonstrated the hatred of the mob toward the Mormon missionary. Elder Clawson was able to return to Salt Lake City with Standing's body. A year later, Clawson courageously returned to Georgia to be a witness at the murder trial. However, the three accused were acquitted. After the trial, Clawson was warned by a stranger, "If you have any regard for your life, permit me to say, you had better get out of here just as quickly as you can."[3] Upon his return to Salt Lake City, Clawson was given a hero status because of his displayed courage. Standing's murder lived on in the life of Elder Clawson. His appointment to the Quorum of the Twelve gave occasion for his life to be reviewed at times by newspapers, including the murder of Elder Standing, and he was often asked to recount the story in his travels to the stakes of Zion.

Clawson was the first practicing polygamist to be convicted and sentenced to prison after the passage of the Edmunds Act. The judge gave him the maximum sentence possible of three and a half years, plus half a year for cohabitation, in the Utah Penitentiary. In a statement prior to his being sentenced, Clawson challenged the constitutionality of the court's verdict, stating that the First Amendment to the Constitution denied Congress the right to pass laws prohibiting the free exercise of religion. His appeal was heard by the US Supreme Court in "Clawson v. United States" but was rejected. He was only twenty-seven years of age at the time of his sentencing. The early part of his imprisonment was difficult, being alone among the criminal element and being inflicted with indignities by prison officials. However, as others began to be sentenced under the Edmunds Act, he found himself among fellow Saints. Even his father and President Lorenzo Snow were fellow inmates. However, since his was the first and therefore the harshest sentence, others came and went while he remained. He was eventually pardoned by President Grover Cleveland and left the penitentiary December 12, 1887. "During my imprisonment of three years, one month, and ten days, I never once felt to murmur or complain," he later said. "I felt to praise and glorify the Lord that He had deemed me worthy to suffer bonds and imprisonment in defense of the right."[4]

On December 23, 1887, Clawson was called as president of the Box Elder Stake and moved to Brigham City. At the October 1898 general conference of the Church, he was called to the apostleship and was later called as Second Counselor to President Lorenzo Snow on October 6, 1901, but President Snow died just four days later and he was recalled to the Twelve. In March 1921, he was sustained as President of the Quorum of the Twelve, which position he held for twenty-two years until the time of his death.

*Reed Smoot*

Born: January 10, 1862, Salt Lake City, Utah
Ordained Apostle: April 8, 1900
Died: February 9, 1941, St. Petersburg, Florida, at age 79

Reed Smoot was born January 10, 1862, in Salt Lake City. Approximately ten years later, his family moved to Provo, Utah, where his father served simultaneously as mayor and stake president. In April of 1876, he was one of twenty-nine students who attended the first term at the newly opened Brigham Young Academy. Much of his studies were along commercial lines, and during vacations, he worked in the Provo Woolen Mills, which were started by his father and others. While thus employed he determined that one day he would manage the mills. Upon graduation, Reed went to work with the Provo Cooperative Institution where he literally started at the bottom sacking fruit, sorting potatoes, and doing various odd jobs. One day, he overheard his father say to the store superintendent, "I see you have Reed here, but I guess he won't stay with you very long." At that point, Reed said to himself, "I will stay here until I am superintendent of this institution."[1] Less then eighteen months later, his prediction was fulfilled. He held this position for nearly four years until April 1884, when he was made manager of the Provo Woolen Mills, thus fulfilling his earlier personal ambition.

In 1880, Reed received a mission call. However, the call was rescinded because his services were needed in the cooperative store. In March 1884, he was called on a second mission, but he was stopped from going abroad by President John Taylor, in order for him to manage the Woolen Mills. In September of that same year, he was married. During these years, Reed's interests were centered in business and becoming a man of financial means more than in religious matters. While becoming prosperous in business, some acquaintances feared that Reed was drifting away from religion and probably would not accept another call to serve a mission. But their fears were ill-founded. When a call came in 1890 to serve in the European Mission, he immediately left. During his mission, there came a great change over him in his relation to things of the spirit. He spent much of his time in the Liverpool office as bookkeeper and emigration clerk, but he also had the opportunity of traveling throughout much of Europe in the company of Elder James E. Talmage. He was called home by President Wilford Woodruff due to the serious illness of his father, arriving home October 1, 1891.

Upon his return home, he flung himself again into business enterprises. Among the many business titles he obtained were manager of Provo Lumber Manufacturing and Building Company, manager of Provo Woolen Mills, president of Provo Commercial and Savings Bank, vice president of Grand Central Mining Company, and president of the Victoria Mining Company. Since his mission experience, his efforts were also turned to spiritual service, and in April 1895, he was called as a counselor in the Utah stake presidency, which position he held until his call to the apostleship on April 8, 1900.

On January 20, 1903, Elder Smoot was elected by the Republican State Legislature to be a United States senator from Utah. Being an Apostle, Elder Smoot had obtained a "leave of absence" from his ecclesiastical duties in order to fulfill his duties as a senator. Within six days of his election a formal protest was filed against his being seated in the Senate. The protest came from several non-LDS citizens of the state, including ministers, lawyers, and businessmen. The protest centered around Elder Smoot's being a member of the governing council of the Church, which, according to the protestors, considered itself supreme above any political government, and that members still practiced polygamy in defiance of the laws of the land. Thus, elevating Smoot to the office of senator would place him and the Church in a position "from which to wage war upon the home— the basic institution upon whose purity and perpetuity rests the very government itself."[2]

Hearings began before the Senate Committee on Privileges and Elections on January 16, 1904. Their final report to the Senate was on June 11, 1906, after two and a half years of hearings. During this time Smoot was allowed to occupy his seat in the Senate. Because of the nation's interest in Mormons and polygamy, and because many Church leaders were called to testify before the Committee, the hearings drew national interest in newspapers across the country. Indeed, the Senate hearings went far beyond the question of Smoot himself. It became an inquiry into Mormonism, its history, its theology, and its culture. It was the Church more than Smoot that was on trial before the nation. The Committee's report resolved "that Reed Smoot is not entitled to a seat as a senator of the United States from the state of Utah."[3] The case was brought before the Senate on December 13, 1906, and discussed until the final vote was taken on February 20, 1907. The vote was forty-two to twenty-eight, with twenty not voting, allowing Senator Smoot to retain his seat. Elder Smoot went on to have a long and distinguished career in the US Senate. Due to the seniority system, he became chairman of the powerful Senate Finance Committee and served on the Appropriations Committee. He was recognized as an expert on government finance and public land issues. His politics were conservative and pro-business, leading him to coauthor the famous but oft criticized Smoot-Hawley Tariff Act. He was a delegate to the Republican national convention during five different election years and served as an advisor to several Republican Presidents. Twice he was offered the Republican nomination for President of the United States if he would deny his religion, for a Mormon could not win. He rejected it both times, stating that he would rather be a deacon in the Church of Jesus Christ than President of the United States.

It should be pointed out that one of the facts that surfaced in the Smoot hearings was that plural marriage was still being practiced by some leaders in the Church after Wilford Woodruff's Manifesto, interpreting it to apply only to the United States. Consequently, President Joseph F. Smith issued a second Manifesto prohibiting plural marriages anywhere throughout the Church, the violation of which would result in excommunication.

Senator Smoot was defeated in his bid for reelection in 1932. Many felt that the great depression cost him his senate seat. After thirty years in the Senate, he retired from political and business life, committing his remaining years to his apostolic duties. In February of 1941, he died during a trip to St. Petersburg, Florida, at age seventy-nine.

*Hyrum Mac Smith*

Born: March 21, 1872, Salt Lake City, Utah
Ordained Apostle: October 24, 1901
Died: January 23, 1918, Salt Lake City, Utah, at age 45

**B**orn March 21, 1872, the eldest son of President Joseph F. Smith and Edna Lambson Smith, Hyrum led what one might consider a sheltered life. In his youth, he and his younger brothers were carefully protected by their mother, who seldom let them out of her sight. President Smith took great delight in gathering his family around him and teaching them the principles of the gospel, to shun evil, to be honest and truthful, and to help them see the consequences that came from doing right and wrong. Thus, Hyrum grew up to love and trust his parents and developed an especially close bond with his father. Hyrum graduated from the Latter-day Saints' College in June 1894. In November 1895, he was married to Ida Bowman, and on the evening of the next day, he left for a mission in Great Britain. He did not return until February 1998.

Up until this time, Church fast meetings had traditionally been held monthly on Thursdays. However, Hyrum found that this was to the disadvantage of many of the Saints in England. Members had to get excused from work on that day at a loss of pay. Many of them worked in the coal mines. When they came from the pits they had to go home, bathe, and change clothes before attending their meetings. This resulted in an added loss of time and compensation. Hyrum wrote home to his father, President Joseph F. Smith, asking why it was necessary, under such circumstances, for fast meetings to be held on Thursdays and why they could not be held on Sundays. President Smith took up the matter in his meeting with the First Presidency and Quorum of the Twelve. It was decided that "on the first Sunday of each month . . . the saints . . . should have the privilege of meeting in their meeting houses at 2 o'clock P.M. to observe fast day."[1] Since then, fast meetings have continued to be conducted on the first Sunday of the month. Following his mission, Hyrum was employed at ZCMI and served in his stake as a home missionary, as secretary to the stake quorum of Seventy, and later as secretary of the Sunday School. In October 1901, Hyrum was called to the apostleship. Among his many apostolic duties, in 1913 he was called to preside over the European Mission, arriving in Liverpool, England, on September 30, along with his wife and four children. Shortly thereafter, in June 1914, World War I broke out. At the time, Hyrum was in Germany and was able to return to England only after considerable difficulty. From there, he called the missionaries in and modified their work according to their situations, thus enabling the work to go on with as little interruption as possible.

Elder Hyrum Smith was known for his scholarship in the gospel and in the scriptures. He had a special fondness for the Doctrine and Covenants, feeling that its revelations were specifically directed to our times. "Every phrase, sentence, and paragraph," he wrote, "is so instructive and enlightening; so pregnant with wisdom and purpose, and throws such a flood of light upon the gospel, as to bear convincing witness of their Divine Source, and proclaim them to be the very Word of God."[2]

Consequently, during his time in England, he and Elder J. M. Sjodahl wrote and compiled the *Doctrine and Covenants Commentary*.

Years later, due to the book's popularity, the First Presidency instructed the Publication Committee to revise and prepare it for re-publication. To this day, it remains widely used throughout the Church. Fulfilling a difficult and successful mission, he returned home with his family September 15, 1916, where he resumed his apostolic duties for the next year and a half.

On January 23, 1918, Hyrum unexpectedly died from a ruptured appendix that resulted in peritonitis. He was forty-five years of age. His wife, Ida Bowman Smith, after giving birth to a son, died in Salt Lake City, September 24, 1918, just eight months after the death of her husband. Hyrum's death was especially traumatic for his father, President Joseph F. Smith. Hyrum had been called to the apostleship at the same general conference in which his father had been sustained as the sixth President of the Church. A man of intellect and wisdom, his sermons displayed a deep understanding of gospel doctrine. His father, President Smith, said of him, "His mind was quick and bright and correct. His judgment was not excelled, and he saw and comprehended things in their true light and meaning. When he spoke, men listened and felt the weight of his thoughts and words." President Smith further observed, "He has thrilled my soul by his power of speech, as no other man ever did. Perhaps this was because he was my son, and he was filled with the fire of the Holy Ghost."[3] President Smith considered Hyrum's death one of the most severe blows that he ever had to endure. President Smith's son Joseph Fielding Smith later wrote that President Smith was seriously ill at the time of Hyrum's death "and this shock, without doubt, helped to hasten his own passing some ten months later."[4] It is not improbable that the anguish over the loss of his son may have been a contributing factor leading to President Smith's receiving his vision of the Redemption of the Dead (D&C 138) just eight months after Hyrum's death.

At Hyrum Mac Smith's death, the *Deseret News* wrote: "The finite mind gropes in vain for a reason why one so good and useful . . . should thus be torn away in the very prime and vigor of manhood."[5] What lesson, if any, can we take from his early death? When Hyrum was sick, he was told he should go to the hospital at once for a possible operation. But he declined, stating that he had kept the Word of Wisdom and that the Lord would consequently look after him. As the pain grew worse, his doctor told him he had a one-in-a-thousand chance to live if he would go now. He finally agreed, but by then it was too late. He died on the operating table from a ruptured appendix. At his funeral service, several General Authorities expressed the thought that Elder Smith "was needed on the other side to preach to so many of the youth of the land who died without a knowledge of the gospel." But when the presiding bishop Charles W. Nibley spoke, he declared, "Had it not been for the iron will of Brother Hyrum M. Smith, he might have been with us here today."[6] In thus speaking, he expressed the feelings of many that, had Hyrum gone to the hospital when first spoken to, he might have lived.

## George Albert Smith

Born: April 4, 1870, Salt Lake City, Utah
Ordained Apostle: October 8, 1903
Sustained President of Quorum of the Twelve: July 1, 1943
Ordained President of the Church: May 21, 1945
Died: April 4, 1951, Salt Lake City, Utah, at age 81

One day, as a young boy, George Albert heard a loud crashing noise from another room. Rushing in, he found his mother lying unconscious beneath a large cupboard that had fallen upon her. He immediately prayed to the Lord that if He would save his mother's life, he would devote his life to the Lord's service. His mother recovered and George Albert never forgot his promise. He was further motivated toward a religious life when, at the age of thirteen, he received a patriarchal blessing, which said in part, "Thou shalt become a mighty Apostle . . . none of thy father's family shall have more power with God than thou shalt have."[1] The significance of this blessing becomes apparent when one considers that George Albert was named after his grandfather George A. Smith, who had been an Apostle and a member of the First Presidency. His father, John Henry Smith, would also be called to the apostleship and the First Presidency.

George Albert's young childhood life was no different than that of other pioneer boys. He spent his time herding cows, riding horses, studying, and performing as a musician. Yet he had a serious nature with regard to things of the spirit. In later years he would reflect: "From childhood, I have never been taught to do anything improper, or that would harm one of my Heavenly Father's children; but from infancy I have been taught to acquire industry, sobriety, honesty, integrity, and all virtues possessed by men and women who God delights to honor and bless. I thank my Heavenly Father this day that these teachings have come to me from Him through His faithful servants."[2] Thus, his younger life was one of preparation through obedience and service. It was also a time of refinement through personal suffering—typhoid fever, a severe eye injury, two narrow escapes from death while serving a mission in the southern states, and five years of painful affliction with a serious disease. Out of these experiences came sincere feelings of empathy and compassion toward others who suffered. Indeed, if one attribute were chosen to describe President George Albert Smith, it would be love, love for all mankind.

Shortly after his marriage to Lucy Woodruff in 1892, George Albert was called on a mission to Chattanooga, Tennessee. His bride was almost devastated by loneliness. Consequently, George's father arranged for her to join her husband in the mission field. Following their successful joint efforts as missionaries, they had a belated honeymoon at Niagara Falls before returning home. In Salt Lake City, George returned to work for ZCMI. An active supporter of President William McKinley, in 1896 he was rewarded by an appointment as special disbursing agent of the Land Office of the Department of the Interior. He was later reappointed to that office by President Theodore Roosevelt.

Walking from his office on October 6, 1903, he went to Temple Square to attend general conference, but finding the Tabernacle full, he continued across the street to his own home. There he was surprised to find the house full of well-wishers. When he asked what was going on, he was informed that it had been announced at conference that he was called to the Quorum of the Twelve. He was more depressed than elated. At the age of only thirty-three, he felt unworthy and unprepared for such a high and holy calling. When he later met with his father, Apostle John Henry Smith, his father's first words were, "George, I didn't have anything to do with it."[3] In truth, George Albert's spirit of love and good will made him ideal for his calling. From 1920 to 1923, he presided over the British and European missions. From 1921–36, he was general superintendent of the Young Men's Mutual Improvement Association. In 1922, he became national vice president of the Sons of the American Revolution. And in 1934, the national council of the Boy Scouts of America awarded him the Silver Buffalo.

George Albert was ordained as President of the Church on May 21, 1945. Speaking at the following October general conference, Patriarch Joseph F. Smith, son of Apostle Hyrum Mac Smith, stated, "It is frequently said that the Lord raised up a particular man to perform a particular mission. . . . It is not for me to say what particular mission President George Albert Smith has ahead of him. This I do know, however, that at this particular time in the world's history, never was the need for love among brethren so desperately needed as it is needed today."[4]

President Smith's mission was soon to be revealed. When World War II came to an end, he went to visit the President of the United States to seek support in the Church sending food, clothing, and bedding to destitute people of Europe. "Well, what do you want to ship it over there for? Their money isn't any good," said President Truman. "We don't want their money," replied President Smith. "God has blessed us with a surplus, and we will be glad to send it if we can have the co-operation of the government."[5] Government support was granted in shipping the supplies. Having obtained approval of the President of the United States, 127 train carloads of food, clothing, quilts, and other supplies, as well as substantial sums of cash contributions, were soon on their way. President Smith then turned his attention to the Native Americans and appointed Spencer W. Kimball to oversee the Navajo-Zuni Mission. He also assigned Matthew Cowley to head up the Pacific Mission, where war had also left devastation. He then traveled to Mexico, where twelve hundred members of the Church, who felt that they had been neglected by Church headquarters during the war, had developed their own organization. President Smith's emotional appeal for love and brotherhood brought nearly all of twelve hundred dissenters back into the fold.

President Smith died on his eighty-first birthday, April 4, 1951. At his funeral service, Elder Spencer W. Kimball remarked, "It seemed to me that every act, every thought of our President would indicate that with all of his heart and soul he loved the Lord, and loved his fellowmen. Is there a mortal being who could have loved them more?"[6]

*Charles W. Penrose*

Born: February 4, 1832, London, England
Ordained Apostle: July 7, 1904
Sustained Second Counselor to President Joseph F. Smith:
    December 7, 1911
Sustained Second Counselor to President Heber J. Grant:
    November 23, 1918
Sustained First Counselor to President Grant: March 10, 1921
Died: May 15, 1925, Salt Lake City, Utah, at age 93

Born February 4, 1832, at Chamberwell, London, England, Charles was a naturally studious boy with a remarkable memory. He advanced quickly in school and read the scriptures when only four years old, becoming well-versed in its doctrines and prophecies during the ensuing years. At the young age of eighteen, after thoroughly comparing the teachings of the restored gospel with the Bible, he became the only member of his father's family to join the Church. Shortly thereafter, he was ordained an elder and called on a mission in his native England. Although offered a life situation in a government office on the condition of his remaining home, he chose the mission. Completely penniless and without a change of clothes, he started off on foot and faithfully served as a missionary for nearly eleven years. Upon his release, he immigrated to Utah, eventually settling in Cache Valley. In the spring of 1965, he was called to return to England on a mission, where he served for nearly three and a half years.

In January 1870, he moved to Ogden, where he worked as assistant editor and then as editor-in-chief of the *Ogden Junction* newspaper. In 1877, Brigham Young requested that he come to Salt Lake City to work with the *Deseret News*, eventually becoming its editor-in-chief, a position that he would also hold under Presidents Taylor and Snow. Having become a naturalized citizen of the United States, Elder Penrose was involved in politics, serving on the Ogden City council, the Territorial Legislature, and the Salt Lake County legislature, and helping to frame the constitution of the State of Utah. In 1884, he was called as second counselor in the Salt Lake Stake, followed by another mission to England. He was a prolific writer of books, pamphlets, and poems. Some of his poetical writings were put to music and became well-known hymns throughout the Church.

As stated before, following his conversion, Elder Penrose served as a missionary in England. Toward the later part of his mission, he served in the presidency of the Birmingham Conference, and had brought some of his own furniture to use in his mission office. When he was released from his calling and took his furniture home, he was accused by a member of the Church of stealing Church property for his own personal use. The accusation deeply hurt young Charles and he became very angry toward the person, even to the extent that he considered seeking revenge. Instead, he sat down and wrote in an effort to calm his feelings and control his anger.

> School thy feelings, O my brother;
> Train thy warm, impulsive soul,
> Do not its emotions smother,
> But let wisdom's voice control.[1]

It became popular after being printed in the *Millennial Star*. Years later he wrote, "I was very pleased to know that it was a great comfort to President Brigham Young when he was under arrest. He later told me that he had it read to him several times when he had a deputy marshal guarding him in his house."[2]

To the nineteenth-century Saints, migrating to Zion was as important as building up her stakes is to Church members today. For thousands of European Saints, the Salt Lake Valley was their home psychologically long before it became their actual, physical home. Thus, it is not surprising to find that Elder Penrose penned the following words while still living in England, exulting in a place he had not yet seen.

> O ye mountains high, where the clear blue sky
> Arches over the vales of the free,
> Where the pure breezes blow and the clear streamlets flow,
> How I've longed to your bosom to flee.[3]

Elder Penrose had a profound knowledge of the gospel. His writings included a valuable work entitled *Mormon Doctrine.* In Salt Lake City, he delivered several Sunday evening lectures at the 12th Ward Assembly Hall, speaking on such subjects as "Blood Atonement" and the "Mountain Meadows Massacre," answering anti-Mormon arguments and refuting charges against the Church. Defending the Mormon cause, politically and religiously, he earned the hostility of the anti-Mormons and was singled out as a target under the Edmunds Law. Consequently, he was sent overseas in a protective "exile" from his enemies. In England, he revived the missionary work and contributed editorially to the *Millennial Star.* Accompanying President Daniel H. Wells on his European tour, he preached the gospel in Denmark, Sweden, Norway, Germany, and Switzerland. Although indicted under the Edmunds Law, US President Grover Cleveland issued him full amnesty at the request of a few influential friends.

In October 1892, the Church relinquished control of the *Deseret News,* leasing it to George Q. Cannon and Sons Publishing Company, at which time Charles W. Penrose retired from its editorship, a position he had held for twelve years. In January 1899, when the Church resumed control of the newspaper, Penrose was reinstated as editor-in-chief, which position he held until 1906 when called to preside over the European Mission. During those years, his editorials "defended the Church against the assaults of the world, meeting all comers with the force of logic, with the truth of the scriptures."[4]

In 1896, he was sustained as assistant Church historian. Elder Penrose was ordained to the apostleship July 7, 1904, filling the vacancy left by the death of Abraham O. Woodruff. He went on to serve as Second Counselor to both President Joseph F. Smith and President Heber J. Grant. In March 1921, he was sustained as First Counselor to President Grant, serving in that position until his death four years later on May 15, 1925, at the age of ninety-three.

*George F. Richards*

Born: February 23, 1861, Farmington, Utah
Ordained Apostle: April 9, 1906
Sustained as acting Patriarch to the Church: October 8, 1937
Released as acting Patriarch: October 3, 1942
Became President of the Quorum of the Twelve: May 21, 1945
Died: August 8, 1951, Salt Lake City, Utah, at age 89

George Franklin Richard was born the son of Apostle Franklin D. Richards and Nanny Longstroth in Farmington, Utah. He grew up to graduate from the University of Deseret in English language and literature in June 1881. He continued on in mathematics for a term, but then left school for a position with the Utah Central Railroad, where he was clerk in the lumber, carpentry, and car-building department. In 1882, he took his new family to Farmington to live with his mother, who was ill and in need of help. His life was one of hard farm work with little material returns. On his twenty-third birthday, he lamented over the facts that he had never been on a foreign mission, he was four hundred dollars in debt with interest, and his total assets were a harness, a wagon, six horses, a cow, two calves, and not quite two acres of land. At that time he consecrated his life to the Lord, stating, "That which I have is upon the altar and subject to the direction of those in authority, as is also my time and life if necessary."[1]

In 1885, he purchased a 160-acre farm in what is now the town of Fielding in Box Elder County, where he began to prosper. A man who appreciated education, he continued to self-educate himself at nights, reading books after the children were asleep. He would also make long lists of gospel questions and then research the answers. In 1888, he again moved, this time to Tooele, Utah, to take over the operation of an uncle's ranch. There he served in many important positions, including chairman of the district school board of trustees, chairman of the board of trustees for the Tooele Irrigation Company, director of the Tooele City Water Company, and county representative in the State legislature. He also engaged with his sons in the implement and lumber business, as well as farming.

In 1890, he was set apart as second counselor in the Tooele Stake presidency, and in 1893, he was ordained a patriarch by Elder Francis M. Lyman. On April 9, 1906, George F. Richards was ordained an Apostle. Among his many assignments, he was a member of the General Board of the YMMIA and an advisory member of the General Board of the Primary, as well as a representative of the Quorum in stakes from Canada to Mexico. In 1916, he was called to preside over the European Mission. World War I made the seas dangerous for travel as German submarines patrolled the Atlantic. However, Elder Richards arrived at Liverpool, England, safely. It had been decided that his wife would remain home and care for the children. Two years and eight months after a tearful farewell, they were again reunited. From 1921 to 1938, Elder Richards served as president of the Salt Lake Temple. Then in 1937, President Heber J. Grant asked him to serve as Church Patriarch. Inasmuch as he was not a literal descendant of Joseph Smith Sr., he was sustained and set apart as *Acting* Presiding Patriarch to the Church. He fulfilled this position until 1942.

Elder Richards was a believer in and a recipient of dreams from the Lord. Of one such dream, he recounted, "I was in the presence of my Savior as he stood in mid-air. He spoke no word to me, but my love for him was such that I have not words to explain. I know that no mortal man can love the Lord as I experienced that love for the Savior unless God reveals it unto him. I would have remained in his presence but there was a power drawing me away from him, and as a result of that dream I had this feeling, that no matter what might be required at my hands, what the gospel might entail unto me, I would do what I should be asked to do, even to the laying down of my life. . . . If only I can be with my Savior and have that same sense of love that I had in that dream it will be the goal of my existence, the desire of my life."[2] Two days after this dream he was called to the Quorum of the Twelve.

Many years later, following World War II, he had a remarkable dream in which he found himself standing face-to-face with the Fuhrer Adolph Hitler. Speaking to the Fuhrer, he said, "I am your brother. You are my brother. In our heavenly home we lived together in love and peace. Why can we not so live here on the earth?" Elder Richards then explained, "It seemed to me that I felt in myself, welling up in my soul, a love for that man, and I could feel that he was having the same experience, and presently we arose and embraced each other. . . . I think the Lord gave me that dream. Why should I dream of this man, one of the greatest enemies of mankind, and one of the wickedest, but that the Lord should teach me that I must love my enemies, and I must love the wicked as well as the good? . . . I have tried to maintain this feeling and, thank the Lord, I have no enmity toward any person in this world; I can forgive all men, so far as I am concerned, and I am happy in doing so and in the Love which I have for my fellow man."[3]

Elder Richards died August 8, 1950, from coronary thrombosis at the age of eighty-nine. Elder Ezra Taft Benson said of him: "In my early childhood my father always held up as the ideal family, that of President Joseph F. Smith; but when President Smith passed away, then he held up the family of George F. Richards. It was father's ideal for us."[4] Elder Spencer W. Kimball wrote of him years later, "He was so honest he circled the block and stopped again for a red light he had accidentally run." To Elder Kimball, he was "about as nearly perfect as men get on the earth."[5]

*Orson F. Whitney*

Born: July 1, 1855, Salt Lake City, Utah
Ordained Apostle: April 9, 1906
Died: May 16, 1931, Salt Lake City, Utah, at age 75

O rson's paternal grandfather was Newel K. Whitney, the second presiding bishop of the Church. His maternal grandfather was Heber C. Kimball. Born in Salt Lake City, his earliest recollection was his family's move to Provo in the spring of 1858 to escape the threat of Johnston's approaching army. "I was not then three years old, but I distinctly remember incidents of the journey to and the sojourn at Provo, where my father's family resided until the general return north in the summer."[1] When Orson was thirteen years old, he worked construction on the Union Pacific Railroad as an employee of his uncle. There, for the first time, he experienced the rough side of life but had no taste for it, allowing serious temptations to pass him by. Later, while attending the University of Deseret, he took time off to seek employment in the business world, working as an express driver, a store clerk, and a sewing machine agent. At the university, he and others organized the Wasatch Literary Association. He also became involved in a debating society. He was musically talented, teaching himself to play the flute and the guitar. But he discovered that his real interests were in the theater.

Concerning his school years, Orson wrote, "As a youth I became indifferent to spiritual things, though at the same time I led a moral life. . . . Humorously inclined, fond of fun and amusement, still I was generally serious, and sometimes melancholy."[2] It became his desire to travel to New York in pursuit of an acting career. His mother, finding it impossible to dissuade him, promised that if she could sell a particular parcel of land, she would let him have enough money to make the journey to New York City. But try as she may, she could not find a buyer. Then, at the age of twenty-one, came Orson's call to go on a mission. "Though poorly prepared to preach, I had faith enough to accept the call."[3] No sooner had he accepted the call than the land was sold and the money used to finance his mission. Laboring in Pennsylvania, he had the opportunity of visiting Washington, DC, and other points of interest, which he described in letters to the *Salt Lake Herald*. The spirit of his mission had not yet thoroughly come upon him, when he had a remarkable experience that changed the course of his life.

It was while laboring in Pennsylvania that Orson had a dream in which he saw the Savior as He prayed and wept in the Garden of Gethsemane. Twice the Savior woke His sleeping Apostles, Peter, James, and John, and tenderly admonished them for not being able to watch with Him. "My whole heart went out to Him; I loved Him with all my soul," recounted Elder Whitney. The scene then changed to where the resurrected Christ stood with His Apostles, and all of them were about to ascend into heaven. Orson ran to the Savior, fell at His feet, and begged the Savior to take him with Him. "No, my son; these have finished their work; they can go with me, but you must stay and finish yours." "Well, promise me that I will come to you at the last," pleaded Orson. Smiling sweetly, the Savior replied, "That will depend entirely upon yourself." "I saw the moral clearly," recorded Orson. "I have never thought of being an Apostle, nor of holding any other office in the Church, and it did not occur to me then. Yet I knew that these sleeping Apostles meant me. I was asleep at my post—as any man is who, having been divinely appointed to do one thing, does another."[4] From that time forward, he gave himself to the work, growing in faith and knowledge daily, until his testimony burst upon him.

Returning home, he was employed by the *Deseret News,* where he soon became editor. At the age of twenty-three, he was called as bishop of the 18th ward even though he was still unmarried, a thing unheard of in the Church. This dilemma would be rectified within the year with his marriage. In 1881, he was called on a mission to Europe, where he labored in the editorial department of the *Millennial Star.* While there, he learned of the death of his second child, whom he had never seen. Upon his return home, he resumed his work with the *Deseret News* and as bishop. Becoming involved in politics, he served as city treasurer, as delegate to the Constitutional Convention where he championed woman suffrage, and later as state senator. He taught religion at the Brigham Young College in Logan and was chancellor of the University of Deseret. His literary achievements would include his four-volume *The History of Utah.*

At the April 1906 conference of the Church, Orson was called to the Quorum of the Twelve. President Joseph F. Smith said, "I have wanted Orson in this Council for years. . . . I have long thought that he should stand among the leaders of this people."[5] Elder Whitney would entreat his old friends and associates to continue calling him "Bishop," understandably, since he had spent the previous twenty-eight years a bishop. "I have never wanted to be called 'Apostle' Whitney," he said. "It is exceedingly distasteful to me; that sacred title should not be used thus commonly."[6] Fortunately, custom had recently changed and he had only to accept the title "Elder Whitney." In 1921, Elder Whiney was called to preside over the European Mission. While there, he was challenged to a public debate by an anti-Mormon minister. Whitney declined taking part, citing the counsel of Brigham Young: "Never condescend to argue with the wicked. The principles of the gospel are too sacred to be quarreled over. Bear your testimony in humility, and leave the result with the Lord."[7] And yet, Elder Whitney could be brutally to-the-point when pressed. Asked why the Lord would allow grammatical errors in the Book of Mormon if it were word of God, he answered: "I believe that was left there just to keep you out of the Church." "Doesn't God want me in His Church?" asked the individual. "No!" replied Elder Whitney. "He only wants honest seekers after the truth; and if you think more of a grammatical error than you do of your soul's salvation, you are not fit for the kingdom of heaven, and the Lord doesn't want you."[8] In 1925, the assignment of the Twelve was extended beyond visiting stakes to include visiting missions of the Church. Those missions near Utah were to be visited once a year. Elder Whitney found great enjoyment in these assignments.

Elder Whitney died May 16, 1931. He has been described as a noted historian, poet, orator, and Church leader.

*David O. McKay*

Born: September 8, 1873, Huntsville, Utah
Ordained Apostle: April 9, 1906
Sustained Second Counselor to President Heber J. Grant:
    October 6, 1934
Sustained Second Counselor to President George Albert Smith:
    May 21, 1945
Sustained President of the Twelve: September 30, 1950
Sustained President of the Church: April 9, 1951
Died: January 18, 1970, Salt Lake City, Utah, at age 96

Born in Huntsville, Utah, in September of 1873, his life would stretch over ninety-six years, from the time when the railroad first came to Utah, ending the covered wagon era, to the time when man would land on the moon. And yet, when he died in 1970, over half the Church membership had known only him as President of the Church. When David was only six years old, his two older sisters died within a week of each other and were buried in the same grave. Just prior to his turning eight years of age, his father,

David McKay, was called on a mission to his native Scotland, leaving David O. mainly responsible for the farm work, rapidly maturing him beyond his years. Jennette, David O.'s mother, managed to obtain considerable profit from the grain crop and add a planned addition to their house before David Sr. returned from his mission two years later. When David O. asked his father if he had seen any miracles on his mission, his father replied, "Your mother is the greatest miracle that one could ever find."[1] David would grow up holding a high regard for his mother and for women in general. Following his return home from his mission, David McKay Sr. served as bishop from 1883 to 1905. He often shared his experiences and testimony with his son, leaving David O. to recollect in later years, "As a boy, I sat and heard that testimony from one whom I treasured and honored as you know I treasured no other man in the world, and that assurance was instilled in my youthful soul."[2]

When David O. was twenty-one, he entered the University of Utah, where he debated, played piano in a musical group, was on the football team, and eventually graduated as president and valedictorian of his class. Actively courting Emma Ray Riggs, and accepted as a faculty member of Weber State Academy, all was looking bright when he received an inconvenient mission call at the age of twenty-four. But leaving all behind, he left for Scotland. It was there while attending a conference that Elder James L. McMurrin of the mission presidency stood and said, "Let me say to you, Brother David, Satan hath desired you that he may sift you as wheat, but God is mindful of you, and if you will keep the faith, you will yet sit in the leading councils of the Church."[3] At that moment, David developed deep resolve to keep that faith and serve his fellow man.

Returning home, he took up his position at the Weber State Academy, married Emma Ray Riggs, and served as the superintendent of the Weber Stake Sunday School.

Many of his innovations were adopted by Sunday Schools throughout the Church. Career-wise, he rose to be principal of the academy. At the age of thirty-two, he was in Salt Lake City with his family to attend conference when he was summoned to the office of the Quorum of the Twelve. There he was met by Quorum President Francis M. Lyman. "So you're David O. McKay," said President

Lyman. "Well, David O. McKay, the Lord wants you to be a member of the Quorum of the Twelve Apostles."[4] David was stunned.

In 1916, Elder McKay was in a serious car accident that threatened to leave his face badly scarred for life, but through the blessings of Bishop Olsen and President Grant, both promising that he would not be scarred, he was completely and miraculously healed. In 1920, in company with Hugh J. Cannon, he left on a tour of the worldwide missions, taking him away from home for one year and three weeks, during which time they traveled about 56,000 miles. During his travels, he witnessed many manifestations of the Spirit. Speaking to a Maori branch without using an interpreter, he found that the congregation understood him even though they did not speak English. On two other occasions, he realized his interpreters were not translating him correctly even though he did not understand their language. While sailing toward Samoa, in the dreams of the night, he had a vision of the Savior leading a group of people toward His Eternal City. In answer to his inquiry as to who the people were, he was given to understand that they were those who had "Overcome the World—Who Have Truly Been Born Again."[5] When bidding farewell to a congregation of Samoans, many testified that they saw a bright heavenly halo surround him. In Hawaii, as he and others stood on a shelf looking into Kilauea Volcano, he felt impressed that they should get off the shelf immediately. No sooner had they done so that the shelf fell into the molten abyss. Such were the spiritual manifestations that marked his travels throughout his apostolic ministry.

During the ensuing years, he would serve as counselor to two Presidents of the Church and as President of the Quorum of the Twelve. Then, with the death of President Smith in April of 1951, David O. McKay was sustained as ninth President of the Church. The numerous accomplishments under his administration included the establishment of the Priesthood Correlation Program, the emphasis on "every member a missionary," and the family home evening program. But probably most important was his leading the Church from a mountain west organization into a truly worldwide institution. Almost immediately, he began a series of tours that would take him to countries throughout the world. He traveled over a million miles, more than the combined travels of all the presidents before him. He foresaw temples dotting the world and initiated the building of temples outside of the United States, dedicating temples in Switzerland, London, and New Zealand. So strongly was his influence felt throughout the world that a Secretary of State called him the best goodwill ambassador the United States had.

With his wavy white hair and dignified stature, President McKay gave the very appearance of a prophet. The story is told about the United Press sending their hardened New York crime photographer to take a picture of President McKay arriving at the airport when their regular photographer couldn't go. He was only supposed to take two pictures but emerged from his dark room with a tremendous sheaf of photos. Chided for his waste of time and supplies, he explained: "When I was a little boy, my mother used to read to me out of the Old Testament, and all my life I have wondered what a prophet of God must really look like. Well, today I found one."[6]

Upon his death, President Joseph Fielding Smith eulogized David O. McKay by saying that he had become perfect in life.

*Anthony W. Ivins*

Born: September 16, 1852, Toms River, New Jersey
Ordained Apostle: October 6, 1907
Sustained Second Counselor to President Heber J. Grant: March 10, 1921
Sustained First Counselor to President Heber J. Grant: May 28, 1925
Died: September 23, 1934, Salt Lake City, Utah, at age 82

**B**orn in 1852 in the state of New Jersey, Anthony came west with his parents, Israel and Anna, the following year because they were recent converts to the Church. In 1861, they moved to southern Utah, being one of the group called by Brigham Young to settle the area. In fact, Israel completed the survey of St. George and served as the area's physician. Faithful in his callings as a deacon and a teacher, Anthony was ordained an elder at the early age of thirteen. He later took an active leadership role in the YMMIA. In 1875, Anthony was part of a group called on an exploratory mission by President Brigham Young and under the direction of Dan Jones. They were instructed to explore the area of what is now New Mexico and Arizona as well as current Mexico, for future colonization purposes, and to visit and establish friendly relationships with the various Indian tribes of the area. Traveling 2,400 miles, their exploration resulted in the eventual establishment of several colonies in Mexico. Upon his return from his mission, Anthony was appointed constable of St. George. In 1878, he was again called on a mission, this time to preach to the Navajo and Pueblo Indians of the Arizona and New Mexico areas. That same year he married Elizabeth Ashby Snow, the daughter of Apostle Erastus Snow, having known her from their early childhood.

By 1882, he had become a prominent figure in St. George, having been elected as prosecuting attorney. However, he was once again called on a mission, this time to Mexico City to preach. He returned home in 1884, having spent one year presiding over the Mexican Mission. He became involved in farming and ranching, becoming manager of the Mojave Land and Cattle Company and one of the owners of the Kaibab Cattle Company, the two largest owners of cattle on the Arizona Strip. In 1888, he was called as first counselor in the St. George Stake presidency. He was also very active and prominent in politics, having served in several elected positions, as well as serving as Indian Agent for the Shebits, a band of southern Piutes. He achieved the first government appropriation for the Shebits and moved them from the Shebit Mountains, where they had become a menace to the settlers, and purchased land and established them on the Santa Clara River. He was elected to two terms of the Territorial Legislature and as representative to the Utah State Constitutional Convention. His popularity placed him in a strong position for nomination as Utah's first governor.

Then in 1895 came the call from President Wilford Woodruff for Anthony to go to Mexico to assist in Church affairs and with the establishment of Mormon colonies, and to serve as president of the Juarez Stake. With his successful business interests and his political aspirations, as well as other personal reasons, Anthony did not want to go, but his first loyalty was to the Church, so he accepted the call. In a letter of congratulations over his assignment, Anthony's first cousin, Apostle Heber J. Grant, wrote to him: "The letter which you wrote to them [the First Presidency of the LDS Church] is just such a letter as I should have expected from you, and if you had written any other kind of letter I should have been greatly surprised as well as disappointed. I feel sure that the day will come when you will thank the Lord that you have been selected by His inspiration to preside in Mexico."[1]

In 1896, after residing in Mexico for a year, he brought his family to join him. While in Mexico, he acted as vice president and general manager of the Mexican Colonization and Agricultural Company, under which the Mormon colonies in Mexico were established, making him virtually the final word in the affairs of the colonies. He was also president of the Dublan Mercantile Company, the largest mercantile house in that part of Mexico. He remained in Mexico for twelve years until, in October 1907, he was called to the Quorum of the Twelve. His duties as an Apostle were many and varied, but he continued to have an interest and involvement in the Mormon colonies of Mexico. In Utah his many responsibilities included superintendent of the Church YMMIA, president of the Board of Trustees of the Utah Agricultural College, vice president of Zion's Saving Bank and Trust Company, director in the Deseret Savings Bank and Utah State National Bank, and member of the National Boy Scout Committee. In 1921 he was sustained as second counselor to his cousin, President Heber J. Grant; in 1925, he was sustained as first counselor.

Elder Ivins was a man who was loved for his goodness and kindness and was greatly respected for his integrity. Elder David B. Haight of the Twelve recalled the following incident during the onset of the Great Depression. "I recall the day when all the banks closed and remember vividly walking up Main Street of this city and seeing crowds of people blocking the sidewalk and street in front of Zion's Bank. Anthony W. Ivins, counselor to President Grant, was standing on the steps of the bank. He said to the people, 'There's money here in the bank if you want it. There is no need to cause a run on the bank. There's money here for your deposits.' And the people started to drift away because Brother Ivins was a symbol of integrity and confidence."[2] This respect was perhaps best expressed by the Piute Indians, who sent him a gift in 1932: a leather vest with bead-work which read, "Tony Ivins, he no cheat."[3]

Elder Ivins died September 23, 1934, at the age of eighty-two. Condolences from prominent people of all religions and political persuasions were extended to the family. Funeral services were held for him in the Salt Lake Tabernacle while the Piute Indians held a separate tribal ceremony in his honor.

*Joseph Fielding Smith*

Born: July 19, 1876, Salt Lake City, Utah
Ordained Apostle: April 7, 1910
Sustained acting President of the Quorum of the Twelve:
    September 30, 1950
Sustained President of the Quorum: April 9, 1951
Sustained Counselor in First Presidency: October 29, 1965
Ordained President of the Church: January 23, 1970
Died: July 2, 1972, Salt Lake City, Utah, at age 95

**B**ecause Juliana was first among Joseph F. Smith's three wives, his name had been reserved for her first son; and so her newborn boy was named Joseph Fielding Smith, Jr. With Joseph Sr. going into exile to escape federal marshals and his taking care of his Church responsibilities, he was seldom home. Thus, young Joseph's early years were filled with difficulty. He would remember in those early years marshals entering their house, searching for his father, prowling relentlessly around their home, interrogating women and children, and generally terrorizing and blighting their lives. His later years would also know trials and sorrow as he would marry three times, only to outlive all three of his wives.

From his father, Joseph developed the habit of being an early riser, being up before six a.m. throughout his life. An early start meant a day of accomplishment. His hard work ethic in his later years was seen in his brown-bagging his lunch so that he could continue working uninterrupted through his lunch hour. He claimed that this provided him with an additional 300 hours of work a year. Many of his youthful hours were spent herding cows and working on the family farm. At the age of ten, he helped his mother—who was a midwife—becoming the stable boy and buggy driver, taking her at all hours of the night to where she was needed. On some occasions, as he waited for her outside, he felt that he was going to freeze to death. In his teens he worked at ZCMI, putting in long and exhaustive hours hauling hams and heavy sacks of flour and sugar. "I weighed 150 pounds, but thought nothing of picking up a 200 pound sack and putting it on my shoulders," he would later recall.[1] Work was hard and pay was modest, but jobs were hard to find and the family needed the money. Joseph Jr. grew up enjoying sports and was active throughout his long life. While enjoying a variety of sports, his favorite was handball, and he excelled at it. Many a time he trounced players far younger than he and who had thought they could easily beat him because of his age.

But his first and foremost interest was in studying the gospel and reading the scriptures. By the age of ten he had read the Book of Mormon twice. Years later, as General Authority, he came to be recognized as a leading authority on gospel principles. For many years the church magazine, *The Improvement Era,* contained a monthly feature, "Answers to Gospel Questions," wherein Elder Smith answered question sent to him by Church members. Over his lifetime he authored twenty-five books. His son-in-law, Elder Bruce R. McConkie, himself known as a gospel authority, wrote of him: "Joseph Fielding Smith is the leading gospel scholar and the greatest doctrinal teacher of this generation. Few men in this dispensation have approached him in gospel knowledge or surpassed him in spiritual insight. . . . It was inevitable, therefore, that his sermons and writings should form the basis of a substantial contribution to the literature of the Church."[2]

In 1899, just one year after his first marriage to Louie Shurtliff, he was called on a mission to England where, in two years, he did not have a single baptism. It was a time when missionary work was ineffective in England, even the members being lackadaisical toward the Church. Upon his return home he was employed in the Church Historian's Office. In 1906, he became Assistant Church Historian. After less than ten years of marriage, Louie died, leaving two daughters. Within three years, Joseph married Ethel Reynolds. They were together for twenty-nine years until her death in 1937, at the relatively young age of forty-seven. A third marriage took place to Jesse Evans, a gifted contralto who had been a lead singer with the American Light Opera Company in New York and had been offered a contract with the Metropolitan Opera, but turned it down feeling she should return to Utah, where she met Elder Smith. For thirty-three years she travelled around the world with him, singing her way into the hearts of the Saints, and often getting him to join her in duets, much to his chagrin. "I'm more of a *do it* than a *duet*," he would often say, showing his sense of humor. In August of 1971, a year and a half into Elder Smith's presidency, Jesse Evans Smith passed away, leaving him for the third time without an earthly companion.

In 1910, when a vacancy came in the Quorum of the Twelve, President Joseph F. Smith was hesitant to suggest his son Joseph as a new member since his son Hyrum was already a member of the Twelve and his other son David was a counselor in the Presiding Bishopric. But when he presented Joseph's name to the Twelve, they were immediately receptive. Ordained to the special task of preaching repentance, Elder Smith took the assignment seriously. His sermons were always taken from the scriptures—his being neither a storyteller nor an entertainer—and he spoke with an attitude of solemnity. He was what the world would consider straitlaced in his obedience and his avoidance of the very appearance of evil. Because of these characteristics, he had a reputation of being austere and uncompromising, an image that was contrary to that seen by his family at home, and by his friends and associates. In reality he was a gentle, loving, and forgiving man. When ordaining new bishops, he often advised that if they were to make any mistakes in passing judgment, it was best to err on the side of mercy. Some of his brethren observed that if it was ever necessary for them to be judged for some reason, they hoped it would be Joseph Fielding Smith that was their judge. When sustained as President of the Church, it was this later image that became evident to the Church at large.

Called as president at the age of ninety-three, many came to see this as the Lord's seal of approval upon his life and works. Despite his age he carried on the work with vitality, holding conferences throughout several states, as well as in Mexico and England. Upon his quietly passing away at the age of ninety-six, President N. Eldon Tanner said, "his passing was as near a translation as possible."[3]

*James E. Talmage*

Born: September 21, 1862, Hungerford, England
Ordained Apostle: December 8, 1911
Died: July 27, 1933, Salt Lake City, Utah, at age 70

James Talmage was baptized and confirmed a member of the Church in Hungerford, Berkshire, England, the place of his birth—in June 1873—and in August of that same year, was ordained a deacon in the Aaronic Priesthood. Reflecting back on that event in later years, he recorded,

> As soon as I had been ordained, a feeling came to me such as I have never been able fully to describe. It seemed scarcely possible, that I, a little boy, could be so honored of God as to be called to the priesthood. . . . I felt strong in thought that I belonged to the Lord, and that he would assist me in whatever was required of me. The effect of my ordination entered into all the affairs of my boyish life. . . . The impression made upon my mind when I was made a deacon has never faded. . . . I have been ordained in turn a teacher, an elder, a high priest, and lastly an Apostle of the Lord Jesus Christ, and with

every ordination there has come to me a new and soul-thrilling feeling which I first knew when I was called to be a deacon in the service of the Lord.[1]

In May 1876, the entire Talmage family immigrated to the United States, eventually settling in Provo, Utah.

If there was one characteristic chosen to best epitomize Elder Talmage's life and work, it might well be "scholarship." His early schooling in England led to his being honored as an Oxford diocesan prize scholar. In Utah he attended the Brigham Young Academy and at the age of seventeen taught science and English in that school. From 1882–83, he took selected courses, mainly in chemistry and geology, at Lehigh University, located in Pennsylvania. Though not registered as a candidate for a degree, he did, in that single year, pass nearly all the examinations in the four-year course, and was later awarded a degree. Following his work at Lehigh University, he did advanced studies at Johns Hopkins University, in Baltimore, Maryland. Returning to Utah in the fall of 1884, he went on to become professor of geology and chemistry at the Brigham Young Academy and a member of its board of trustees, president of the Latter-day Saints college in Salt Lake City, and professor of geology and president of the University of Utah. Resigning as president, he continued to retain the chair of geology for ten years, at the end of which time he went into the practical work of mining geology. Talmage traversed this country and Europe many times in the course of his scientific pursuits. As a consequence of his work he was awarded several honorary doctorate degrees as well as being elected to lifetime membership of many distinguished Scientific Societies.

Despite his recognition as a teacher and contributor to the scientific world, to Latter-day Saints he is best remembered for his many theological works, many of which are still standard reading within the Church today. In 1891, twenty-nine-year-old James Talmage was appointed by the First Presidency to write a book on theology for religion classes. However, his busy schedule caused delays. In 1898 the First Presidency pressed him for publication. Basing his writing on a series of lectures he had given, *The Articles of Faith* was published. The first printing of 10,500 copies sold quickly, and it has continued to be a popular book within the Church even to the present day.

Talmage felt it an honor to be able to write for the Church and waived all royalties in order that the book could be sold at the lowest possible cost ($1.00 for the cloth-covered edition).

On September 17, 1911, members of the Church were stunned to learn through the *Salt Lake Tribune* that the interior of the Salt Lake Temple had been secretly photographed. Gisbert Bossard, a disgruntled convert, had gained access to the temple through the aid of a groundskeeper during the temple's closure for renovation. Motivated by money and "revenge," they and another accomplice were demanding $100,000 in ransom for the photographs. Otherwise the photos would be revealed to the public. Talmage proposed to the First Presidency that they commission their own photographs, which idea they accepted. President Joseph F. Smith then suggested that Talmage write a treatise on the temple to accompany the pictures. The result was his landmark book, *House of the Lord*. It was at this time that Talmage was called to the Quorum of the Twelve Apostles.

From September 1904 to April 1906, Elder Talmage gave a series of lectures on the life and mission of Christ, attended by hundreds of students. During this series, he was requested by the First Presidency to publish these lectures in book form. However, his busy schedule and work on other writings prevented him from pursuing the task for several years. In September 1914, the Brethren again asked him to prepare the book "with as little delay as possible." To assist him in this assignment, he was given space in the council room of the Twelve Apostles on the fourth floor of the Salt Lake Temple, where he might work without interruption. With the time and seclusion, *Jesus the Christ* was finally completed. Upon its completion he wrote, "Had it not been that I was privileged to do this work in the Temple, it would be at present far from completion. I have felt the inspiration of the place and have appreciated the privacy and quietness incident thereto."[2]

A humorous story exemplifies Elder Talmage's preoccupation with his studies. President Heber J. Grant felt that Elder Talmage needed a means of relaxation from his continual studies, and that golf would be just the thing. He struck up a deal with Talmage that if he would come out to the golf course and learn to swing a club and practice until he hit a ball that would be satisfactory to President Grant, President Grant would stop nagging him to play. President Grant was confident that by that time Elder Talmage would be hooked. To the course they went, along with other General Authorities who played golf and who had joined in the fun. After being shown how to grip and swing the club, Elder Talmage teed up a ball and took a swing. To the amazement of all, he connected with the ball and sent a good, straight drive down the center of the fairway. The spectators were momentarily dumbstruck, then burst into applause with President Grant commenting that it was a very fine shot. "Thank you," replied Elder Talmage. "If I have carried out my part of the agreement, then I shall call on you to live up to yours. . . . Now I should like to get back to the office, where I have a great deal of work waiting." With that, Elder Talmage laid down his golf club and went back to his office, apparently never to attempt to play golf again.[3]

*Stephen L. Richards*

Born: June 18, 1879, Mendon, Utah
Ordained Apostle: January 18, 1917
Sustained First Counselor to President David O. McKay: April 9, 1851
Died: May 19, 1959, Salt Lake City, Utah, at age 79

**B**orn June 18, 1879, at Mendon, Cache County, Utah, Stephen L. Richards was the grandson of Willard Richards, close friend and associate of the Prophet Joseph, and member of the Quorum of the Twelve Apostles. Stephen's maternal grandfather was Arthur Stayner, a prominent businessman in the early history of the West who was largely responsible for the establishment of the sugar industry in Utah. Stephen was baptized at about fourteen years of age, and from his youth he took a great interest in Church activities. His education took him to the University of Utah for a short time. He then moved to Ann Arbor, Michigan, where he attended the University of Michigan. While there his home became the meeting place for students who were members of the Church. Transferring to the University of Chicago, he became the first Utah student to earn a Bachelor of Law degree from that institution, graduating *cum laude* in 1904.

In 1900, Stephen married Irene Merrill of Fillmore, Utah. They were blessed with nine children. Following his schooling, Stephen passed the bar exam in Utah and eventually entered into a private practice in civil law. His sound counsel led to a successful legal practice. He served two terms as secretary of the Utah State Bar Association and became an officer and director of some of the largest and most important corporations in the state. He also served for a time as a member of the law faculty at the University of Utah. Much of his Church service was in the Sunday Schools: teacher, stake assistant superintendent, member of stake and general Sunday School boards, and assistant to the general Sunday School superintendent.

In January of 1917, Elder Richards was called to the Quorum of the Twelve Apostles by President Joseph F. Smith. While deeply admired by his coworkers, he had an austere side. When a young Gordon B. Hinckley was employed as executive secretary of the newly formed Church Radio, Publicity, and Mission Literature Committee, over which Elder Richards presided, he was warned, "You'll never be able to work for him—nobody can. He's too exacting, too demanding."[1] Yet he proved to have a profound influence on Gordon as his mentor. In 1918, when Elder David O. McKay was assigned as Superintendent of the Deseret Sunday School Union, he chose as his first assistant his close and lifelong friend, Elder Stephen L. Richards. Years later, in 1951, when Elder McKay became President of the Church, he again looked to his friend and called Elder Richards as his first counselor in the First Presidency. At the time of his being sustained, Elder Richards observed: "I have often felt that the only reason for my being in the presiding councils of the Church is in the devotion of Willard Richards to the Prophet Joseph Smith. I believe there are councils on the other side. We have had testimonies of them, and while I cannot understand, I can believe that the Prophet, out of consideration for his friend, has had a voice in bringing me into the Council of the Twelve through President Joseph F. Smith, and also in that which has brought me to this position."[2]

Throughout Elder Richards's life, he had success as a student as well as in careers in law, politics, business, and the Church. With such a wide variety of successful experiences, the following statement by him takes on added significance. "I believe," said Elder Richards, "that as high an order of intelligence is required to understand and interpret the things of the spirit as is required to comprehend the truths of science and other secular matters. I believe that accomplishments and achievements in the field of religion are just as worthy and commendable and great as are accomplishments in the field of science, in the domain of business and commerce, and in all other worldly affairs."[3]

Unknown to many church members, Elder Richards's legacy to the Church stands in the rotunda of the North Visitors Center on Temple Square. Sometime around 1912, Elder Richards met and became friends with Hubert Eaton, the owner of Forest Lawn Cemetery in Glendale, California. Over the years, their friendship continued to grow. Several decades later, in 1950, while in Copenhagen, Elder Richards saw and was deeply moved by Bertel Thorvaldsen's statue of Christ, the *Christus*. Inspired by its image, the idea was planted in his mind that a copy of this magnificent statue needed to stand on Temple Square.

In 1955, plans were approved by the First Presidency to build a new visitors center on Temple Square. It was at a planning meeting that Elder Richard L. Evans, an Apostle and president of the Temple Square Presidency, commented, "you know, the world thinks we're not Christians because they see no evidence of Christ on our square. They hear the words, but they see no evidence." As they discussed what might be done to portray the Church's belief in Christ, a marble copy of Thorvaldsen's *Christus* was suggested. The First Presidency accepted the proposal. As the Presidency further discussed the idea, President McKay said to President Richards, "Don't you have access to acquire a statue through your association with Hubert Eaton and Forest Lawn?" President Richards contacted his old friend and obtained one of the Forest Lawn copies of the *Christus*, which was sent to Italy as the model for a marble replica made for the Church. The finished product was eleven feet high, and weighed approximately 12,000 pounds. Because of his fondness for the statue, Stephen L. Richards had taken a personal interest in the project and consequently took care of all the preliminary work. He then donated the statue to the Church as his personal gift. Unfortunately, he became seriously ill and died just a few days before the *Christus* arrived at Temple Square. He never saw the statue that would stand as his legacy to the Church.[4]

Richards died of a fatal heart attack on May 19, 1959. Upon hearing of Elder Richard's death, President McKay wept as he told associates, "He was as dear to me as a brother. A true and loyal friend. A wise counselor with one of the greatest minds in the Church. Oh! How I shall miss him!"[5]

*Richard R. Lyman*

Born: November 23, 1870, Fillmore, Utah
Ordained Apostle: April 7, 1918
Excommunicated: November 12, 1943
Rebaptized: October 27, 1954
Died: December 31, 1963, Salt Lake City, Utah, at age 93

Richard Lyman's father was Francis Lyman, president of the Quorum of the Twelve for thirteen years and a member of the Quorum for thirty-six years. His grandfather Amasa Lyman was a member of the Quorum of the Twelve for twenty-eight years and served as a counselor to Joseph Smith for a short time. It has been reported that as a child Richard was never known to smile, though he would jump with excitement. When only eight years of age, he was put in charge of his father's fine horse team and Concord buggy. Although he was too small to hitch the team, he took great pride in keeping the horses, buggy, and harnesses clean and in excellent condition. At around the age of eleven he drove the team for his father, and then for Heber J. Grant, who replaced his father as Tooele Stake president.

Francis Lyman was a strong believer in the importance of hard work for his children and the training gained therefrom. Consequently, Richard grew up spending his summer months working such jobs as herding cattle and hauling lumber out of the mountains. While riding herd he would read the New Testament, which he carried with him. His mother had given it to him with instructions that he was to read it, which he did again and again. In 1888, he attended Brigham Young Academy in Provo. Here he met Amy Brown, whom he would court over the next eight years; they were married in 1896. A friend of Richard's described Amy as the most popular girl he had ever known. She would go on to become a noted sociologist and to serve as general president of the Relief Society during the war years of 1940–45. Richard always credited whatever success he had in the business world, in education, and in the Church to his wife.

In the year of 1889, Richard began studies at Brigham Young College in Logan, Utah. Then in 1891, with the help of a loan from his father, he went east to attend the University of Michigan. On his way east he stopped in Manassa, Colorado, to spend several days with his mother and her other children who had been "on the underground" from the anti-polygamist crusades. It would be the last time that Richard would see his mother alive. The following year he came from Ann Arbor to attend her funeral in Tooele, Utah. At the University, Richard was elected as president of his sophomore class, and two years later as president of his senior class. He continued to work hard during the summer months to help support himself, and eventually graduated with a degree in civil engineering. Following his marriage to Amy, he was employed at the University of Utah where he became a full professor and head of the civil engineering department, which position he held for eighteen years. His work would be briefly interrupted for graduate studies at Cornell University, where he earned a masters of civil engineering degree and a PhD. Richard's secular successes in his field were numerous. He was chairman of the Utah Road Commission, vice chairman of the Utah Water Storage Commission, and a consulting engineer for the Grand Coulee Dam in Washington, the Columbia Basin Water Project, and the Metropolitan Water District of Los Angeles, to mention just a few of the positions he held. His 1915 essay on the flow of streams won the

James R. Coe gold medal, the highest award given in civil engineering in the United States.

Richard Lyman was a large man, standing six feet, four inches tall and weighing 250 pounds. In photographs his face had a gentle look. Within the Church he was involved for several years as superintendent of stake YMMIA, then as supervisor of parent's classes. In 1918, he was ordained an Apostle and set apart in the Quorum of the Twelve. Among his assignments as an Apostle was second assistant in the general YMMIA and president of the European Mission from 1936–38. Elder Spencer W. Kimball's fond memories of Elder Lyman included Elder Lyman's offering the prayer at Elder Kimball's ordination to the apostleship and then inviting Elder Kimball to a luncheon at the Lion House to welcome him into the Quorum. Sadly, within the month, Elder Lyman lost both his apostleship and his membership in the Church. Concerning the meeting of the Council of Twelve on November 12, 1943, Elder Kimball left the following account:

> Our hearts stood still as we heard that Richard R. Lyman, for twenty-six years a member of the Council of the Twelve, was accused of immorality. His written confession was read and he being present did not deny the accusation nor the confession. He told also of the situations. He had little to say. He was as pale as could be. . . . It was a terrible ordeal. To see great strong men such as the members of this Quorum all in tears, some sobbing, all shocked, stunned by the impact, was an unforgettable sight. No tears from him, but plenty from the rest of us, and what a heart-rending experience.

Following the pronouncement of excommunication, "he said goodbye and shook hands with each of us and left the Temple, his quorum, his Church. Still stunned almost beyond recovery, the members seemed to be yet unable to believe the terrible truth."[1] A one-sentence announcement was presented to the newspaper only stating that the ground for excommunication was violation of the Christian law of chastity.

Elder Kimball, with Elder LeGrand Richards, continued to have interviews with Richard Lyman and finally recommended him for rebaptism in 1954. Elder Kimball recorded: "I kept hoping through the years that he would make another serious attempt to receive his [priesthood and temple] blessings back, but apparently it did not seem important enough to him, or he didn't have the energy or the courage or something. At any rate, he died as a lay member of the Church without Priesthood, without endowments, without sealings, and it was sad indeed."[2] And yet his faith had not altogether abandoned him. Writing in 1958, Richard recounted how his mother had impressed upon his mind the law of tithing. He then wrote: "That lesson I have never forgotten nor has God the Eternal Father ever forgotten me. With no salary and no business for the last fifteen years this Great Provider has certainly 'opened the windows of heaven' and He has poured out upon me many marvelous, greatly needed and greatly appreciated blessings"[3]

Richard Lyman died December 31, 1963, at the age of ninety-three. Of the four General Authorities who attended his funeral, only Elder Kimball had been in the Quorum when Elder Lyman was excommunicated.

*Melvin J. Ballard*

Born: February 9, 1873, Logan, Utah
Ordained Apostle: January 7, 1919
Died: July 30, 1939, Salt Lake City, at age 66

Margaret McNeil Ballard had become ill during her pregnancy and was confined to bed. She had already lost two children in infancy and had had several miscarriages. One day when her husband had taken the other children to see a parade, she crawled to the door and locked it so she would be alone and knelt in prayer to ask the Lord for help and to know her standing before Him. In answer to her pleas, a voice spoke plainly to her, saying, "Be of good Cheer. Your life is acceptable, and you will bear a son who will become an Apostle of the Lord Jesus Christ."[1] She soon bore a son who was named Melvin Joseph Ballard. She never revealed this experience to anyone. The written account was found among her personal papers after her death in 1919. Melvin J. Ballard was called to the Quorum of the Twelve Apostles a year after she died.

Born in Logan, Utah, to Bishop Henry and Margaret Ballard, Melvin grew up working on his father's farm and attending school as time and means allowed. Being studious in nature, he managed to obtain a common school education even amid difficulties. Melvin seems to have had a feeling from a very young age that he had a life mission to aid in the salvation of his fellow man. Attending to his Aaronic Priesthood duties with diligence, he found special delight in service projects; cleaning the chapel; chopping fire wood for widows and the poor; and especially distributing gifts to widows, orphans, and those in need on Christmas Day. Melvin was talented in music and had a beautiful singing voice that was well-known throughout the area and was sought after for funerals and other special occasions. He took special delight in opportunities to preach and over the years became a gifted speaker and teacher.

Continuing his schooling, Melvin graduated from Brigham Young College with the class of 1894. In June of 1896, he married Martha Jones in the Logan Utah Temple. The following month he was ordained a Seventy and sent on a mission to the eastern cities and then to the Northern States Mission. He returned in December 1898. In 1899, along with Joseph Cardon, he organized the Logan Knitting Factory, which became one of the leading manufacturing institutions in the state. In 1900, he was set apart as second counselor in the bishopric, which calling he fulfilled until 1906. This calling was briefly interrupted when, in 1902, he was called to go to Boise to assist in organizing the scattered Saints into a branch of the Church. In Logan he was also ward chorister for many years as well as chairman of the Cache Stake tabernacle choir. In 1909, he was called as president of the Northwestern States Mission, presiding for the next ten years.

It was toward the end of his presidency that Elder Ballard had a remarkable vision. He reported it as follows:

> When I was doing missionary work with some of our brethren, laboring among the Indians, seeking the Lord for light to decide certain matters pertaining to our work there, and receiving a witness from Him that we were doing things according to His will, I found myself one evening in the dreams of the night, in that sacred building, the Temple. After a season of prayer and rejoicing I was informed that I

should have the privilege of entering into one of those sacred rooms, to meet a glorious Personage, and as I entered the door, I saw, seated on a raised platform, the most glorious Being my eyes ever have beheld, or that I ever conceived existed in all the eternal worlds. As I approached to be introduced, he arose and stepped towards me with extended arms, and he smiled as he softly spoke my name. If I shall live to be a million years old, I shall never forget that smile. He took me into his arms and kissed me, pressed me to His bosom, and blessed me, until the marrow of my bones seemed to melt! When He had finished, I fell at His feet, and as I bathed them with my tears and kisses, I saw the prints of the nails in the feet of the Redeemer of the world. The feeling that I had in the presence of Him who hath all things in His hands, to have His love, His affection, and His blessings was such that if I ever can receive that of which I had but a foretaste, I would give all that I am, all that I ever hope to be, to feel what I then felt.[2]

In January 1919, Melvin J. Ballard was called to the apostleship by President Heber J. Grant. During previous years when President Grant was a member of the Twelve, he had consistently submitted the name of a good friend to fill vacancies that arose in the Quorum, but his friend was never called. Elder Grant was consequently reported to have said that if he ever became president of the Church and there was a vacancy in the Twelve, he would call his friend because he was so well qualified. When that time came, he went to the Lord for the approval of his friend, but the name of Melvin J. Ballard kept coming into his mind, a man whom President Grant hardly knew. So impressive was the spirit, that Melvin's name was presented to the Twelve and accepted.

On Christmas day in 1925, in Buenos Aires, Argentina, Elder Ballard dedicated South America for the preaching of the gospel. At that time there were only four members of the Church in all of that land. Missionary work among the native Argentines was difficult and only one person was baptized in the following eight months. Nonetheless, on July 4, 1926, Elder Ballard prophesied,

The work of the Lord will grow slowly for a time here just as an oak grows slowly from an acorn. It will not shoot up in a day as does the sunflower that grows quickly and then dies. But thousands will join the Church here. It will be divided into more than one mission and will be one of the strongest in the Church. The work here is the smallest that it will ever be. The day will come when the Lamanites in this land will be given a chance. The South American Mission will be a power in the Church.[3]

In the summer of 1939, after a grueling tour throughout the eastern states, Elder Ballard drove his car from New York to Salt Lake City. In the driveway of his home he collapsed and was rushed to the LDS Hospital where he was found to have acute leukemia. He never left the hospital but went in and out of a coma. According to his son, Elder Ballard rose up on one elbow, and as if looking out over a congregation, said, "And above all else, brethren, let us think straight."[4] These were his last words and are inscribed on a plaque in the office of his grandson, Elder M. Russell Ballard of the Quorum of the Twelve.

*John A. Widtsoe*

Born: January 31, 1872, Dalloe, Island of Froyen, Norway
Ordained Apostle: March 17, 1921
Died: November 29, 1952, Salt Lake City, at age 80

When John was born, his wrist was attached to his head and there was some doubt that he would live. But crude surgery released his wrist and he survived. When he was about two years of age, the family moved to the mainland of Norway, where his father died, leaving his mother, Anna, to struggle as a seamstress for the care of her children. Following her conversion, she emigrated to the Utah with a group of Norwegian Saints in 1883. Settling in Logan, Anna continued as a seamstress and saw that her children got a proper education.

Having always had a great desire for knowledge, John attended Brigham Young College at Logan, graduating in 1891. He then entered Harvard University, graduating with highest honors in biochemistry in 1894. From 1894 to 1898, he was a professor of chemistry in the Agricultural College at Logan (now Utah State University).

He then went to Germany where, in 1899, he obtained a PhD from the University of Gottingen. Returning to Utah, he again became employed in the field of education. As an educator, Professor Widtsoe acted as director of the Utah Agricultural Experiment Station from 1900 to 1905, director of the Department of Agriculture in the Brigham Young University from 1905 to 1907, president of the Utah Agricultural College from 1907 to 1916, and president of the University of Utah from 1916 until his calling to the Quorum of the Twelve in 1921.

In launching the agricultural experiment station in 1900, Widtsoe's aim was to improve the agricultural potential of the Great Basin area through three goals: examining irrigation from a scientific point of view, studying the possibilities of dry-land farming, and conveying information to farmers and housewives. Consequently, he wrote two books, one on the principles of irrigation and a second on dry-farming. Both books won international acclaim and were used throughout the arid regions of the world, being interpreted into many languages. As a result he was appointed to serve as president of the International Dry-Farming Congress in 1912. Recognized as the father of scientific irrigation practices and dry-farming, he was later called by the US Secretary of Interior to revise the reclamation laws and policies of the United States. As an advisor on the Colorado River Commission, he urged that the whole Colorado River Basin be developed independent of state lines, which proposal was accepted. He thus became a key voice in the development of the Hoover and Glenn Canyon Dams.

His efforts to bring updated information to the farmers, however, was not so immediately successful. Widstsoe recorded of these early attempts: "Up in Heber, a leading citizen, examining my hands, looked heavenward and remarked, 'Oh Lord, that the time should come that a man with such hands should teach us how to farm.'" At a farmers' institute held in Springville, "Only two men came out. Nevertheless we practiced on them. After the meeting we discovered that one of the two was stone-deaf, and passed time by attending meetings, and the other was the janitor who had to be present. Eight years later when our agricultural train reached Springville, we were met by the mayor, city council with a brass band, and the meeting hall was crowded to capacity. It did not take long to convert the people of Utah."[1]

As the twentieth century progressed, scientific reasoning increasingly confronted religious beliefs. Within the Church, Dr. Widtsoe's knowledgeable voice joined ranks with other distinguished individuals, such as James E. Talmage and B. H. Roberts, in advancing reconciliation between science and religion. Widtsoe taught that Joseph Smith's teachings were in harmony with scientific principles and that the universe was controlled by law. Widtsoe believed that the earth was created in an undetermined period of time, the terms *day* and *night* being figurative, and that we need not accept a six-day or a 6,000 year creation, although he felt people were free to come to their own interpretation. Regarding evolution, it was his feeling that all things are in ceaseless change, moving toward a state of increasing complexity; however, that change is directed by the Spirit of God and not by natural selection as proposed by Darwin. He believed that God was nature's master and worked in a natural manner. However, Widtsoe, along with Talmage and members of the Twelve, reviewed and approved the draft of an article written by Orson F. Whitney under assignment from the First Presidency, entitled "The Origin of Man." It maintained that Adam was the first man and was created in the image of God. Man was never something other than what man is today. Throughout his career Widtsoe wrote many books on both science and gospel doctrine, maintaining there was harmony in all "truth." Elder Widtsoe did not enjoy confrontation, so in the early 1930s when a controversy arose among some of the leading brethren over questions relating to the creation, Elder Widtsoe wrote in a letter, "I have been afflicted with these questions for a generation of time. It does seem high time that the Church answer them definitively or declare that it does not know, so that more important questions may engage the minds of young and old."[2]

On March 17, 1921, President Heber J. Grant told Widtsoe that he was being called to the Twelve. Would he accept the call? "There flashed before my mind the probable result," recorded Widtsoe, "The laying aside of many a cherished desire; the constant service to the end of life; the complete change in life from that for which I had been trained. But, the biggest thing in my life was the restored gospel of Jesus Christ. It had full claim upon me. . . . Then, without hesitation I answered, yes."[3] His duties as a member of the Twelve included President of the European Mission for nearly six years, editor of the *Improvement Era,* and Commissioner of Education.

He died at the age of eighty of uremia while in the comfort of his home with family present. At his funeral, President J. Reuben Clark said of him, "where other men saw blind forces at work and at play, he saw God. And throughout his life, as I see it, he brought to bear the full treasure house of his great knowledge in the field of science, to advance the cause of our Heavenly Father. That was the key to his work throughout life."[4]

*Joseph F. Merrill*

Born: August 24, 1868, Richmond, Utah
Ordained Apostle: October 8, 1931
Died: February 3, 1952, at age 83

**B**orn August 24, 1868, in Richmond, Cache County, Utah, Joseph was the son of Apostle Marriner Merrill and Maria Kingsbury. He grew up assisting his father in farming and railroading. In later years he recounted how, following his twelfth year, he spent several summers working in grading camps along the railroad his father was constructing in northern Utah and Idaho. The men working these camps were rough and crude and all of them smoked and drank. They often tried to tempt young Joseph and his brothers to do the same, but they would not. One evening when the dinner bell rang, one of the workers threw down a lighted cigarette of which hardly any had been used. Wondering what a cigarette tasted like, young Joseph waited until everyone had left and went and picked up the cigarette. As he put it between his lips, he looked around to make sure he was alone and saw the foreman a short distance away, looking at him. Joseph threw down the cigarette and ran. The foreman never said a word about it to anyone, but Joseph learned from that experience "that everything I did from then on should be openly and above board, which I have endeavored to do since that time."[1] Interestingly, years later as an Apostle, he was chairman of the Anti-Liquor-Tobacco Committee of the Church, bringing to the attention of Church members the latest scientific research and findings on the evils of tobacco and liquor.

In Richmond, Joseph attended the common schools until, in 1887, he entered the University of Deseret. Graduating in 1889, he attended the University of Michigan, where he studied chemistry; he received a bachelor of science degree in 1893. He then became an assistant professor of chemistry and physics at the University of Utah, but soon returned east where he obtained a PhD from Johns Hopkins University, majoring in physics. In 1920 he would also receive an honorary doctor of science degree from the University of Utah. Following graduation from Johns Hopkins, Dr. Merrill returned to the University of Utah, where he organized the School of Engineering and served as dean of the College of Mines and Engineering for twenty-five years. During his lifetime, Elder Merrill outlived two wives. He was married in June 1898 to Annie Laura Hyde, who died in 1917. In June 1918, he married Emily Traub, who died in October 1941. Elder Merrill was not interested in obtaining wealth but was greatly interested in serving others. When one of his sons died in World War I, resulting in his receiving insurance money, he took the major portion of that money and contributed it to student loan funds in order to help others receive an education. His personal motto was "cheerful service."

While doing undergraduate studies at the University of Michigan, Joseph Merrill was president of the Ann Arbor Branch. He went on to serve as a member of the YMMIA general board, Salt Lake Stake YMMIA superintendent, and counselor in the Granite Stake presidency. When the call came to serve as Commissioner of Church Education, Dr. Merrill was not too well pleased over leaving the University of Utah, but the Church had called and he responded, resigning as dean of engineering. As commissioner he inaugurated, in large measure, the seminary and institute programs of the Church, which began in the Granite Stake when he was in the stake presidency. He was also one of the first men to give encouragement to the "home evening" program.

Elder Merrill was called as an Apostle October 8, 1931, and served in that calling for twenty years until the time of his death. As an Apostle he visited nearly every stake in the Church and traveled extensively throughout Europe, where he served as president of the European Mission from 1933 to 1936. Because of his eastern education, he became an example to other Latter-day Saints who desired to obtain a higher education. A nephew of his recalled how he wanted to go to Harvard but was warned by many against such a venture. "One day my father said to me, 'Son, do you want to go to Harvard?' 'Yes, father, I do,' I replied. 'Well, then, don't pay any more attention to what they are saying. Look at Uncle Joseph. Remember him. His scholastic work in eastern universities did not affect him in his Church work.' Oh, what a guide that was for me throughout my entire life."[2] Along with such men as James E. Talmage and John A. Widtsoe, Elder Merrill became a voice for truth as found in science as well as in religion. In his series of radio talks in 1945, he spoke of the wonders of the universe discovered by physicists and astronomers, and told of how they supported the existence of God. For many, it was good to know that Elder Merrill, familiar with both Mormonism and science, considered that science fit in well with Mormonism.

Eighty-three years of age at the time of his death, he was reported to have the vitality of a man in his fifties. On a Saturday evening he conducted the first session of the Ensign Stake quarterly conference. Afterward he returned to the home of his son where he was living. Around ten p.m., after visiting with family members, he retired to his bed. Sometime during the night he quietly passed away. The family did not discover his death until around nine o'clock in the morning when they checked to see why he was not getting ready for Church. He was the eldest member of the General Authorities at the time of his death.

## Charles A. Callis

Born: May 4, 1865, Dublin, Ireland
Ordained Apostle: October 12, 1933
Died: January 21, 1947, Jacksonville, Florida, at age 81

The story is told by Elder James E. Faust of a young man, who as he concluded his mission to the British Isles, said, "I think my mission has been a failure. I have labored all my days as a missionary here and I have only baptized one dirty little Irish kid. That is all I have baptized." Many years after his return home to Montana, he was visited one day by a gentleman who asked if he had served a mission in the British Isles in 1873. "Yes," he replied. The man then asked, "And do you remember having said that you thought your mission was a failure because you had only baptized one dirty little Irish kid?" "Yes." The gentleman then put out his hand and said, "I would like to shake hands with you. My name is Charles A. Callis of the Council of Twelve of the Church of Jesus Christ of Latter-day Saints. I am that dirty little Irish kid you baptized on your mission." Elder Faust concluded by saying that

Elder Callis served for twenty-five years as a mission president and thirteen years in his apostolic ministry and that he felt "privileged to have known this great Apostle of the Lord when I was a young man."[1]

Charles Albert Callis was born May 4, 1865, in Dublin Ireland, and knew extreme poverty from an early age. He was baptized at the age of ten, and that very same year immigrated to America with his widowed mother. Eventually they settled in Centerville, Utah, where his mother remarried. Due to continued poverty, Charles left home and moved to Coalville at the age of sixteen, where he began working in the mines. For eleven years he labored underground, during which time he drifted for a short while from the Church. He was reclaimed when Elder B. H. Roberts of the Council of Seventy took a personal interest in him. In December 1892, he was called on a mission to Great Britain and spent part of his time in his native Ireland. Returning to Coalville, he determined to further his education and make something of his life. In 1896, in Utah's first national election as a state, Charles ran for state representative and won. He consistently voted to better the conditions of the common laborer, especially coal miners and railroaders. During this time he studied law and was eventually elected as county attorney, which position he won for three consecutive terms. He also met and married Grace E. Pack of Kamas, Utah, during this time.

But Brother Callis's life took a new direction when, in December 1905, he was called on a mission to the eastern states, which assignment was changed to the southern states in March 1906. Permission was granted for him to take his wife and two daughters with him. The southern states was a difficult area for the Church. Four years previous, the missionary force had been reduced from 466 to 154, due in part to the sufferings that had been inflicted upon missionaries, including whippings, tar and featherings, forcible ejection from communities, attempted murders, and even the murders of some missionaries. Attitudes were beginning to change when Elder Callis arrived, but it was still difficult for Mormon missionaries and the Church in general. Becoming a member of the Florida Bar, Elder Callis was able to defend the Church in court, and through his associations with judges and community leaders, and with his sense of justice and his persuasive powers, he was able to improve the image of the Church and spread goodwill. Two years later he returned home, only to be immediately recalled to the South, this time to serve as mission president, which position he held continuously from 1908 to 1933. During that time, he helped make the South a safer place for missionaries and church members in general. In October 1933, he was finally released, only to be called to the Quorum of the Twelve.

As a mission president Elder Callis has been seen as a transitionalist, bridging the gap between nineteenth century missionary work and that of modern day uses of referrals, mass media, and public relations. Yet he was still a firm believer in tracting. He urged his missionaries to be clean and to live frugally. Though not a taskmaster, he did expect hard work from his missionaries. His style of leadership can perhaps be seen in an incident recalled by Apostle Delbert L. Stapley. As a young missionary in the Southern States Mission, Elder Stapley rode on the train to his newly assigned area with his mission president, President Callis. Upon arrival at the station, they put their luggage in the back of a buggy that only had room for two people. President Callis got in the buggy alongside the driver and told the missionary to follow. As the horse kicked up the dust ahead, the missionary began to resent President Calllis. After a mile he had lost respect for his leader altogether. Then the buggy came to a halt and President Callis traded places with the elder. For two miles President Callis followed in the dust. "I grew to love him with every step" said Elder Stapley. "I thought he was about the greatest man who had lived."[2]

Though a truly blue-collared Apostle who grew up knowing poverty and hard labor, he was a deeply spiritual man. Speaking of Elder Callis, President Harold B. Lee said, "There are a few whom I have heard pray who did talk with God, one of whom was the late [Elder] Charles A. Callis. I never heard him pray at the holy altars in the temple, I never heard him when we knelt together in prayer when we were out on a difficult mission, but what he seemed, as he talked, to be reaching right into the portals of our Father's holy dwelling place, and he talked with divine beings."[3] President Lee further illustrated this point on another occasion when he told of being on assignment with Elder Callis. It seems that the two were unable to agree over a knotty issue. "That was always a rather serious thing not be in agreement with Brother Callis," reflected President Lee. "He was a man of strong, vigorous, and powerful thinking. He had said finally, 'I will have to sleep on it.'. . . The next morning, he called me into his room; and as he pulled his chair alongside mine, he said to me with an impressiveness which I shall never forget, 'Last night I talked with God, and He has given me to understand that you are right and I am wrong.'"[4]

Sister Callis died in October 1946. Her passing was a terrible blow to Elder Callis from which he never fully recovered. In January of 1947, he traveled to Jacksonville, Florida, to take part in the organization of the first stake in his beloved South. To his daughter he wrote that evening, "I am being treated well but it is very lonely without your mother. . . . The Lord gave me strength to go through with the organization. With his aid I am battling through. I feel that your mother is not far from us."[5] Within twelve hours of his writing, Elder Callis had passed away.

## J. Reuben Clark Jr.

Born: September 1, 1871, Grantsville, Utah
Sustained Second Counselor to President Heber J. Grant: April 6, 1933.
Sustained First Counselor to President Heber J. Grant: October 6, 1934
Ordained Apostle: October 11, 1934
Sustained First Counselor to President George Albert Smith:
    May 21, 1945
Sustained Second Counselor to President David O. McKay: April 9, 1951
Sustained First Counselor to President David O. McKay: June 12, 1959
Died: October 6, 1961, Salt Lake City, Utah, at age 90

A s a printer, young Thomas S. Monson got to know President
Clark fairly well. One evening, delivering some press proofs to
President Clark in his home office, he found President Clark
reading the scriptures. He was in a quiet and reflective mood. He turned,
looked at Brother Monson, and started to read: "Let us hear the conclu-
sion of the whole matter: Fear God, and keep his commandments; for
this is the whole duty of man" (Ecclesiastes 12:13). He exclaimed, "A
treasured truth: And profound philosophy!" President Monson stated
that that lesson has ever remained a bright memory in his life.[1]

Joshua Reuben Clark Jr. was born about three miles north of Grantsville, Tooele County, in a rock house that his father had built. J. Reuben, the eldest of ten children, grew up accustomed to hard work and was actively involved in Church programs. He also had a deep thirst for learning, and his father, though a poor man, would find occasions to buy books of interest for his son. At the age of nineteen, J. Reuben left home to attend the Latter-day Saint College in Salt Lake City. At the age of twenty-three he entered the University of Utah, where he became student body president, managing editor of the student newspaper, and valedictorian of his graduating class. At the age of thirty-two, he left the faculty of the LDS Business College and entered Law School at Columbia University, receiving his Law Degree in 1906.

In addition to conducting a private law practice, he went on to have a distinguished career as a civil servant, serving as, among other positions, Solicitor of the Department of State, Major in the Judge Advocate General's Office during World War I, legal adviser to the Ambassador to Mexico, Undersecretary of State, and Ambassador to Mexico. During these years he wrote many important papers on the legal system, probably his most noteworthy being his treatise on the Monroe Doctrine. His career can best be summarized in the words of the Hon. Philander C. Knox, who served as Secretary of State and US Senator, who said, "I have not in a long professional and public service met his superior and rarely his equal."[2] The Hon. Hunting Wilson who was Acting Secretary of State, declared, "I never knew a man whose high character, sound judgment, and splendid ability won for him a more extraordinary position in the absolute confidence of those in charge of the department and of all with whom he was associated."[3]

Even though he had no Church leadership experience on ward, stake, or mission levels—he, himself, stating that his church experience had been relegated almost entirely to teaching Sunday School—yet, in December of 1931, J. Reuben Clark was issued a call to the First Presidency. It had been over a half century since someone had been called to the First Presidency who was not already a General Authority. Although it meant giving up all his political aspirations, he accepted the call. However, because he was in the midst of sensitive negotiations with Mexico, it was mutually agreed that announcement of his call would be postponed until the negotiations were completed. He was sustained as second counselor to Heber J. Grant in April of 1933. At the October conference of 1934, he was sustained as first counselor to President Grant as well as an Apostle and member of the Quorum of the Twelve. David O. McKay was second counselor. They both continued in these positions under the later presidency of George Albert Smith.

When President Smith died, David O. McKay, as senior Apostle, became president of the Church. He then called Stephen L. Richards as first counselor and J. Reuben Clark as second counselor, referring to Elder Richard's seniority in the Twelve as the reason for this reversal of President Clark's position. Never before had such a change taken place in the First Presidency. Elder Spencer W. Kimball recorded that when the announcement was made to the Quorum of the Twelve, "I was stunned. . . . I looked around and found the other brethren stunned. . . . We had been wholly unprepared for this shock."[4] It was equally shocking to President Clark, for in the world in which he had lived and operated, such an action was seen as a demotion and a question of competence. Yet, at general conference, following the sustaining votes, President Clark spoke his famous words which have since become a standard in the Church: "In the service of the Lord, it is not where you serve but how. In the Church of Jesus Christ of Latter-day Saints, one takes the place to which one is duly called, which place one neither seeks nor declines."[5]

Perhaps Elder Marion G. Romney, then an Assistant to the Twelve, summed up the significance of these events when he recorded in his diary: "His performance in this conference in [his] taking what most people consider a demotion and [in his] presenting the authorities in the solemn assembly, had endeared him in the hearts of the people more than anything he has ever done. It must be that he is being tempered for a greater glory. Perhaps some of the rest of us must be trained to step down gracefully, and President Clark is the only man great enough to give us a demonstration of how to do it."[6] President Clark's daughter wrote to him, "I believe your spirit grew to a new height that day—perhaps one to which you might never have attained without this experience."[7] Eight years later, with the death of President Richards, President Clark again became first counselor.

President Clark left his mark upon the Church. Many of his classic talks have been printed in booklet form. His charge to the Church Educational System still directs Church education to this day. His Bible scholarship is seen in such books as *Our Lord of the Gospels* and *Why the King James Version*. As a counselor in the First Presidency, he made many proposals in church management that have left an impact upon various programs of the Church even today. As Elder Spencer W. Kimball wrote to him, "What leadership you have given to the Church! What power! What vigor! You have been an example to all the people and will be long remembered and quoted."[8] President Clark died after twenty-eight years in the First Presidency, at the age of ninety.

*Alonzo A. Hinckley*

Born: April 23, 1870, Cove Fort, Utah
Ordained Apostle: October 11, 1934
Died: December 22, 1936, Salt Lake City, Utah, at age 65

Alonzo was born at Cove Fort, an outpost at least twenty miles from the nearest village. He would live to become the uncle of Gordon B. Hinckley, inasmuch as Gordon's father, Bryant, was Alonzo's brother. As a youth, on more than one occasion, Alonzo narrowly escaped death. Working on a ranch, he was dragged along the stony ground by a runaway horse. In answer to his prayer for deliverance, his boot came off, freeing him from the horse. On another occasion, he was playing in the upstairs of an unfinished house when the roof collapsed. A hole in the roof intended for the chimney, encircled the area where he sat, preserving him from being crushed by the roof.

Following graduation from the public schools, Alonzo went on to attend Brigham Young University, after which he taught in the public schools for two years. He then turned his attention to farming and merchandizing. Called on a mission to the Netherlands, he came to experience spiritual gifts in miraculous ways. He records that when he arrived in Holland in 1897, he was unable to learn the language. One day a woman stepped out of her house to loudly rebuke him. So loud did she speak that a workman across the street came over to the house, thinking that the young elder might be abusing the woman. "I did not realize for the moment, that I was understanding Dutch as clearly as though she had been speaking English." When she was through, he calmly bore testimony of the restored gospel in her own language. The workman put his arm across Elder Hinckley's shoulders and said to the woman, "The Mormon Church may have its black sheep, but this is a man of God." The woman, her bitterness gone, replied, "I know it." Running to the mission home, anxious to tell of the experience, he found that the language had left him. But that evening at a conference, he was called upon to speak, and the ability to speak Dutch again returned to him.[1]

While in Holland, his wife, Rose May Robinson, whom he had married in 1892, gave birth to their second son. In answer to his anxiety over them, he saw them in a dream, seeing that they were well and cared for. On another occasion, a woman, suffering from tuberculosis, was told by the doctor that she only had a few months to live. Calling on the missionaries to bless her, Elder Hinckley told her that if she would be baptized and have faith, she would recover and live to have children. She joined the Church, immigrated to Utah, and lived to have eleven children.

When Alonzo returned from his mission in 1901, he succeeded his father as president of the Millard Stake, and then the Deseret Stake, following a stake division. He served as stake president for twenty-seven years. President Heber J. Grant would say of him years later, "these two men [Anthony W. Ivins and Alonzo A. Hinckley], when they were presidents of Stakes, one in the United States and one in Mexico, fed me the bread of life and had more of the spirit of the living God and of the Gospel of Jesus Christ than any of the other Stake Presidents that I knew."[2] During this time, Alonzo also served as a representative in the State Legislature. Having had some negative thoughts about a legislative colleague, Charles R. Mabey, that he later found to be unjustified, he came to Mabey and apologized although he had never expressed his feelings to anyone else. "His conscience was of so fine a texture," said Mabey, "that it wouldn't let a wrong, known only to himself, go uncorrected. That conscience had to be satisfied. Is there any wonder that I formed a deep and lasting regard for him?" Consequently, when Mabey became governor of Utah, he called Alonzo to be State Secretary of Agriculture, a newly established department. "He organized that department and had it functioning in perfect order within the minimum of time," recalled Mabey.[3]

While serving as president of the California Mission in October 1934, Alonzo was called to the Quorum of the Twelve. Years earlier in October of 1903, he received a blessing from a stake patriarch in which he was promised that "If you continue to labor with the zeal with which you have started, you will be numbered with the Twelve Apostles of the Church of Jesus Christ of Latter-day Saints."[4] Alonzo never mentioned this blessing until thirty years later when ordained an Apostle.

At the time of his calling he was not in the best of health and lived for slightly more than two years thereafter. Prior to his death, he was visited by heavenly beings. Having gone to Southern California for his health, he was visited one night by his father, Ira, who had been dead for over thirty years. His father told him that he was greatly in need of his help on the other side, having more work than he could do. Alonzo told his father that he had work he yet needed to finish in this life and wished to stay. The next night his father appeared again and the conversation continued from the night before. On the third night, his father came and said he would have to have Alonzo. That was the final word, and Alonzo returned home to Salt Lake City. There, one evening shortly before his death, when his daughter came into his room to check on him, he told her that he had had a wonderful afternoon in the company of three heavenly beings dressed in the robes of the Holy Priesthood. He told of their teaching him to sing a hymn. President Heber J. Grant said, "although he had a terrible disease, the Lord saw fit to let him suffer but very little."[5] He died of stomach cancer on December 22, 1936, at the age of sixty-five.

There appeared to be no doubt in Elder Hinckley's mind as to what the next life held for him. Upon hearing from his doctor that his illness would be fatal, Elder Hinckley wrote a letter to the First Presidency. Included in the letter were words reminiscent of Enos's farewell in the Book of Mormon (Enos 1:26–27). He wrote,

> I assure you that I am not deeply disturbed over the final results. I am reconciled, and I reach my hands to take what My Father has for me, be it life or death. With a spirit of thanksgiving and I trust free from vanity or boastfulness, I look over the past with satisfaction. I would not turn the leaf down on any chapter of my life. So far as I know I have honored my Heavenly Father with my time, my humble talents, and all the means that he has blessed me with and I have dealt justly with all men. I have fought, but I have fought fairly. As to the future, I have no misgivings. It is inviting and glorious, and I sense rather clearly what it means to be saved by the redeeming blood of Jesus Christ and to be exalted by his power and be with him ever more.[6]

*Albert E. Bowen*

Born: October 31, 1875, Henderson Creek, Idaho
Ordained Apostle: April 8, 1937
Died: July 15, 1953, Salt Lake City, Utah, at age 77

Born October 31, 1875, at Henderson Creek in southern Idaho, Albert was the seventh son of David and Annie Bowen. His first home was a log cabin and he grew up knowing the hard labors of farm life. As a young boy barely old enough to drive a team, he helped his father freight grain to Ogden, Collinston, and Corrine, all railroad points in northern Utah. When he was only about ten years of age, he spent a hard winter with his elder brother, John, homesteading in Star Valley, Wyoming, during which time their diet consisted almost entirely of venison. During these younger years he had a deep desire to grow in knowledge. Consequently, as he approached the age of twenty, a family council was held and it was decided to send Albert to Logan, Utah, where he completed his high school courses and attended Brigham Young College. He was able to partially support himself by working as a part-time teacher.

Graduating with a bachelor of arts degree in 1902, he then married Aletha E. Reeder of Hyde Park, Utah. But just when they were getting started in their married life, there came a mission call to the Swiss-German Mission. Now separated, Aletha was left to support her husband's mission with her meager earnings.

Upon returning from his mission, Albert joined the faculty at Brigham Young College in Logan. But in 1905, tragedy struck when his young wife died after giving birth to twin sons. It would be eleven years before he would marry again. Obtaining a law degree from the University of Chicago in 1911, Albert returned to Logan, where he practiced law for four years, also serving as superintendent of the Cache Stake Sunday School. He then moved to Salt Lake City, where he became a law partner with J. Reuben Clark, Jr. In 1916, he married Emma Lucy Gates. A renowned singer, she was a popular opera and concert artist throughout the major cities of Europe, sang with the Chicago Opera until establishing her own opera company, and had a highly successful recording career with Columbia Records. Following her marriage to Albert, she continued to sing professionally until 1934, when her husband was called as a General Authority.

In Salt Lake City, Albert served for about twelve years on the Deseret Sunday School general board and was chairman of the board's missionary training committee. In January 1935, he was called as general superintendent of the YMMIA, becoming the first person to head a Church auxiliary that was not a General Authority. Then, in April 1937, Albert Bowen was called to the quorum of the Twelve. As an Apostle he traveled to stakes throughout North America, visited military installations during World War II, helped start the Church servicemen's program, served on the Church expenditures committee, and championed the welfare program. When Elder Bowen became a member of the board of directors of the Deseret News Publishing Company, he knew nothing about the newspaper business. But he was determined he was not going to get into something that he knew nothing about. And so, at the age of sixty-five, he began to learn the newspaper business. He also began to learn about the printing business, that being a part of the Deseret News Company. Later, when he was called upon to negotiate with paper mills and publishing companies, he learned all he could about paper manufacturing and publishing. This thirst for knowledge and desire to be well informed in the businesses he dealt with, earned him the respect of those with whom he worked as well as those who worked under his direction. When faced with a problem, he was known to say, "What are the facts? Get all the facts, for there is no substitute for facts."[1]

Elder Bowen died July 15, 1953, following a stroke and a year of suffering from arteriosclerosis. "When he was stricken," said a friend and associate, "as soon as he could speak again, he said, 'I am ready. I am ready to go.' But the Lord made him wait. Throughout all that waiting he still was the obedient, the faithful, the patient man he had always been."[2] Speaking at Elder Bowen's funeral, Elder Richard L. Evans, then a member of the First Council of Seventy, summed up his life in these words:

> His life in some ways would seem to be a sermon to a generation of young people who face serious uncertainties, and are sometimes impatient with the delays of life. His was a late start. . . . He was twenty years of age before he began his high school work; twenty-seven before he received his first college degree; married before he went on his mission; twenty-nine when he returned; a widower at thirty with two infant sons; thirty-three before he started the study of law; thirty six before he received his degree in jurisprudence, with highest honors, at the University of Chicago. And with that late start, years behind what most young men would these days consider essential, with all of this, he rose to unusual eminence, professionally and personally; with all of this he proved a great point and principle; that hard work and high purpose are more important than traveling fast in deviating directions.[3]

*Sylvester Q. Cannon*

Born: June 10, 1877, Salt Lake City, Utah
Sustained as Presiding Bishop: June 4, 1925
Sustained as Associate to the Quorum of the Twelve: April 6, 1938
Ordained Apostle: April 14, 1938
Sustained member of the Quorum of the Twelve: April 6, 1939
Died: May 29, 1943, Salt Lake City, Utah, at age 65

**B**orn the son of George Q. Cannon and Elizabeth Hoagland, he was the youngest of eleven children born to the couple. His younger years were spent on the Cannon farm and attending a private school maintained by his father. Following three years at the Latter-day Saints College and year at the University of Utah, he attended the Massachusetts Institute of Technology, graduating in 1899 with a bachelor of science degree in mining engineering. Shortly after graduation he was called on a mission to the Netherlands. Having previously studied French and German quite extensively, he became mission president after a year of service, which position he held until his release in 1902. In 1904, he was called as first counselor in the Pioneer Stake presidency. In that same year he married Winnifred Saville. His service in the stake presidency was interrupted from 1907 to 1909, when he again served as president of the Netherlands Mission. In 1917, he was called as president of the Pioneer Stake, which position he held until 1925, when he was called as Presiding Bishop of the Church. In 1938, he was ordained an Apostle and sustained as Associate to the Twelve. A year later, upon the death of Elder Melvin J. Ballard, he was sustained as a member of the Quorum of the Twelve.

Professionally, Elder Cannon worked as a mining engineer from 1902 to 1905, mainly on Cannon family properties. He then supervised hydrographic and irrigation surveys of the Weber River system for the Utah State Engineer's Office until 1907. After returning from his second mission in 1909, he was employed by Salt Lake City as water supply engineer and then as the city engineer, which position he held until called as Presiding Bishop in 1925. But even then he remained active, serving in such positions as on the Salt Lake City Planning Commission, chairman of the Chamber of Commerce Smokeless City Committee, and chairman of the Special State Flood Commission.

During his lifetime, Elder Cannon was involved in several significant events in the history of this country and of the Church. Having arrived in San Francisco the night of April 17, 1906, he was awakened in his downtown hotel room the next morning by a violent shaking of his bed, falling plaster and deep rumbling sounds as the city was hit by a great earthquake. Catching a train home that afternoon, he wrote, "The last I could see of San Francisco was a mass of flame and smoke. The difference between its condition to-day and that of yesterday afternoon when I saw it for the first time, is simply appalling. Our train proceeded slowly as the wires were down and the condition of the track uncertain. . . . I have felt my nerves under tension all day as a result of this morning's fearful occurrence."[1]

In the very early days of radio, when the public was still uncertain what to make of this invention, the Church saw in it the possible fulfillment of the gospel being taken to all nations. General conference was first broadcasted in 1923, and has continued to be so ever since. Of course, in the early days this was not without glitches. At one early October conference, members sitting in the Tabernacle on Temple Square were suddenly surprised to hear the World Series over the public address system. Someone in the station had pulled the wrong switch. For seven minutes the Tabernacle was flooded with the play-by-play broadcast of the game while Presiding Bishop Sylvester Cannon ran frantically to the top of the Union Pacific Building to reverse the switch and restore order to the conference.

On October 29, 1929, the United States was hit hard by the Great Depression. By 1932, the unemployment rate in Utah was a staggering 35.9 percent. With the establishment of President Franklin D. Roosevelt's New Deal, a sense of apathy seemed to be creeping into the Church. President Heber J. Grant noted, "Many people have said, 'Well, others are getting some [government relief], why should not I get some of it?' I believe that there is a growing disposition among the people to try to get something from the government of the United States with little hope of ever paying it back. I think this is all wrong."[2] Prior to this time the Church had a welfare program but it was not standardized. The Presiding Bishopric and the Relief Society General Board were busily trying to help people find employment, were maintaining a storehouse, and were helping in whatever ways they could. Church leaders wanted to help Church members, but in a way that was in agreement with gospel principles. Sylvester Cannon, who was Presiding Bishop during this critical time, explained that their goal was "to see that none of the active members of the Church suffers for the necessities of life. . . . The effort of the Church . . . is to help people to help themselves. The policy is to aid them to become independent . . . rather than to have to depend upon the Church for assistance."[3] In 1935, the newly developed welfare program was introduced to the entire Church.

During the early part of the twentieth century, when the country was becoming more conscious of the need for city development planning and the consequences of environmental neglect, Elder Cannon was in the forefront of activity in Salt Lake City and Utah. Through the positions he held, he helped plan improvements in water storage and supply, sewage disposal, and clean air. He promoted the establishment of zoning laws to control the locations of businesses, industrial sites, and residential homes. He advocated controlled grazing and watershed protection as well as federal government land purchase and regulations, and strong limits on the use of private property. Though an environmentalist, he was also a pragmatist who believed in protecting the environment while still using its natural resources for the benefit of man. Thus, he endorsed the construction of dams, aqueducts, and pipelines. Much of what he promoted and accomplished is enjoyed today by residents of the Salt Lake area and of Utah in general.

Elder Cannon died May 29, 1943, at the Salt Lake Hospital, following a long illness that had kept him from his office and official duties for several months.

*Harold B. Lee*

Born: March 28, 1899, Clifton, Idaho
Ordained Apostle: April 10, 1941
Became President of the Quorum of the Twelve and First Counselor to
President Joseph Fielding Smith: January 23, 1970
Sustained President of the Church: July 7, 1972
Died: December 26, 1973, Salt Lake City, Utah, at age 74

**B**orn in the small community of Clifton, Idaho, on March 28, 1899, Harold grew up knowing the rigors of hard farm work. By worldly standards, the family was poor, leading Elder Lee to observe in later years, "We had everything that money could not buy."[1] In their earlier school years, the Lee children were taken two miles to school in a two-wheeled cart pulled by a small pony driven by their mother. When the Lee boys finished their local schooling, they rode horseback fifteen miles to the Oneida Stake Academy in Preston, Idaho, to complete their high school education. There Harold was known for his musical talents on the piano, his basketball playing, and his skills on the debate team. Following graduation, he went on to pass his teacher certification exams and became teacher and principal of a one-room school house at the age of seventeen. The following year he was hired as principal of a larger school. Though some of the students were older than Harold and had reputations of being ruffians, he gained their respect by playing basketball with them during lunch break.

After four years of teaching, Harold went on a mission to the Western States Mission. Upon his return home, he went to Salt Lake City to court Fern Lucinda Tanner, whom he had met in the mission field, but admired from a distance. They were married November 14, 1923, and would go on to have two daughters. The special relationship that existed between them was described by their daughter Helen, who wrote, "There is no doubt but what Mother had a most profound influence on my father's life. When one recalls that he grew up in a very small farming community in Idaho, it is easy to understand that he needed the refining influence of a loving companion to introduce him to gracious, genteel living. She incorporated those values, as well as spiritual dimensions, into their home."[2] While attending the University of Utah, Harold worked several part-time jobs, including salesman for the Foundation Press. In 1928, he was appointed intermountain manager for the firm. But in 1932, he resigned from his position when he was appointed and later elected as Salt Lake City commissioner.

As a young boy, Harold had what he called his "first intimate touch with divinity." Playing about the farm, he saw over the fence some broken-down old buildings and decided to go explore them. As he started over the fence, an audible voice said, "Harold, don't go over there." Looking about, he could see no one. Realizing he was being stopped from unseen danger, he turned around from the buildings. What that danger was, "I don't know," he later recounted. "But from that time on, I accepted without question the fact that there were processes not known to man by which we can hear voices from the unseen world, by which we can have brought to us the visions of eternity."[3] This faith would carry him through many challenges that lay ahead.

Many years later, as a young married man, Harold was called to the Pioneer Stake High Council. Then, at the age of thirty-one, he was called as stake president, the youngest stake president in the Church at that time. It was the time of the Great Depression and most of the stake presidency's time was spent in trying to find ways to provide for the numerous unemployed. His efforts did not go unnoticed. On April 20, 1935, the First Presidency called him to head the Church welfare movement. Resigning as city commissioner and released as stake president, Harold took charge of the development of what we know today as the Church Welfare Program. Then, on April 6, 1941, he was sustained as a member of the Quorum of the Twelve Apostles.

In 1961, his unique leadership skills were again called upon as the First Presidency gave the General Priesthood Committee, which was under Elder Lee's direction, the assignment of refining the Church Priesthood Correlation Program. In the following year, President David O. McKay appointed Elder Lee as chairman of the Church Correlation Committee. In introducing the correlation program to the Church at the October 1962 general conference, Elder Lee said of its importance, "Don't you ever let anybody tell you, the membership of the Church, that the Lord is not today revealing and directing and developing plans which are needed to concentrate the entire forces of this Church to meet the challenge of the insidious forces at work to thwart and to tear down and to undermine the church and kingdom of God."[4]

Elder Lee's wife, Fern, died in September of 1962. Her death was especially hard on Elder Lee. Recognizing Elder Lee's heavy burden of grief, President McKay sent him on a European assignment, hoping that the preoccupation with work would do him good. Brother Stover of the Welfare Committee, who traveled with him, later recounted: "When his beloved wife, Fern, passed away, President Lee and I were assigned to go to Germany, Austria, and Switzerland for four weeks. We held many conferences. At that time he was in deep sorrow for the loss of his beloved eternal companion and I have seen him weep on many occasions, and it was very difficult for me to cheer him up. . . . In Berlin he was so depressed he had to go to his hotel room and turn the conference over to me."[5]

The following year he would marry again to Freda Joan Jenson, a longtime friend of the Lees, who had been especially close to Fern and who had served on the Church Primary and Young Women's general boards. But in August of 1965, tragedy would come again to Elder Lee with the death of his daughter Maurine, at the young age of thirty-nine and while expecting her fifth child. He would teach throughout his later ministry that no greater trial can come to us than the loss of a loved one.

In 1970, Elder Lee was called to the First Presidency, and two years later was sustained as President of the Church. However, President Lee's administration lasted only eighteen months, due to his suddenly passing away on December 26, 1973, at the age of seventy-four. Many felt his death was untimely, but his contributions to the kingdom of God over his lifetime had a profound influence and left a lasting impact upon the Church. At his funeral, Elder Spencer W. Kimball eulogized, "A giant redwood has fallen and left a great space in the forest."[6]

*Spencer W. Kimball*

Born: March 28, 1895, Salt Lake City, Utah
Ordained Apostle: October 7, 1943
Became President of the Quorum of the Twelve: July 7, 1972
Ordained President of the Church: December 30, 1973
Died: November 5, 1985, Salt Lake City, Utah, at age 90

Growing up in Thatcher, Arizona, young Spencer experienced a normal childhood. Following a mission to the central states, he spent twenty-five years serving his stake as clerk, counselor in the presidency, and finally as stake president, which position he held until his call to the apostleship. In business, he was successful in banking, insurance, and real estate. He was also very active in his community and civic organizations. However, his life also knew personal pain and suffering. He underwent brain surgery, the removal of throat cancer, and open heart surgery, to mention just a few of his many struggles. He later observed, "Suffering contributes to sainthood in People."[1]

Spencer's call to the Quorum of the Twelve came by way of a telephone call from President J. Reuben Clark on July 8, 1943. Spencer was overwhelmed with feelings of unworthiness and inadequacy. For several days and nights he pled with the Lord for an affirmation of his calling. Traveling to Boulder, Colorado, to visit his son, he went for an early morning walk in the mountains. He may have fallen asleep, for he knew not if it was a dream or a vision, but he saw his grandfather, Heber C. Kimball, and became conscious of the great work he had done. With that vision "A calm feeling of assurance came over me, doubt and questionings subdued. It was as though a great burden had been lifted . . . and I felt nearer my Lord than ever at any time in my life. . . . I felt I knew my way, now, physically and spiritually and knew where I was going."[2]

As a new Apostle, Elder Kimball was assigned by President George Albert Smith to take responsibility for the Church's attention to Native Americans. As a consequence, the Indian Placement Program was officially established in 1954. The purpose of the program was to place Indian children in foster homes during the school year, where they could obtain a better education than that obtained in reservation schools. By 1970, the program reached a peak of 5,000 participants. But by 1977, the number had dropped to 2,750 due to a combination of factors. Critics believed that participating children suffered psychological trauma from being separated from their parents. Reservation schools began to show improvement. And most significant, the American Indian Movement (AIM) objected to Indian children being indoctrinated away from their native culture and even insisted on removal of Church missionaries from the reservations. Representatives marched on Temple Square and demanded a million dollars in reparations. Elder Kimball felt both betrayed and angry that his efforts and the unselfish motives of Church members were so misrepresented and unappreciated.

At the time of President Harold B. Lee's sudden passing in December 1973, Elder Kimball was president of the Quorum of the Twelve. His feelings at that time are shown in his words at President Lee's funeral service. "President Lee has gone. I never thought it could happen. I sincerely wanted it not to ever happen. I doubt if anyone in the Church has prayed harder and more consistently for a long life for President Lee than my Camilla and myself. . . . I have expected that I would go long before he did."[3] Many may have wondered what lay ahead with this pint-size man with the weak and raspy voice at the helm. They soon found out. President Kimball's watch-words became "lengthen your stride." And lengthen his he surely did, for no man could match his giant steps.

President Kimball entertained an expansive vision of missionary work. Up to this time, most missionaries came from the United States. He envisioned missionaries from foreign lands taking care of the missionary needs in their own lands; of every young man feeling the responsibility to serve a mission; of potential missionaries being better prepared and committed. At the beginning of his presidency, there were 17,000 missionaries. In time, with his vision established in the hearts and minds of Church members everywhere, the missionary force would grow to over 50,000.

In 1979, the Church published for the first time its own edition of the Bible. Two years later it published a new edition of the triple combination. The project had actually begun during the administration of President Joseph Fielding Smith, but as acting president of the Quorum of the Twelve, Elder Kimball had called the committee and specialists responsible for the work, and had taken personal interest in seeing that the project moved forward. It was only fitting that the project came to fruition under his presidency.

Of all of President Kimball's many accomplishments, he will undoubtedly be best remembered for extending the priesthood to all worthy males in the Church. As President Gordon B. Hinckley is reported to have said, "Here was a little man, filled with love, able to reach out to people. . . . He was not the first to worry about the priesthood question, but he had the compassion to pursue it and a boldness that allowed him to act, to get the revelation."[4] Aware of the many problems that priesthood restriction brought upon the Church, as well as the growing acceptance of the gospel by black populations of Africa, President Kimball pursued the issue by studying the scriptures and church history, and through continual prayer and fasting in the Temple. Eventually, at a meeting of the First Presidency and Quorum of the Twelve in the Temple, he announced his decision to lift racial restrictions on the priesthood. All expressed agreement. Then, as they knelt in prayer, with President Kimball being voice, there followed what Elder McConkie called "another day of

Pentecost."[5] With the official news release, the way was opened for the gospel, with all its priesthood blessings, to truly be taken to all nations.

How was this man able to accomplish so much? What was the key to his success? In the mid-1960s, President Baird of the Southwest Indian Mission related the following incident: Conducting a series of leadership training meetings across the reservation with Elder Kimball, President Baird was sleeping in the front seat of the car as they were driven to their next location. Awaking late at night, he looked to see Elder Kimball in the back seat working under a portable light. President Baird, himself a very vigorous man, asked, "Elder Kimball, how do you do it? How do you keep up this exhausting pace?" Elder Kimball replied, "President Baird, this is my magnificent obsession."

Following a long illness that left him mostly incapacitated, President Kimball died November 5, 1985, at the age of ninety.

*Ezra Taft Benson*

Born: August 4, 1899, Whitney, Idaho
Sustained Apostle: October 7, 1943
Became President of the Quorum of the Twelve: December 1973
Ordained President of the Church: November 10, 1985
Died: May 30, 1994, Salt Lake City, Utah, at age 94

The first of eleven children, Ezra began life in a one-room adobe farmhouse in Whitney, Idaho. Growing up on a farm, he knew the meaning of hard work. He was just twelve years old when his father was called on a mission. Being the eldest of the children, he assumed much of the responsibility for the farm and dairy herd. Ezra also loved music and played the trombone and the piano, and also performed vocal solos in the community and later at college.

Just a few weeks before his twenty-second birthday, Ezra left on a mission to the British Isles. Upon his return home, he graduated from Brigham Young University, married Flora Smith Amussen, and obtained a master's degree from Iowa State University. Returning to Whitney, Ezra became county agricultural extension agent. At the age of thirty-one, he took his family to Boise, Idaho, where he became head of a newly organized Department of Agriculture Economics and Marketing for the Extension Service of the University of Idaho and was eventually called as stake president. At thirty-nine, he accepted a position as executive secretary of the National Council of Farmer Cooperatives in Washington, DC. There he became the first stake president of the newly formed Washington, DC Stake.

In the summer of 1943, Ezra was told that President Heber J. Grant wanted to see him. Of that visit, he later recounted, "Then he took both of my hands in his and looked me in the eye. He said, 'Brother Benson, the Lord bless you. You have been chosen as the youngest member of the Council of the Twelve Apostles.' I just could not believe it. It just seemed as though the whole world had caved in on me."[1] In December 1945, Elder Benson was appointed to preside over the European Mission in the aftermath of World War II. His specific assignment was to reopen the missions throughout Europe and to distribute food, clothing, and bedding to the suffering Saints. Travels in war-torn Europe were difficult and time-consuming. Many times when it seemed near impossible to enter countries or distribute supplies, Elder Benson would go to the Lord in prayer, and barriers would dissolve. During his year in Europe, he traveled 60,000 miles and distributed thousands of tons of supplies to the Saints scattered throughout thirteen nations. On one occasion Elder Benson was accompanied to a warehouse by a German member of the Church, Richard Ranglack. When Richard saw the food and supplies, he wept and said, "Brother Benson, it is difficult for me to believe that people who have never seen us before could do so much for us."[2] Also during this year, Elder Benson dedicated Finland for the preaching of the gospel.

In 1952, Elder Benson received a phone call from President-elect Dwight D. Eisenhower, a man he had never met, wanting to talk to him about becoming US Secretary of Agriculture. Farm leaders had recommended Benson to Eisenhower as the best man for the job. Upon inquiring of President McKay, he was told, "Brother Benson, my mind is clear in the matter. If the opportunity comes in the proper spirit, I think you should accept."[3] Upon his meeting with President

Eisenhower, he was told that the country needed a spiritual tone in government and was assured by Eisenhower that he need never endorse a policy that he did not agree with. Besides, argued Eisenhower, "You can't refuse to serve America."[4] Elder Benson accepted the post. The task before him was enormous. He recalled that after moving into his Washington apartment, where he would live alone for five months until his family was able to join him, "for the first time, it was suddenly more than I could bear. The job ahead seemed too big, the load too heavy, loneliness too sharp a pain. I broke down and wept aloud."[5] Eisenhower had asked that Elder Benson remain in his Cabinet for the entire period that he occupied the White House. Consequently, Elder Benson served for eight years. During those years he merely did what he thought was right, not what might have been politically expedient. A plaque on his Washington desk read, "O God, give us men with a mandate higher than the ballot box."[6]

After his swearing-in, Elder Benson made it known that he would not take part in any secular activities on Sunday except in case of emergencies. He and his wife felt no qualms about refusing social invitations when it interfered with such family activities as a school concert or a daddy-daughter night. It became known that he did not smoke or drink but was comfortable in the presence of those who did. At his suggestion, President Eisenhower began his cabinet meetings with prayer as did Elder Benson in his staff meetings. Ever mindful of his apostolic calling, he found opportunities in his world travels to bear witness of Christ. One memorable experience came in Russia when he asked to visit a church where Christians were still allowed to meet. Entering the church, he bore testimony of Christ through an interpreter as people wept. When he left, hands reached out to him as the congregation sang "God be with you till we meet again." Even the hardened press correspondents that accompanied him were moved to tears.

Recognition came to President Benson in the form of numerous awards, honorary degrees, and the nation's highest Scouting awards. Attempts to draft him as a candidate for Utah Governor and President of the United States were both turned down by him.

On December 30, 1973, Elder Benson became President of the Quorum of the Twelve, and twelve years later, on November 10,

1985, he became President of the Church. Three months into his administration, the First Presidency extended the opportunity to receive temple endowments to those whose spouses are not endowed. In his conference addresses he stressed to members the power of the Book of Mormon as an instrument of conversion and a means of uplifting their own personal lives. Members were challenged to read it and to give it to friends and relatives not in the Church, with their written testimonies inside the cover. Starting in 1990, all Church programs—including the construction of buildings—were to be paid for from General Church funds, relieving members from ward budgets, construction contributions and money-making projects. Outspoken against communism, he saw the dissolution of the USSR and the opening of the way for the gospel to be taken to Eastern Europe. President Benson died of heart failure on May 30, 1994, at the age of ninety-four.

*Mark E. Petersen*

Born: November 7, 1900, Salt Lake City, Utah
Ordained Apostle: April 20, 1944
Died: January 11, 1984, Salt Lake City, Utah, at age 83

Mark and his twin sister, Mona, were born November 7, 1900. Their father was a carpenter and builder who worked with his boys and taught them his skills that Mark loved throughout his life. When nineteen, Mark served a mission in Canada. Upon his return, he served as chorister in his ward. The accompanist was Emma Marr McDonald. They were married August 30, 1923. Mark worked as a bookkeeper and then as a checker of railroad cars, but his interests were elsewhere. One day, he went to the city editor of the *Deseret News* to inquire if they had any openings. There were none. Nearly every day for the next six months, he inquired, with the same answer, until one day he was told there was an opening. The salary was $90 a month, less than he had been making with the railroad, but he wanted to be a newspaper man. He became a reporter, then a copy reader, news editor, managing editor, editor, and eventually general manager. He would later become president of the company and chairman of its board of directors. Shunning the limelight, he insisted that his name and picture never appear in his paper, but he was generous in sharing all credit with others. To him, his employees were family and he insisted he be called by his given name. It was not unusual for him to visit the homes of employees, often leaving a gift behind. He was first at the bedside of employees who were hospitalized, and visited the home of retired staffers. He was also heavily involved in his community, serving in leadership positions in various civic organizations.

During those years, Mark served on the stake high councils and as counselor in the stake presidencies of two different stakes. Since the beginning of the *Church News* in 1931, he wrote virtually every editorial for fifty-three years. He was also the author of more than forty books, plus other books written jointly with his wife, she also being an author in her own right. No wonder President Thomas S. Monson eulogized, "Few men are given the opportunity to influence the Church in the manner Elder Mark E. Petersen influenced it for nearly forty years as one of the Lord's special witnesses."[1]

Offered a management position with a San Diego newspaper with triple the pay he was presently getting as general manager of the *Deseret News,* a family council was held and a vote taken, which was in favor of San Diego. About that time, hard work drove Mark to his bed for a week of recuperation. While resting, he read the scriptures. Strangely, every time he opened the scriptures, he found himself reading about the Apostles and their ministry. He concluded that he must be receiving some sort of message, but was not sure what it was. Then one night, he dreamed that the headline of his paper read that Elder Richard R. Lyman had died and that he, Mark E. Petersen, had been called to the Twelve. So troubled was he by the dream, that he sent someone to check discretely on Elder Lyman's health. His heath was fine. But the inner promptings were strong enough that San Diego was no longer an option. It was not long before news came of Richard Lyman's excommunication. When President Grant sent to see Mark, he knew what was ahead. At the April conference of the Church, he was sustained to the Quorum of the Twelve Apostles. After the *Deseret News* was published announcing his calling, a second, "employees only" edition was printed, which headlined, "Quorum of the Twelve Goes to the Dogs. They chose a Great Dane."

Among his many apostolic responsibilities, he directed the Church's public information program for many years, and also directed the establishment of numerous visitors centers at Church historical sites and temples. He served on the Military Relations Committee and was an adviser to the Music Committee and to the Relief Society. For over six years he supervised Church activities in Western Europe and South Africa. His spirituality can be seen in an incident told by President Gordon B. Hinckley. During a meeting of the First Presidency and the Twelve, they joined in prayer in behalf of President Kimball, who was hospitalized. Elder Petersen was called upon to be voice. President Hinckley recalled, "There was nothing lofty in his speech. The words were simple, the sentences short. . . . As he spoke in prayer, it seemed to me that there was a conduit opened to the heavens from that little group in the temple to him who sits on high, the God and Father of us all. Tears welled in my closed eyes and ran down my cheeks. Every man there was touched in his heart. The Lord heard that prayer uttered by a man of faith."[2]

It was at the Tokyo Temple dedication in 1980, that Elder Petersen had what he considered to be one of the most spiritual experiences of his life. The temple was small, the room crowded, the choir subsequently small but a good blend of voices. Following the services, as the choir sang "Hosannah, Hosannah, the House of the Lord is Completed," a large number of additional voices was heard joining in the song. All in the room, including the choir as it continued singing, were in tears. Elder Peterson believed that they were hearing the voices of the Asian people on the other side of the veil, who were rejoicing with them over the building of the temple.

Tragedy struck when Emma Marr died on April 15, 1975. Earlier she had had a melanoma removed from her head and had worn a wig ever since. Then she suffered a series of strokes; with each episode came increased dementia. By the time she passed away she was living in her past as a young girl. Elder Petersen's daughter recorded that, for her dad, it was as though part of him died with her. Some time later he was assigned to a seminar for mission presidents and their wives. Elder Boyd K. Packer recounted, "The first day, being without his wife, his loneliness was so overwhelming he thought he could not bear it. Then, something happened. He became aware that she was with him, there by his side. And she stayed with him for days. And he was greatly comforted."[3]

While Elder Petersen was able to continue with his apostolic duties throughout most of his remaining years, those years were filled with physical pain and suffering. For nearly ten years he went through cycles of surgery, therapy, radiation, treatment, then surgery again. He died January 11, 1984, from longstanding complications of cancer. He was eighty-three years of age.

*Matthew Cowley*

Born: August 2, 1897, Preston, Idaho
Ordained Apostle: October 11, 1945
Died: December 13, 1953, Los Angeles, California, at age 56

Upon completion of their substantial rock home in Preston, Idaho, Matthias and Abbie Cowley invited Apostle Moses Thatcher, who was in town on Church business, to come and dedicate their new house to the Lord. In his dedicatory prayer, Elder Thatcher prayed that "herein might be born prophets, seers, and revelators to honor God."[1] Into this home would be born Matthew Cowley. Unfortunately, neither parent would live to see the fulfillment of Elder Thatcher's prophetic prayer. Just a few days after Matthew's birth, his father was called to the Quorum of the Twelve. Consequently, the family moved to Salt Lake City the following year where they obtained a home on West Temple Street in the block just north of Temple Square. As Matthew grew older, he had a great desire to serve a mission in Hawaii since his brother, Moses, had served there. Consequently, he was called to the Hawaiian Mission.

But shortly thereafter his call was changed to New Zealand. The Cowley family's next door neighbor, President Anthon H. Lund of the First Presidency, came to their home and explained to Matthew, "I was having dinner tonight, and the spirit told me you should go to New Zealand instead of Hawaii. I don't know why. That's the way I feel."[2] The following years of Matthew's life would explain the "why."

Matthew was only seventeen years of age when he left on his mission. His travels in New Zealand were by whatever means he could obtain: horseback, boat, bike, and walking. The Maori language came to him as a gift of tongues. And though he was young, the natives respected and honored him because of the priesthood he bore as manifested in the power to bless them and heal their sick. He, in turn, developed a great love for Maori people. As his knowledge of the language grew, the mission president, with the approval of President Joseph F. Smith, assigned Matthew to retranslate the Book of Mormon and then to translate the Doctrine and Covenants and the Pearl of Great Price. Because of the time involved in this work, his mission was extended to five years. In later years, as he would look back on those translations he would "marvel that I was the one that was supposed to have done the translating. The language surpasses my own individual knowledge of it."[3]

Upon his return home, Matthew found work at the Federal Reserve Bank while attending the University of Utah. He then enrolled in the George Washington University Law School. During this time he married Elva Taylor. While a student at George Washington, he also worked as a special assistant to Senator [Apostle] Reed Smoot and came to know Washington, DC, quite well. His opinion of politicians left something to be desired. In his diary he wrote, "how bold men in politics are when their incumbency in office is about to terminate. It seems that it is then only that they will say what they really believe and not confine their remarks to the pleasure of their constituents. Love for public office tends to make cowards of men."[4] As in Salt Lake City, he also came in demand as a speaker at various Church meetings. Upon his return to Utah, he passed the state bar and began practicing law. He was a good lawyer, but too honest and too much of a humanitarian to accumulate any wealth. If people were guilty of a crime, he would try to get them to plead guilty. If they would not, "I defended them, but when I knew they were wrong, my duty was to help them, but not to make them plead their innocence."[5] In divorce trials, he would try to get the couple to reconcile, acting more as a counselor than a lawyer. In 1938, while working on the best case he ever had, one that involved oil land in Wyoming and would have made him enough money to live comfortably for several years without making another penny, he was called to return to New Zealand as mission president. He turned the case over to a friend and never received a penny from it.

Back in New Zealand he was given the Maori title, *tumuaki*, meaning great leader, big chief, or president. The mission numbered about nine thousand members; eight thousand were Maori and a thousand were European. In 1940, with the approach of war, all the missionaries from the United States were ordered out of New Zealand by the First Presidency. Matthew stayed on to look after the Church. When he told his wife she had better pack up and go home, she replied, "I've been with you this long in all your troubles, and this is no time to leave you. I'm staying with you."[6] He was released as mission president in the fall of 1945, having spent the war years in New Zealand. One Maori member said of President Cowley's leaving, "There's nothing to worry about. When President Cowley gets home, he'll fill the first vacancy in the Council of the Twelve Apostles, and we'll still have a representative among the Authorities of the Church."[7] Matthew had too much faith in the spirituality of the people to take this as an idle statement. Shortly after their arrival home, he was called to the Quorum of the Twelve.

As a newly ordained Apostle, Elder Cowley threw himself into the work and within a few months suffered a heart attack, but eventually recovered to where he could resume his apostolic duties. In December of 1946, the First Presidency created the new position of president of the Pacific Missions of the Church, which was filled by Elder Cowley. His first trip was in February of 1947. Over the following three years he would travel to all the island groups. Church members would throng at his arrival and to hear him speak. Lines of people would form to receive his blessings and have their sick healed. They brought the blind, the halt, the barren; he never refused and many were healed. Elder Cowley, always a believer in the importance of education for the Polynesians, was asked by the Brethren to study the advisability of establishing Church Schools in the Pacific. Many schools would later be built as a result of his study and recommendations. As he traveled the Pacific Islands, he never failed to look in on LDS servicemen. In November of 1949, Elder Cowley was released from his Polynesian assignment. The First Presidency had decided that the missions of the Pacific would be visited at intervals by General Authorities. Elder Cowley was now free to visit stakes and missions of the Church, but he would never be forgotten by the Polynesian people.

On Friday, December 11, 1953, Elder and Sister Cowley attended the cornerstone ceremonies for the Los Angeles temple. The following day they bid good-bye to many of Elder Cowley's associates who were returning to Salt Lake City, while they stayed to visit family members. Early the next day, about 4:45 Sunday morning, Elder Cowley died quietly and peacefully in his sleep in his hotel room. Just about seven hours earlier, family members had told him to take care of himself so that he might have a long life. He had laughingly replied, "Life is eternal."[8]

*Henry D. Moyle*

Born: April 22, 1889, Salt Lake City, Utah
Ordained Apostle: April 10, 1947
Sustained Second Counselor to President David O. McKay: June 12, 1959
Sustained First Counselor to President McKay: October 12, 1961
Died: September 18, 1963, Deer Park, Colorado, at age 73

Henry Dinwoodey Moyle was born in Salt Lake City on April 22, 1889. Although he grew up in a conventional upper-middle-class home, his father believed that hard work was character-building. And so the barn, with its many animals and chores, became Henry's training ground. Following graduation from the University of Utah in 1909, with a degree in mining engineering, he was called to the Swiss-German mission, serving in both countries. Upon completion of his mission, he stayed in Germany and enrolled at the University of Freidberg, where he studied geology for a year. Returning home, he then pursued a law degree, studying at the University of Utah, the University of Chicago, and Harvard University.

In 1916, he began a law practice in Salt Lake City, and soon learned that corporate law gave him a higher-paying clientele. His practice was soon interrupted by World War I. Applying for a military commission, he gained the rank of captain and served as an instructor in the officers' school at The Presidio in San Francisco, and was in charge of ROTC at Utah State University. Years later, when World War II broke out, he again served his country; this time as director of the Petroleum Industry Council, and as chairman of refining for the Rocky Mountain area. In 1919, Henry married Alberta Wright. They went on to have six children—four daughters and two sons. Money interested Henry Moyle, but he enjoyed making it more than owning it. Apart from his law practice, his business interests led him into various enterprises, including mining, real estate, financing, freighting, livestock, and oil. By the time he was called to the apostleship, he was a millionaire. He was also involved in politics and rose to state party chairman for the Democratic Party. But when he lost his bid to run for governor in 1940, he retired from the political limelight.

In 1927, Henry D. Moyle was called as president of Cottonwood Stake, which position he held for ten years. During the end of his tenure, in 1936, the Church initiated what would become the Church Welfare Program. When the announcement of the program came, Elder Moyle did not wait for further instructions or to see if it applied to his stake, but within a couple of months had set up a storehouse and had established the program within his stake. He was consequently called as a member of the general welfare committee, and, in 1937, was called as chairman of the committee. By the time he was sustained to the Quorum of the Twelve on April 6, 1947, he was already well-known throughout most of the Church, having visited and spoken at their stakes on behalf of the Welfare Committee. In 1959, when he was called as a counselor in the First Presidency, he was also given responsibility as chairman of the Missionary Committee. During the three and a half years he served in that capacity, the number of missions increased from forty-seven to seventy-one, and 267,669 converts joined the Church, more than ten percent of the total Church membership.

President David O. McKay observed that Elder Moyle "was an indomitable worker. He was not one who performed merely the task given him. If he saw work beyond that assigned him, he labored with equal zeal in completion of the extra labor, as he did to his assigned task. No trip was too long, no assignment too unexpected, no responsibility so great, but he would fill the assignment without question, and perform his duty to his utmost ability."[1]

Gordon B. Hinckley gave a glimpse at just how involved Elder Moyle's life was. Following Elder Moyle's death, Elder Hinckley sat in his friend's then-empty office.

> I glanced at [his appointment book]. The appointments began at seven-thirty in the morning, and lasted until six-thirty in the evening. They included board meetings of the Brigham Young University and a radio and television corporation; committee meetings on the budget of the Church; discussion on a new mission home in one of the distant missions of the world; a marriage in the temple; an appointment with a mother whose son was ill in one of the missions of Europe; the funeral of an old friend; an interview with a government official from Germany; a ground-breaking for a new chapel that evening. Such was the unrelenting pace of his day.[2]

Members of the Church of Jesus Christ pledge their willingness to consecrate all that they have and all that they are to the building up of the kingdom of God. Nowhere is that willingness demonstrated more readily than in the life of Elder Moyle. In spite of his many business interests and investments, it was all secondary to the gospel of Jesus Christ in his life. Speaking at his funeral services, Elder Harold B. Lee told of when Henry Moyle was called to the apostleship. He had been in New York City for several days negotiating with Phillips Petroleum Company for the sale of two oil and gas companies when he received a phone call from President George Albert Smith informing him that he had been called to the Twelve. President Smith "asked him if he could manage to get home by Sunday because he was to be sustained as a member of the Council of the Twelve at the General conference," recalled Elder Lee.

> Characteristically, he had for days and days prior to this, been in conferences with the Phillips Petroleum officials, trying to drive an exact bargain, and trying to do the best possible for the stockholders of Wasatch Oil and Idaho Refining Companies. After the call came he walked in to meet the officials by appointment the next morning, and

he said, "Gentlemen, I accept your offer of last night. I must leave at once for home." Surprised because he had thus yielded, because they expected more days of discussion and conference before he would yield, he said, "I have been called to a high position in the Church, and the President has called me to be home. I must leave at once."[3]

Elder Lee continued, "His call to the Twelve superseded all other things in life. He began to dispose of his business interests, and he tells, and his associates say, that he never went back into his law office to consider one case. He merely said, 'I have turned my back on that. I have other work more important.'"[4]

President Moyle died while on a Church assignment in Florida, passing quietly in his sleep from heart failure at the age of seventy-three.

*Delbert L. Stapley*

Born: December 11, 1896, Mesa, Arizona
Ordained Apostle: October 5, 1950
Died: August 19, 1978, Salt Lake City, Utah at age 81

D elbert Leon Stapley was born in Mesa, Arizona, and was one of nine children, having five brothers and three sisters. He grew up having a love for sports, and was a consistent golfer throughout his adult years. He also enjoyed music and played the violin in the school orchestra. Delbert's first recollection of his father was at the age of three when his father returned home from a two-year mission. At the time of Delbert's birth, his father had a forty-acre ranch, which was replaced early on by a family hardware business known as the O. S. Stapley Company. The family business dealt in the sale of hardware, appliances, trucks, and farm implements. Consequently, Delbert learned to work at an early age. He would later recall, "I started working in the warehouse. I loaded out the freight wagons and eventually graduated into the selling part of the business."[1]

Graduating from Mesa High School in 1915, Delbert was invited at the age of eighteen to try out for a major league baseball team, but turned down the offer to accept a call to the Southern States Mission. Though a relatively young missionary, he showed his leadership abilities and was called to preside over the Kentucky Conference for a year. Upon returning home, he married his childhood sweetheart, Ethel Burdett Davis, on January 14, 1918. He then joined the US Marine Corps and served as a recruiter at Mare Island, California, for eight months until World War I ended. In 1925, he would join the Arizona National Guard, remaining in the guard for nine years and retiring as a major.

Upon his return home, he became Scoutmaster and Superintendent of the YMMIA. His association with the Boy Scouts would continue over the years. He would be the recipient of the Silver Beaver, the Silver Antelope (the highest regional award in Scouting) and the Silver Buffalo, the National Scouting Council's highest award. In 1970, he received a diamond pin commemorating fifty years of service in Scouting. He was still a scout leader at the time of his death. Regarding his work in YMMIA, business pressures soon became so great that he resigned his position, but soon found himself so unhappy and miserable not being involved in the Church, that he went to his leaders and asked for another calling, any calling. He was immediately reinstated in the MIA. He would serve in that calling for seventeen years while serving simultaneously as first counselor in the Phoenix Stake Presidency during twelve of those years. Upon Elder Stapley's death, the First Presidency issued a statement which included, "the youth of the world have had no greater champion than this rugged but tender man."[2]

When the family business moved its headquarters from Mesa to Phoenix, he moved with it. There he served as first counselor in the Phoenix Stake Presidency for ten years. Then, in December of 1947, he was called as stake president, serving in that position until his call to the apostleship three years later. At the time of his calling to the Twelve, Elder Stapley was in Salt Lake City to attend general conference. Reflecting back upon that day, Elder Stapley recalled: "I received a very strong feeling that I would be called to fill the vacancy in the Twelve. . . . I was embarrassed that the thought would enter my mind. And so, not understanding, I started to make myself scarce so I wouldn't run into any of the General Authorities. . . . As I came out of the elevator (in the Hotel

Utah) I met President George Albert Smith face on."³ "And so here he was, blocking my way," he further recalled on another occasion. "He said, 'President Stapley, you are just the man I am looking for.' There in the lobby of Hotel Utah he told me that it was the wish of the Brethren that I come on the Council. Well, . . .I went up to the room and called my wife. . . . I just couldn't speak, I was so overcome with emotion."⁴ In his first address as a General Authority, Elder Stapley referred to two promises given in his patriarchal blessing—that he "would be called into positions of responsibility and trust," and that he "would travel much for the gospel's sake." Then, paying homage to the patriarchs of the Church for their ability to lay out before us the pattern of our lives, he testified, "I know if we keep in the way of God's commandments, we will realize that pattern of life."⁵

Elder Stapley taught that those who are not ashamed of the gospel of Christ will not be ashamed to testify of it. His joy in teaching and testifying of the gospel is seen in a story told by President Thomas S. Monson. Elder Monson attended a stake conference in the southern states area where Elder Stapley had served as a young missionary. Following conference, a sister came up to Elder Monson with an old, worn copy of the Book of Mormon and asked if he knew the person who had inscribed it and given it to her grandmother years ago. Looking at the signature in the front of the book, Elder Monson said yes, that he served with Elder Stapley. The sister then asked Elder Monson, "would you please take this book to Elder Stapley with our love and tell him his testimony and this book guided my entire family to become members of the Church?" Elder Monson readily agreed to do so, but upon his return to Salt Lake City, he waited for a time when neither he nor Elder Stapley was pressed for time. Entering Elder Stapley's office one day, he told him the story and handed him the book. Turning to the title page and reading his inscription of years before, "great tears came to his eyes and coursed down his cheeks," said Elder Monson. "Teaching through testimony had brought to him indescribable joy and profound gratitude."⁶

On August 19, 1978, Elder Stapley died of cardiac arrest while on a walk near his home. He was eighty-one years of age.

*Marion G. Romney*

Born: September 19, 1897, Colonia Juarez, Mexico
Sustained Assistant to the Twelve: April 6, 1941
Ordained Apostle: October 11, 1951
Sustained Second Counselor to President Harold B. Lee: July 7, 1972
Sustained Second Counselor to President Spencer W. Kimball:
    December 30, 1973
Sustained First Counselor to President Kimball: December 2, 1982
Became President of the Quorum of the Twelve: November 10, 1985
Died: May 20, 1988, Salt Lake City, Utah, at age 90

Marion G. Romney was born September 19, 1897, in Colonia Juarez, Mexico, in a community of Latter-day Saints who had fled from the United States years earlier to escape persecution and had come to consider Mexico their home. When Marion was only eight days old, his father, George Romney, was called away on a two-year mission for the Church. Growing up in the Mexican colonies was a hard frontier life. "We raised our own food, everything we ate. We worked hard, even as children,"[1] Elder

Romney later recalled. But in 1912, as the Mexican Revolution swept back and forth across the country, the Mormon colonists found it necessary to flee from their homes for safety. George Romney sent his family to the United States. Young Marion, fifteen years of age, was placed in charge of the move as the family traveled by wagon to El Paso, Texas, to be joined by his father later. A family with seven children, they left Mexico with all their possessions contained in a single trunk. At one point they were confronted by soldiers who took all their money—twenty pesos—and aimed their guns at them. "I think one of the most exciting moments of my life was when I looked up the barrels of those rifles," Elder Romney recalled. "For some reason, these Mexicans did not fire, and we continued on safely. . . . For the preservation of my life on this occasion I have always been very grateful to the Lord, and this experience has given me a desire to live in such a manner as to demonstrate to the Lord my appreciation."[2]

The family eventually settled in Rexburg, Idaho. Young Marion, the oldest of ten children, learned the carpentry trade from his father and helped support the family as his father finished a university degree. Marion went on to serve in the US Army and to graduate from Ricks Normal College. He was then awarded a scholarship to continue his schooling, but turned it down to serve a mission in Australia. Following his mission, he worked his way through school, obtaining a Law degree from the University of Utah. He then practiced law in Salt Lake City, where he served as assistant county attorney, assistant district attorney, assistant city attorney, and state legislator. In September 1924, he married Ida Jensen. They first met when Marion's father, then president of Rick's Normal College, hired her as an English teacher. "I have never seen any girl since that time that I cared about," said Elder Romney fifty nearly years later.[3] They went on to have four children; one lived only six days, and another was stillborn. Two sons survived.

Elder Romney served as a bishop and a stake president. He was the first of five men sustained to the new position of Assistants to the Twelve in 1941. In that same year he was called as assistant managing director of the Church Welfare Program, which position he occupied until 1959, when he was called as general chairman. In October 1951, he was called to the Quorum of the Twelve, and went on to serve as counselor in the First Presidency to Presidents Lee and Kimball. With the death of President Kimball, Elder Romney became president of the Quorum of the Twelve. Among his many responsibilities, one of his greatest thrills was to organize Mexico's first stake in 1961.

Some of the words used to define Elder Romney's character can best be illustrated through statements from those with whom he associated over the years. The first is compassion: President Ezra Taft Benson referred to him as *Mr. Welfare.* "To that assignment he brought two remarkable traits. First, he had a philosophy that one should work for what one receives. Second, he had a natural compassion and sympathy for those who have met with misfortune." These traits were "born out of struggle and independence."[4] The second word is scholar. President Hinckley paid the following tribute: "He had a remarkable power of concentration as he read and studied. He was gifted with a rare capacity for scholarship. . . . No one among his brethren was an abler student of the Book of Mormon. He read it scores of times . . . deliberately, carefully; he pondered it and prayed over it."[5] The third is communication. Elder Romney told the following: "Some fifty years ago . . . one evening as I was walking with Elder [B. H.] Roberts to the temple, he said something to me which I have remembered through the years. It was, 'Brother Romney, never say anything so people can [just] understand you. Always say it so they cannot misunderstand you.'"[6] He tried to live by that standard. The fourth is humor. Everyone spoke of his keen sense of humor. In an interview, his wife, Ida, told of how he tried to bring something home that was funny and cheerful at the end of each day, adding, "He has always felt it important to make me laugh. We laugh and enjoy each other. That's our dessert in life."[7] The fifth word is faith. President Benson said, "you have never heard a man pray until you have heard President Romney pray."[8] In a tribute to his friend and counselor, President Kimball said of Elder Romney, "His prayers are so earnest . . . that we know the Lord is listening. His sincerity is of such quality that it touches the listeners, and all of us feel that because President Romney is praying, we are all closer to our Father in Heaven. . . . All is holy where this man kneels."[9] The sixth is testimony. Speaking to his brethren of the Twelve on a Thursday morning, he said: "I know that this is God's work. I know that Jesus is my Redeemer, I know it with as much certainty as I shall know it when I meet him. I know as well as Joseph Smith knew, that Jesus and the Father appeared to him."[10] The seventh word to describe him is love. Elder Boyd K. Packer told of an evening, not long after the death of Ida Romney, when he and Elder Romney were driving home from a day of meetings. Both were quiet in their own thoughts when Elder Romney enthusiastically said, "Boyd, when I think that in a few years, 25 at the outside, I will be on the other side with Ida, that we will be together and the frailties we know here will be gone and that we will not be separated again, I am filled with such joy that I can hardly contain myself."[11] He rejoined Ida eleven years after her death. The eighth and last word is devotion. Elder Packer tells of how, just a day or two before Elder Romney's death, having been in bed enfeebled and not able to speak for several weeks, he spoke out and said "Joseph, Joseph," over and over again. "There is no Joseph in the Romney family," said Elder Packer, "and I can see this great, venerable leader of ours, this man of great mind and powerful spirit, now rejoicing in the presence of those who have gone before in the leadership of this Church and the kingdom of God."[12]

*LeGrand Richards*

Born: February 6, 1886, Farmington, Utah
Sustained Presiding Bishop: April 6, 1938
Ordained Apostle: April 10, 1952
Died: January 11, 1983, Salt Lake City, Utah, at age 96

L eGrand Richards was the third Apostle of direct descent
in the Richards family. Both his father, George F. Richards,
and his grandfather, Franklin D. Richards, served as presidents of the Council of the Twelve. LeGrand was born February 6,
1886 in Farmington, Utah, one of fifteen children of George F. and
Alice Robinson Richards. The family soon moved to Tooele, Utah,
where LeGrand grew up on the family farm. While still a young man,
he went to Salt Lake City, where he attended the Salt Lake Business
College. Upon completion of a business course, he was offered a
position with a prominent business firm, but declined it in order to
accept a mission call to the Netherlands. On his mission, LeGrand
felt such a pressing need to master the Dutch language that he would
walk to the cattle market and preach to the animals and the trees.

Apparently he was successful, for at a conference attended by President Heber J. Grant, he spoke and bore testimony with such power that many nonmembers who were in attendance remembered him long afterward because of it, and one joined the Church.

Upon his return home, he married Ina Jane Ashton in 1909. They would become the parents of eight children. Following their marriage, they moved to Portland, Oregon, where he was employed as assistant secretary of the Portland Cement Company. Two years later he returned to Salt Lake City with his family to go into the lumber business, but he eventually settled into real estate. In the course of his Church career, Elder Richards served as a branch president, a bishop of three wards, a member of two high councils, a stake president, and president of two missions. In April 1938, he was called as the presiding bishop of the Church, which position he filled for fourteen years until he was called to the Quorum of the Twelve in April 1952. At the time of his death, he had been a General Authority for nearly forty-five years.

Anyone who heard Elder Richards speak could not forget his enthusiastic, extemporaneous style or the love he conveyed for the gospel. The First Presidency, in paying tribute to him upon his death, wrote: "Elder Richards was a man of great faith and eternal optimism. He seldom, if ever, spoke from a written text. His discourses were filled with scriptural quotations, anecdotes, and personal experiences. His listeners hung on his every word and thrilled with him as he bore fervent testimony of the truth of the restored gospel and the divine mission of Jesus Christ, whose special witness he was."[1] The story is told, whether true or not, that Joseph Fielding Smith followed LeGrand Richards as speaker at general conference. Elder Smith is reported to have begun, "I feel like I have just been through a whirlwind."

Despite his many Church callings and his many years as a General Authority, Elder Richards will best be remembered as the consummate missionary. As a young missionary in Holland, the spirit of missionary work rested upon him "almost to the consuming of my flesh,"[2] he recorded. He was often on his knees in prayer, thanking the Lord for the opportunity to be a missionary and pleading that he would always be worthy to preach the gospel. When he was bishop of the Sugarhouse Ward, President Grant asked for a thousand missionaries, one from each of the thousand wards in the Church, emphasizing that he wanted mature men with experience in preaching the gospel. Bishop Richards went to his stake president and said he could think of no one in his ward better qualified than himself. The matter was taken by the stake president to President Grant, who replied, "Send him." Elder Richards left his ward and his family for the eastern states in January 1926, where he served a mission for six months.

It was this missionary zeal that led to the writing and publishing of his well-known book, *A Marvelous Work and a Wonder.* As president of the Southern States Mission, he prepared, at the request of his missionaries, a concise and logical outline on how best to present the gospel to investigators, entitled "The Message of Mormonism." With time, this outline began to spread in its usage. During his years as presiding bishop, he received many letters concerning it. One day he thought, "Why don't I develop these outline subjects the way I would present them if I were going into a home one night a week for six months?" How much more valuable might it be to missionary work if so developed and published, he thought. It soon became an obsession to him. In spite of his busy schedule, he spent every spare moment he could find in writing it. "I wrote it in longhand," he recorded. "On my assignment to Portland I don't think I looked out of the window once going up or coming back. . . . I sat in the motel writing until my eyes were so tired that I was sick to my stomach."[3] Eventually it was completed. From 1950 to 1981, the book sold more copies than any other Church book save the Book of Mormon—going through twenty-three printings, selling nearly two million copies, and being translated into eighteen languages. Elder Richards never accepted a penny of royalty on the book. It was his contribution to the Lord's work. Many wrote to him over the years to express the great effect the book had had upon their lives.

Elder Richards's missionary zeal also stemmed from his love for people. When he was bishop of the Glendale Ward, there was a gifted man in his ward he wanted as a counselor, but the man had a Word of Wisdom problem. Still, the man was anxious to serve in some way. "Would you take over the ward finances, other than tithes and offerings?" asked Bishop Richards. "I will," was the reply. And he did. The ward debt was paid off, maintenance payments were met on time, ward socials were financed without charging members for admission—the ward prospered socially and spiritually. Elder Richards later reflected, "What a waste of manpower it would have been to keep that talented man from performing so important a service just because of a physical weakness he had not yet found strength to overcome."[4] Such was his love in reaching out to help others realize their potential and to lift them up.

Upon his death in the home of his daughter, at the age of ninety-six, a Church News editorial read,

> An incomparable man has left us. Who in all of Israel was like unto him? . . . Who can measure the stature of such a man? Who would even try? He resembled Paul of old. He was like Alma, and Nephi, and in many ways like the great founding fathers of our Church who so loyally supported the Prophet Joseph Smith in the rise of this latter-day work. That is where he fits in the categories of the Lord. . . . He put on the "whole armor of God" and he used it tirelessly and fearlessly in defense of truth.[5]

*Adam S. Bennion*

Born: December 2, 1886, Taylorsville, Utah
Ordained Apostle: April 9, 1953
Died: February 11, 1958, Salt Lake City, Utah, at age 71

A dam S. Bennion, known as "Ad" by his friends in later years, was born December 12, 1886, in Taylorsville, Utah. He was one of seven children, two of whom died in their infancy because medical attention was not available where they lived. When Adam was not quite two years old, his father died, leaving his widowed mother to raise her five children to maturity. Adam was born during the lifetime of many of the early settlers, and grew to appreciate their hardships. In spite of his later attainments in life, he was always proud of his humble beginnings and of his pioneer heritage. In his acceptance speech as an Apostle, he said, "Often, during the last twenty-five years I have had opportunity to bring eastern people to Temple Square. I always take them to the log cabin in the southeast corner of the Square. I show them the little log cabin and ask them to behold it, and then turn from the cabin to the temple.

I want them to understand the poverty of the pioneers who lived in long cabins, but still dreamed dreams of a temple."[1]

Elder Bennion was described as having "a never-ending thirst for knowledge in order to achieve and to become serviceable in the world of men."[2] Obtaining a BA from the University of Utah in 1908, Adam taught English at the LDS high school in Salt Lake City. During this time, he married Minerva Young; they would become the parents of five children—three sons and two daughters. He then went on in post-graduate work, obtaining an MA from Columbia University in New York City in 1912. Returning to Utah, he was head of the English department and then principal of Granite High School. From 1917 to 1919, he was an assistant professor at the University of Utah. In 1919, he left the university faculty to become superintendent of Church Schools, which position he held until 1928. During this time he returned to graduate studies, obtaining a PhD from the University of California, Berkeley, in 1923. These years were not spent in academic pursuits only. Years later, when the Church historian's office sought to complete his biographical information by asking for the time and location of his mission, he wrote, "No formal call, but active in New York 1911–1912, Chicago 1916, Berkley 1922–1923."[3]

In 1928, Elder Bennion shifted careers, accepting a position as personnel director for Utah Power and Light Company In 1934 he was named assistant to the president, and later vice president in charge of employees, stockholders, and public relations departments. He was highly involved in civic activities and organizations, including the American Red Cross, Community Chest, and Rotary International. He was also named head of an important study group on federal education to make recommendations to the White House. In 1944, he ran for US Senate on the Republican ticket but was defeated by the incumbent. Much of his Church service was focused on the Sunday School program, serving thirty-eight years as a member of the general board of the Deseret Sunday School Union.

Elder Bennion was known as a great and gifted teacher. President Harold B. Lee liked to tell the story of a time when Elder Bennion visited and spoke to the inmates at the Utah State Penitentiary. Said Elder Lee,

This great teacher stood before them and said, "Now, I'm going to talk to you. I am going to ask you some questions, and I want you to get up and answer me. What was it that brought you here as inmates in this penitentiary? I am frequently a speaker at various gatherings of young people and at graduation exercises, and I would like you to tell me so that I can warn them." With the adroitness of a skilled teacher, he finally had them on their feet, and they began to answer. Do you know what they said, almost without exception? "We are here in the state penitentiary because there came a time in our lives when we were made to feel that nobody cared what happened to us."[4]

In 1915, as teaching began to be a formal part of the Sunday School program, Adam was appointed to write teacher training lessons for the coming year. In the following years there would be a series of teacher training textbooks written, two of them by Bennion.

Elder Bennion was gifted in other areas. As a public speaker he was in constant demand, both by Church and non-Church groups. Elder Harold B. Lee said, "I have often wondered at his popularity as a speaker at conventions of businessmen, bankers, civic leaders, and insurance executives."[5] His pen, like his voice, was active in the betterment of education and the work of the Lord, having written numerous manuals and books. He used to remind people that "good reading is a great guarantee of spiritual enrichment."[6] Music was also an important part of his life. As a boy he learned to play the piano and became proficient enough that he gave lessons and played in an orchestra, which aided him in going to college. In later years, he was director and president of the Salt Lake Oratorio Society, and a vice president of the Utah symphony organization. But probably his greatest gift was his genuine love of all men. Elder Lee wrote of him, "he seemed to have almost a divine quality of feeling others' heartaches and sorrows as though they were his own." Regardless of who or what the circumstances, "it was all the same. In him was an intuitive urge to do something about it and not to just feel sorry—and he did it."[7]

Elder Bennion was called to the Council of the Twelve at the April 1953 general conference. He lived less than five years as an Apostle. Of his many assignments, a highlight in his ministry was a five-month tour of the ten missions in Europe in 1956. During that time he traveled thirty-one thousand miles, meeting with missionaries, Church members, and servicemen. He summarized that trip by saying, "Those five months have been the most enriching and inspiring months of my life."[8] Another highlight came that same year when he visited the Holy Land. As they stood before the tomb of Jesus, the guide told his group that that tomb was different from all others because "this one is empty." Recalled Elder Bennion, "It was worth all my effort in visiting the Holy Land to hear that one statement."[9]

On February 11, 1958, six days following a cerebral hemorrhage, Elder Bennion died with family members at his bedside.

*Richard L. Evans*

Born: March 23, 1906, Salt Lake City, Utah
Sustained to First Council of Seventy: October 7, 1938
Ordained Apostle: October 8, 1953
Died: November 1, 1971, Salt Lake City, Utah, at age 65

B orn in Salt Lake City on March 23, 1906, the youngest
of nine children, Richard was only ten weeks old when his
father was accidentally killed, leaving his widowed mother to
care for her children. After completion of early grades, Richard always
held an outside job of some sort while attending school. Being a
member of his high school championship debating team earned him
a scholarship to the University of Utah, where he became manager of
the freshman debating team. But after one year, in 1925, he accepted
a mission call to Great Britain. After six months of missionary work,
he was called into the European Mission office by James E. Talmage
to serve as associate editor of the *Millennial Star*. Here he began a
history of the British Mission, which would later be completed and
published for the one hundredth anniversary of the founding of the

Mission. Under the mission presidency of John A. Widtsoe, Richard was called as secretary of the European Mission, which provided him the opportunity of visiting all the missions in Europe, visiting eleven countries in a trip that lasted over six months.

At the end of a nearly three-year mission, Richard returned to Salt Lake City where he was employed by KSL as an announcer. Working evenings, he was able to complete his schooling, earning a BA in English in 1931, and an MA in Economics in 1932. The following year he married Alice Ruth Thornley—they would become the parents of four sons. At KSL, he rose through successive positions until he eventually became director of the radio station, and later the television station. However, in 1936, he left full-time radio work to become managing editor of *The Improvement Era*. In time he became senior editor of the magazine and was one of those mainly instrumental in the development and supervision of the three current Church publication, the *Ensign*, the *New Era*, and the *Friend*. During his professional years, Elder Evans also served as a General Authority of the Church. In 1938, at the age of thirty-two, he was called to the First Council of Seventy, and in 1953, he was called to the Council of the Twelve Apostles. At the time of his death he had been a General Authority for thirty-three years.

Elder Evans was one of the most widely known and recognized leaders of the Church throughout the world. This was due partly to his involvement in Rotary, which led to leadership in local and district offices and the international board of directors, to chairmanship of Rotary Foundation Fellowship, to the office of president-elect in 1965, and eventually to president of Rotary International in 1966. With such responsibilities, he toured the world, speaking before hundreds of clubs throughout numerous nations. He continued his activity in Rotary until the end of his life.

But his larger claim to fame began in 1930, when he became producer and announcer of the recently established Tabernacle Choir nationwide broadcast. For nearly forty-one years up to the time of his death, he personally wrote and delivered his weekly messages that were always "timely, provocative, and uplifting."[1] His sermonettes eventually evolved into the world-famous *Spoken Word*, which was heard by millions of people of all faiths across the country, and were compiled into fourteen volumes of widely read books. Indeed, for many he was the only religion they knew. However, Richard L. Evans, Jr. tells us that his father's calm, smooth delivery somewhat belied what went on behind the scenes. There was the constant pressure of doing a "live" broadcast. Once on the air, he could not cough, sneeze, hesitate, or stutter over a word. Timing had to be exact, and even though the choir, organist, and Elder Evans rehearsed individually, their time on the air was their first time together. As for his part, "he confided to his family that he had never done the broadcast without feeling great tension, nervousness, even fright—the fear of making a mistake."[2]

The program did not start out as we have come to know it today. Elder Evans was constantly evaluating and changing the format. For example, it took twenty years to refine the wording of the *opening*— "Once more we welcome you within these walls with music and the spoken word from the Crossroads of the West,"—and the *sign-off*— "Again we leave you within the shadows of the everlasting hills. May peace be with you, this day and always."[3] We are also informed by his son that Elder Evans seemed to work better under pressure and, consequently, did not start work on the next Sunday's sermon until two or three days before, and that he continued to work and refine it up to the time of the broadcast. "There is no use saying a piece of copy is final if you can improve it on or off the air," Elder Evans liked to say.[4] Consequently he would walk into the Tabernacle with his script containing crossed-out words and so many marginal notes and insertions that only he could have read it at the time he went on the air. In this way his messages were always current and relative to the day. Also, one of the main attractions of the *Spoken Word* was that it was prepared for a general audience. While it was inspirational, motivational, and practical, it was neither preachy nor missionary-oriented. Yet the sermonettes brought many inquiries to his office concerning the Church. These he answered personally, and when appropriate, he put the inquirer in touch with LDS missionaries. Many of these inquirers eventually joined the Church.

Elder Evans felt a deep sense of responsibility toward the *Spoken Word*. Consequently, family vacations and assignments were planned around it. He shunned the use of prerecording broadcasts and did so on only a few occasions over his forty-plus years. On Saturday night, October 23, 1971, he was admitted to the hospital with a viral infection in the central nervous system. The next morning, although he could not speak and appeared only partially rational, he kept checking his watch as the time approached for the *Spoken Word*. He was repeatedly restrained from his attempts to get up and went into convulsions. It was, wrote his son, as if "his extraordinary sense of duty and his habitual weekly pattern was subconsciously impelling him toward his place at the microphone at the appointed time."[5]

His condition deteriorated until his death early Monday morning, November 1, 1971, at the relatively young age of sixty-five. The day before, on his last Sunday in mortality, the *Spoken Word* broadcasted his message by recording, encouraging all to endure, even in times of adversity.

George L. Morris

Born: February 20, 1874, Salt Lake City, Utah
Sustained Assistant to Quorum of the Twelve: October 6, 1951
Ordained Apostle: April 8, 1954
Died: April 23, 1962, Salt Lake City, Utah, at age 88

**B**orn February 20, 1874, In Salt Lake City, young George always had a love for the Church and is said to have "never neglected his meetings or church responsibilities. He grew up learning the value of hard work. His first employment came at the age of twelve, beginning his days at three a.m. to work at the Home Bakery. He later worked at a brickyard where the men he worked with were so rough and crude that his work area was changed so that he might escape their bad influence. Work in the "Marble Yard" was hard, and often, in the winter season, had him standing in slush and snow polishing stone till his hand seemed near frostbitten. He would often fight the monotony and harsh conditions by reciting to himself Milton's *Paradise Lost.*

As a young man George worked his way through university in his father's tile and monument business, graduating from the University of Utah in 1899. He was soon after called on a mission to Great Britain. Upon his return to Utah in 1902, he entered the field of business, managing his father's business, Elias Morris & Sons Company, for many years. He also became vice president of Prudential Federal Savings and Loan Association, and member of the Salt Lake City Chamber of Commerce. When he was a student at the University of Utah, George and a fellow student and friend, David O. McKay, were walking across campus one evening, discussing, among other things, how they would know when they had fallen in love. David remembered George offering the following advice: "My mother once told me that when I met a girl who awakened in me the highest and noblest feelings of manhood, who inspired in me a desire to be worthy of a woman such as she, then that would be a feeling of true love."[1] George later met such a girl and in 1905 married Emma Ramsy, a talented musician. They would go on to have three daughters.

Elder Morris always had a love for sports and the outdoors, a love that kept him involved throughout the duration of his life. During the summer of 1897, when he was twenty-three years of age, he and a friend swam from Garland to Saltaire in the Great Salt Lake, a distance of seven miles. His daughter Marian remembered that during her childhood, her father was a "magnificent horseman, always controlling his mount with gentle firmness, an excellent marksman, an ardent hiker, generally of unfrequented trails, and a marvelous swimmer and diver."[2] In later years, during a softball team's warm-up at the beginning of a tournament, Elder Morris donned a baseball cap, grabbed a mitt, and went out on the field to join the players catching fly balls—he was eighty-five years old. Following his death, a *Deseret News* editorial stated that Elder Morris did not seem to become old despite his extended life. During his years as chairman of the Priesthood Softball Program of the Church, he found enjoyment in sitting and watching a good game. In 1956, when the Church built a recreation and multiple-unit ball park in Salt Lake City, it was named the George Q. Morris Park in honor of his devotion to youth. Elder Morris suggested the park contain playground equipment as well as picnic tables and ornamental plants so that it could be a place of entertainment for the entire family.

Elder Morris's church service focused greatly upon the youth of the Church. For thirty-five years he served in the Young Men's Mutual Improvement Association [YMMIA]. Upon his return from his mission, young George was called into the Salt Lake Stake YMMIA Association Board, and then as stake superintendent. During the ensuing years, there were interruptions as he served as a counselor in a bishopric, as a bishop, and as a counselor in the stake presidency. But he always returned to the YMMIA, culminated by eleven years as general superintendent over the Churchwide YMMIA. He was also involved in Scouting and provided leadership in integrating the Boy Scouts more closely with the YMMIA. Through his work with the Explorers, he became chairman of the Explorer Committee of the National Council. In his YMMIA work he was also instrumental in the development of Church cultural festivals, in which thousands of youth participated.

In 1948, Elder Morris was called as president of the Eastern States Mission. In October 1951, he was sustained as an Assistant to the Council of the Twelve, and in April 1954, he was ordained an Apostle and sustained in the Quorum of the Twelve, which position he held for eight years. He died peacefully April 23, 1962, at the LDS Hospital in Salt Lake City, with family members at his bedside. He was eighty-eight years of age.

Speaking at his funeral services, Elder Richard L. Evans commented, "Never have I seen him put his own business or his own interest before the business of his Father in Heaven. Never have I seen him put any question before the question: What is the right thing to do? . . . Never have I seen him make a display of anger or impatience. Never have I seen him deviate from a principle or a high and proper purpose."[3]

*Hugh B. Brown*

Born: October 24, 1883, Granger, Utah

Sustained Assistant to the Quorum of the Twelve: October 5, 1953

Ordained Apostle: April 10, 1958

Sustained Counselor in First Presidency: June 22, 1961

Sustained Second Counselor to President David O. McKay:
    October 12, 1961

Sustained First Counselor to President McKay: October 4, 1963

Released at death of President McKay: January 18, 1970

Died: December 2, 1975, Salt Lake City, Utah, at age 92

Showing his sense of humor, Hugh B. Brown wrote, "it is alleged that I was born in Granger, Utah, in 1883, on October 24. I was there but do not remember the event. However, my mother was a honest woman and I must take her word."[1] Hugh was fourteen when his father decided to move the family to western Canada. Taking his eldest son with him, Homer Brown left Hugh to take care of the farm for over a year before Hugh joined him at their new home. Though Hugh would enjoy dual citizenship, he came to consider himself a Canadian. As a young man he moved to Logan, Utah, to attend Brigham Young College, but shortly after his arrival he was called on a mission to England. Elder Brown was assigned to Cambridge, where mobs had driven out the last pair of elders. Without a companion, and after tracting for several days without any success, he returned to his lodgings deeply discouraged. That evening a man came and explained that his family, along with sixteen other families, had left the Church of England. They were looking for a pastor and came across a tract that Elder Brown had left. Would Elder Brown come to his home and be their pastor. Though ill-prepared and frightened at the prospect, Elder Brown accepted the invitation. That first meeting, "As I spoke the name of God, I lost all fear, all worry and all concern and felt sure that He would take over, which He did in a miraculous way,"[2] recalled Elder Brown. Within three months, every person he taught in that meeting that night was baptized.

Returning to the United Sates, he married Zina Card, whom he had loved from his youth, and moved back to Canada. Rising in the military reserves to the rank of Major, Hugh served overseas during World War I. He considered a full-time military career, but that idea was aborted when he was denied further promotion due to religious discrimination. Following the war he obtained his law degree and was called as president of the Lethbridge Stake. In 1927, he moved from Lethbridge to practice law in Utah, where he was again called as a stake president, to the Granite Stake. During the war years of 1939–1946, he was recalled to England to serve as Mission President twice and as coordinator of the nearly 100,000 LDS servicemen in Europe. He also came to know personal tragedy and disappointment. Stricken with tic douloureux, an agonizingly painful disease of the nervous system also known as trigeminal neuralgia, he eventually underwent surgery that resulted in paralysis of the right side of his face. He was unsuccessful in seeking the nomination for US Senator. In World War II he lost his eldest son, who was a fighter pilot, over the English Channel. Due to a series of strokes, his wife, Zina, was bedridden and speechless for seven years before her death in December 1974. Through it all he was a man of faith. His family often heard him pray, "Oh Lord, if in order to be humble we must be humiliated, give us the courage to say, let it come."[3]

In 1950, Hugh became president of an oil development firm in Alberta, Canada. Yet it was at this time, with his family enjoying good health and with the future prospect of prosperity, that he hit what was probably the low point of his life. He felt uncertain about where his life was going and what the Lord would have him do with it. A spirit of depression came over him. Going into the mountains one day in October 1953, he prayed and asked the Lord that if it was not good for him and his family to become rich, as it looked like they were going to be through his oil venture, that "I hoped He would put an end to it." Arriving home that evening, he told his wife that he needed to be alone for the night and went into the bedroom alone. "All night," he records, "I wrestled with the evil spirit. I was possessed with the spirit of wishing that I could be rubbed out of existence. I had no thought of suicide, but wished the Lord would provide a way for me to cease to be. The room was full of darkness and an evil spirit prevailed, so real that I was almost consumed by it." About three o'clock in the morning, Zina, hearing him move about, came into the room and, closing the door behind her, exclaimed, "Oh Hugh, what is in this room?" He replied, "It is Satan."[4] Together they knelt and prayed. The next day at his office, he continued to pray until finally a spirit of peace came over him. That night he received a phone call from David O. McKay, calling him as an Assistant to the Council of the Twelve. Based upon the earnings of those who replaced Elder Brown in the Oil Company, his prayer that day in the mountains cost him nine million dollars.

Elder Brown served as an assistant to the Twelve until 1958 when he was sustained as a member of the Council of the Twelve. In 1961, he was called as a counselor in the First Presidency, serving with Presidents J. Reuben Clark, Jr. and Henry D. Moyle, all three counselors to President David O. McKay. He became second counselor with the death of President Clark, and first counselor upon the death of President Moyle, N. Eldon Tanner becoming second counselor. With the death of President McKay, Elder Brown resumed his seat as an Apostle. A few months later he confided in his nephew, President N. Eldon Tanner, that he missed his involvement in the First Presidency. With his health failing and unable to attend Quorum meetings regularly, President Tanner became his regular contact with the

General Authorities. Following one visit, President Tanner recorded in his journal, "I am sure it is difficult to adjust after being in the First Presidency." He then wrote of an incident Elder Brown had which helped him in his adjustment to declining responsibility. "He said it was not a vision, but the Lord appeared to him, very informal, the same as I was sitting talking to him. The Lord said, 'You have had some difficult times in your life.' Uncle Hugh responded, 'Yes, and your life was more difficult than any of us have had.' In the conversation Uncle Hugh asked when he would be finished here, and the Lord said, 'I don't know and I wouldn't tell you if I did.' Then He said, 'Remain faithful to the end, and everything will be all right.'"[5] Elder Brown died of natural causes following a long illness, at the age of ninety-two.

*Howard W. Hunter*

Born: November 14, 1907, Boise, Idaho
Ordained Apostle: October 15, 1959
Set apart as President of the Quorum of the Twelve: June 2, 1988
Sustained President of the Church: June 5, 1994
Died: March 3, 1995, Salt Lake City, Utah, at age 87

**B**orn November 14, 1907, in Boise Idaho, Howard's only sibling was his younger sister, Dorothy, born two years later. Howard's father, Will, was not a member of the Church and forbade his children's being baptized at the age of eight, feeling that they needed to be old enough to decide intelligently for themselves. When Howard wanted to be ordained a deacon with the other boys in his ward, his father gave in to his son's wishes and Howard was baptized in an indoor swimming pool at the age of twelve. Howard became the second boy to reach Eagle Scout in Boise, and when the Boise Saints discussed building a tabernacle, fifteen-year-old Howard was the first to pledge a donation: twenty-five dollars, which he worked hard to earn. At a young age he displayed a compassionate attitude. He would win other boys' marbles then decline to keep them. He once turned down a job when he learned it would cause another boy to be let go. Though color-blind and not inclined toward organized sports, Howard was academically and socially successful and was musically talented. He learned to play the piano and violin in his childhood and later took up the drums, saxophone, clarinet and trumpet. His sister observed that he had perfect pitch and a beautiful singing voice. At the age of around sixteen he organized a dance band called the Croonaders. After high school graduation, the Croonaders were contracted to provide music for a two-month cruise of the Orient aboard a passenger liner. Upon his return he found that his father had been baptized. On Howard's forty-sixth birthday, they would be sealed as a family.

In 1928, Howard moved to California, where he obtained work at a bank and became drummer for a local dance band. It was there, under the influence of a Sunday School teacher, that he began to study the gospel seriously and "the truths of the gospel commenced to unfold," he later wrote.[1] At a Church dance, he met Clara [Claire] May Jeffs, a former fashion model; they married in 1931 in the Salt Lake Temple. Prior to their marriage, Howard decided that the life of a musician was not conducive to what he pictured as family life, so he packed away his instruments and never played professionally again. The couple would have three sons. Sadly, the first one died at the age of six months. After losing his banking job due to the Depression and working a succession of jobs, Howard decided to enter law school. Graduating from Southwestern University in 1939, he began a very successful law practice in California. Always compassionate when clients could not afford to pay, he would offer free legal advice. As a corporate attorney in Los Angeles, he was asked to serve on the boards of many companies. Offered a position as judge in a state court, he declined the prestigious position in favor of the freedom to serve in the Church and spend time with his family.

At the age of thirty-two he was called as a bishop, then later as president of the Pasadena Stake. Being in Salt Lake City for the October 1959 general conference, he was called to President David O. McKay's office, where he was informed that he would be sustained the following day to the Council of the Twelve. From that time forward his time was fully devoted to his apostolic ministry, which included such assignments as president of the Genealogical Society and Church Historian. Elder Hunter was especially interested in Jerusalem and was responsible for obtaining the land for the building of the Orson Hyde Memorial Garden and the BYU Jerusalem Center of Near Eastern Studies. The mayor of Jerusalem during that time, Teddy Kollek, in speaking of his relationship with Elder Hunter, said:

> I know there were many people involved in this [the building of the BYU Jerusalem Center]. . . . But Elder Hunter was no doubt the moving spirit and the one who stuck with it even during periods when he didn't feel well physically. He thought about this all the time and just gave it a real push. . . . Without Elder Hunter, I am sure this would not have come about. . . I have a slight suspicion that he didn't quite appreciate the fierceness of the arguments that were fought here. . . . but he dealt with them in a sensible, a nice way. . . . With all my high regard for the Mormon Church and its members and the way you all behave . . . he is even quieter, if possible, more simple, more direct than all of you. And that is very impressive.[2]

Upon the death of President Ezra Taft Benson on May 30, 1994, Elder Hunter became president of the Church. His emphasis was on Church members becoming more Christlike, and becoming temple worthy. Unfortunately, his tenure lasted only nine months.

In 1981, Claire suffered a cerebral hemorrhage that left her severely incapacitated. He personally cared for her until a second episode necessitated more intense care. She died in 1983. In 1990 he married Inis Stanton, an old acquaintance from California.

Elder Hunter's life truly led him through the refiner's fire: polio in his youth leaving him with life-long back pains, the death of an infant son and his wife, surgery to remove a benign tumor, a heart attack and bypass surgery, continual lower back pain from spinal bone deterioration, a close brush with death when a bleeding ulcer required nine pints of blood during surgery, kidney failure, gall bladder surgery, back surgery leaving severe pain in his legs, and eventually prostate cancer that moved into his bones, resulting in his death at the age of eighty-seven. Through it all he retained his sense of humor. To those helping him to the podium, he said, "Brethren, I hope next time you won't need my help."[3] To those helping him back to his seat, he whispered, "Just drop me off anyplace." The courage he displayed in handling personal tragedy was shown in other ways. At BYU, a man rushed on stage with what he claimed to be a bomb, and demanded that President Hunter read a prepared statement. President Hunter calmly refused. After the man was subdued and led away, President Hunter began his prepared talk. "Life has a fair number of challenges," adding spontaneously, "as demonstrated."[4]

Upon his death, President Gordon B. Hinckley observed, "Much has been said about his suffering. I believe that it went on longer and more sharp and deep than any of us really knew. He developed a high tolerance for pain and did not complain about it. That he lived so long is a miracle in and of itself. His suffering has comforted and mitigated the pain of many others who suffer. They know that he understood the heaviness of their burdens. He reached out to these with a special kind of love."[5]

*Gordon B. Hinckley*

Born: June 23, 1910, Salt Lake City, Utah

Sustained Assistant to the Twelve: April 6, 1858

Ordained Apostle: October 5, 1961

Set apart as Counselor in First Presidency: July 23, 1981

Set apart as Second Counselor to President Spencer W. Kimball:
    December 2, 1982

Set apart as First Counselor to President Ezra Taft Benson:
    November 10, 1985

Sustained President of the Church: March 12, 1995

Died: January 27, 2008, Salt Lake City, Utah, at age 97

**B**orn June 23, 1910, Gordon grew up in a well-educated family. His father had been president of the LDS Business College and his mother a teacher of English and shorthand. In his childhood his parents purchased a small farm outside Salt Lake City. Consequently, Gordon grew to love books and appreciate hard work. He later attended the University of Utah, earning a BA degree in 1932. But his plans to study journalism at Columbia University in New York City were interrupted by a mission call.

It was during his mission in England that Gordon had what he considered a pivotal experience in his life. After having his missionary efforts met constantly with rejection and a lack of interest, he became extremely discouraged. In a letter to his father, he wrote, "I am wasting my time and your money. I don't see any point in my staying here." Bryant Hinckley, a wise father and always a teacher, wrote back, "I have only one suggestion. Forget yourself and go to work. With Love, Your Father." Having read the letter, Gordon returned to his apartment where "I got on my knees and made a covenant with the Lord that I would try to forget myself and go to work."[1] He often referred to that time as "my day of decision. . . . Everything good that has happened to me since then I can trace back to it."[2] With his renewed dedication, Gordon became an assistant to Elder Joseph E. Merrill of the Quorum of the Twelve. The young missionary showed his growing talents, writing articles for the *Millennial Star* and in the *London Monthly Pictorial* magazine. When President Merrill sent him to visit with the head of a large publishing company responsible for a book that contained falsehoods about the Church, the man agreed to include a disclaimer in the book from that time on. Returning home, President Merrill had him report to the First Presidency on the mission's needs. Impressed with the young man, the First Presidency hired Gordon as secretary of the Radio, Publicity, and Mission Literature Committee. On April 29, 1937, he married Marjorie Pay, whom he had known since childhood. They were married for nearly sixty-seven years until her death on April 6, 2004, and were the parents of five children.

When World War II broke out, Gordon was rejected by the military due to allergies. Feeling he should be involved in the war effort, he accepted a management position with the Denver and Rio Grande Railroad in Denver, managing rail shipments. When the war ended, the Railroad offered him a promotion and a very lucrative salary, but his heart was with the Church. He returned to his former job in Salt Lake City, where he remained employed until the April 1958 general conference, when he was sustained as an Assistant to the Quorum of the Twelve. In 1961, he was sustained to the Quorum of the Twelve. He became well-known for his contributions in public affairs and was often called upon to express Church positions on controversial issues to the media. In July 1981, he was called as a third counselor to an ailing President Kimball. He went on to serve as counselor to Presidents Benson and Hunter. With the death of President Hunter, he became the fifteenth president of the Church.

The magnitude of responsibility that rests upon the president of the Church, as well as the humility of those men called to that position, is well demonstrated in Elder Hinckley's call as president. When President Hunter died, Marjorie Hinckley observed, "[Gordon] was numb. And he felt lonely. There was no one left who could understand what he was going through."[3] Soon afterward he wrote, "Though I had served in the First Presidency for fourteen years . . . I had no idea how overwhelming it would feel."[4] Following President Hunter's funeral services, he recorded, "The burdens of leadership of the Church rest on my narrow shoulders. It is an awesome responsibility and even a terrifying thought to think of it. However, it is the Lord's Church. My responsibility will be to stand strong and listen for the quiet voice of the Spirit."[5] On Thursday, he went to the presidency's meeting room in the temple to be alone. Looking at a painting of the crucifixion he contemplated what the Savior had gone through to pay for his redemption. Then, looking upon the portraits of all the previous presidents of the Church, it seemed as though they were looking at him and pledging their support, assuring him that he need not fear, that he would be blessed and sustained in his presidency. Afterward he wrote, "With the confirmation of the Spirit in my heart, I am now ready to go forward to do the very best work I know how to do."[6]

And go forward he did. Among the numerous accomplishments of his administration were the dedications of sixty-four temples—including those at Palmyra, Nauvoo, and Winter Quarters; more than ninety visits to countries outside of the US, totaling over a million miles of travel; the construction of the magnificent Church Conference Center; the establishment of the Perpetual Education Fund; the publication of *The Family: A Proclamation to the World*; appearances on national television broadcasts—*60 Minutes* with Michael Wallace, and *Larry King Live*; and growth in Church membership from just over nine million to thirteen million. It is significant that on his ninety-fourth birthday, in 2004, he received from President George W. Bush the Presidential Medal of Freedom.

With his many accomplishments, President Hinckley was also a man of the people. "I wish to mingle with the people I love," he stated.[7] His warmth, spontaneous humor and common-man approach endeared him to the people. Elder Russell M. Nelson related that at a Midwest Regional Conference, when it was President Hinckley's turn to speak, "He stood and said, 'It's good to be in Indiana. I don't know why, but it's good to be here,' and everyone roared. If I had said that, it wouldn't have been funny. But he has an uncanny way of making an audience feel as though he is one of them."[8] As he reached out to others, so did he encourage Church members to do the same. "Let us be a friendly people. Let us be neighborly people. Let us be what members of the Church of Jesus Christ of Latter-day Saints ought to be."[9] He wanted this because he cared for people, regardless of background or religion. President Hinckley died at the age of ninety-seven, making him the oldest Church president in this dispensation.

*N. Eldon Tanner*

Born: May 9, 1898, Salt Lake City, Utah
Sustained Assistant to the Quorum of the Twelve: October 8, 1960
Ordained Apostle: October 11, 1962
Sustained Second Counselor to President David O. McKay:
    October 4, 1963
Sustained Second Counselor to President Joseph Fielding Smith:
    January 23, 1970
Sustained First Counselor to President Harold B. Lee: July 7, 1972
Sustained First Counselor to President Spencer W. Kimball:
    December 30, 1973
Died: November 27, 1982, Salt Lake City, Utah, at age 84

Following the marriage of Eldon's parents, Sarah Edna Brown and Nathan William Tanner, in the Salt Lake Temple, they moved to Aetena, a small Latter-day Saint settlement in southern Alberta, Canada, where they made a one-room dugout home in the side of the hill and homesteaded. Because there were no doctors in the area, Sarah went to Salt Lake City when Eldon was due to be born. After his birth, she returned home with her new baby. There, Eldon grew up the eldest of eight children. He had a happy childhood, though farm life presented him with many responsibilities and taught him to value hard work. Once when his father, a bishop, had to be gone, he outlined several tasks for the boys to take care of, but the boys took to riding calves. When their father returned home, he said to Eldon, "My boy, I thought I could depend on you."[1] The words cut so deeply that young Eldon determined that his father would never again have cause to repeat those words to him. On another occasion, when the entire family was sick with smallpox, Eldon went three days and two nights without sleep, caring for the family.

Eldon's parents were determined he would get an education despite many interruptions due to farm work. Consequently, in 1919 he was able to accept a position as teacher and principal at Hill Spring, near his family's home. There he met a schoolteacher named Sara Isabelle Merrill, whom he married December 20, 1919. One student later remembered Eldon entering the classroom on the first day of school and announcing, "Boys and girls, we'll be together for seven hours a day for the next year. In that time I only want to teach you one thing." He then wrote on the blackboard in two-foot high letters, "THINK."[2] By introducing boxing, wrestling, and basketball to his students, he greatly improved the conduct of the young boys. Later, when called as a deacon's quorum adviser, he found that many boys did not come to Church because they were embarrassed to be seen in overalls, which was all they had to wear. By agreeing to wear overalls with them, Eldon helped the boys soon became 100 percent active. Eldon moved his family to Cardston to accept a new teaching position. Because teaching did not pay much, Eldon found it necessary to have additional employment such as operating a general merchandise store and selling insurance. In Cardston, he also served as bishop of the Cardston First Ward.

In 1935, Eldon's life suddenly began to skyrocket into the public eye. Encouraged to become a political candidate, he was elected to the Alberta legislature, which necessitated moving his family to Edmonton. Then, though never having attended a legislative session, he was named speaker of the house. The following year, he was appointed to a cabinet post as Minister of Lands and Mines, making him responsible for administering all the natural resources for the province of

Alberta. He became known as "'Mr. Integrity' because he refused to compromise by accepting gifts of any kind and was strictly honest in his dealings."[3] Consequently, he won the admiration and respect of many influential people in Canada and in Great Britain, even dining with British royalty. During his seventeen years of government service in Edmonton, he also served as president of the Edmonton Branch, seeing membership grow from 15 to 350 members. Involved in Scouting, he eventually became provincial Scout commissioner and was awarded the Silver Wolf, Canada's highest honor to a Scout. In 1952, he left government service, becoming president of Merrill Petroleum. Around this time he was called as president of the new Calgary Stake. In 1954, he was invited to head Trans-Canada Pipelines Ltd., which was bogged down in the construction of a two thousand mile pipeline across five provinces. He was seen as the only man who could bring the various rivaling interests together and complete the project. He agreed to the assignment but insisted that headquarters be established in Calgary where he could continue on as stake president. Upon the pipeline's completion, one authority observed, "It was the greatest undertaking since the building of the transcontinental railroad and was accomplished in less than four years."[4] Eldon went on to serve on the board of directors and as director of several important companies.

In the same manner that Eldon quickly rose in positions of public service, so also came a rapid sequence of callings in the hierarchy of the Church. The Tanners were completing their dream home when the call came for Elder Tanner to serve as an Assistant to the Twelve. He resigned from all his positions and moved his family to Salt Lake City. "It's just a home," he commented, "we'll go where the call requires."[5] Shortly thereafter he was called to preside over the West European Mission. Two years after his call as an Assistant to the Twelve, he was called to the Council of the Twelve, and the following year he was sustained in the First Presidency. He became the first person to serve as a first or second counselor in the First Presidency of the Church to four different presidents. In 1966, he became a citizen of the United States, stating that "we need to be practicing citizens of the nation which shelters us."[6]

Elder Tanner's great value to the Church can be seen in statements made following his death. A collective tribute from the Quorum of the Twelve stated, "clearly, President Tanner's management genius and his many talents were especially suited for this particular time to serve the needs of a growing, worldwide Church. . . . The death of a righteous individual is both an honorable release and a call to new labors. We say, from rich experience, how blessed are they who will now be served directly by this spiritual giant."[7] Presiding Bishop Victor L. Brown observed, "His decision-making resulted in almost flawless judgment. He gathered all possible facts before making a decision, never making an impetuous or off-the-cuff decision." Nor was his judgment warped by bias or pet projects, observed Bishop Brown. A favorite saying of his was, "It isn't important *who* is right. What is important is *what* is right."[8] Elder Ezra Taft Benson said of him, "Nathan Eldon Tanner was one of the great and noble men of our time. He was recognized as a giant among men. In the annals of Church history he will be remembered as one of the most influential counselors in the First Presidency of the Church."[9]

Elder Tanner suffered from Parkinson's disease during the last several years of his life but continued to fulfill his responsibilities until just before the Thanksgiving holidays of 1982. He died of cardiac arrest at the age of eighty-four. Perhaps one of the most important lessons we might learn from his successful life is found in his personal observation that his whole life seemed to have been largely a series of assignments for which he was not prepared, each one causing him to reach beyond his grasp.

*Marvin J. Ashton*

Born: May 6, 1915, Salt Lake City, Utah
Sustained Assistant to the Twelve: October 3, 1969
Ordained Apostle: December 2, 1971
Died: February 25, 1994, Salt Lake City, Utah, at age 78

**B**orn May 6, 1915, Marvin was the son of Marvin O. Ashton, who would later serve in the Presiding Bishopric of the Church. One of six children, Marvin grew up in the depression years learning to work hard and save money. He raised rabbits and pigeons, worked on the family's two-acre produce farm, and learned his father's hardware and lumber business. Because there were only four boys of Scouting age in his ward, they rode three miles on horseback to a neighboring ward that had a Scout troop, earning them the nickname, "The Mounted Patrol."

Marvin's father encouraged him to serve a mission, but told him he would have to save enough to pay his own way. By working half days at his father's hardware store, Marvin was able to earn his way through the University of Utah School of Business and save for a mission. Following graduation at the age of twenty-one, he was financially ready to go.

At that time in England, missionary activities were designed to help improve the Church image. Marvin was captain of a missionary basketball team that won the British National title. In London, he took on the leadership of a Methodist boy's group who had lost their minister and could not afford another one. No conversions came of it, but many friends were made. He was also assigned by his mission president, Hugh B. Brown, as managing editor of the *Millennial Star*. Upon his return home in 1939, he married Norma Bernston. They had been long-time friends and had often played tennis together on her parents' tennis court. They became the parents of two boys and two girls. During World War II, Marvin procured lumber for government use. Following the war, he went on to develop a successful wholesale lumber business.

In 1948, he was called to serve in the Church YMMIA, serving ten years on the general board, and eleven years as a general superintendent. During that time he was heavily involved in promoting Churchwide athletic programs. Then, in October of 1969, he was called as an Assistant to the Twelve. Two years later, in December 1971, he was ordained to the Quorum of the Twelve. Looking back on that day, he observed, "You wonder why the call has come to you, but you get busy and persevere."[1] Elder Ashton had a keen business mind and as an Apostle headed several major Church corporations. But he was best known for his genuine warmth and his love for all people, regardless of their walk in life. "I've always tried to find the best in everyone," he said. "If you don't have faith in people, they won't change for the better."[2] Serving four years in the state legislature, he pushed for the development and improvement of juvenile detention facilities. During his years as a General Authority he worked with Church Social Services, supervising programs that dealt with foster children, adoptions, Indian student placement, counseling, and other welfare concerns. In counseling couples with marital problems, he placed the burden on both individuals rather than one. He'd ask "What are *you* doing individually to make things better with your spouse? No matter how innocent you may feel, have you done your part to resolve the problem?"[3] To those with moral issues, he did not review the circumstances or reasons leading up to their behavior, but would say, "I'm not so concerned with what you've done or where you've been as I am with where you're going."[4]

He especially found great satisfaction in working with prison inmates, stating that "If I didn't have anything else to do, I would like to be a liaison to the prison system."[5] Once, while at the Jordan River Temple, a young man who was about to get married approached Elder Ashton and reminded him that they had met at the Utah State Prison where Elder Ashton had spoken to a gathering of inmates. Surprised, Elder Ashton asked, "What did I say to help you?" "I don't remember what you said," replied the young man, "but afterwards you came down among us and shook *my* hand! When I realized that an Apostle of the Lord would shake the hand of a man like me, then I knew that I must be worth something."[6] That was the beginning of his road to repentance.

Elder Ashton was equally comfortable with prominent people of the world. In 1984, the premier of the People's Republic of China came to the United States for the first time since the Republic's founding in 1949. Stopping in Hawaii en route to Washington, DC, Premier Zhao Ziyant was taken to the Church's Polynesian Culture Center. As he stepped out of the helicopter, the man delegated to officially greet him on behalf of the president of the United States was Elder Ashton. There followed a tour of the Culture Center and a luncheon. Elder Ashton decided he would not mention the Mormon Church since he wanted the premier's first exposure to Americans to be positive. A White House official worried that the premier might be offended if not offered tea, but Elder Ashton said, "We'll just serve him fruit punch and see how it goes." It went well and the premier asked for a refill. Elder Ashton wondered if prayer should be offered before his atheistic guest, but decided to do so and had a stake president offer prayer. The premier bowed his head in respect. During the meal, the premier said to Elder Ashton, "I want you to know I've appreciated everything you've done today being natural. You've gone ahead as usual and have presented everything the way it is." That evening at a reception in Honolulu, honoring the premier, Elder and Sister Ashton stood three or four rows back among three hundred people in attendance. As the premier began walking down the line, he spotted the Ashtons and broke through the lines to shake their hands. "He recognized us as friends and wanted to greet us promptly," said Elder Ashton.[7]

Elder Ashton once quoted Elder Howard W. Hunter, who said of those called to the apostleship, "It is required of us that despite our age, infirmity, exhaustion, and feelings of inadequacy, we do the work he has given us to do, to the last breath of our lives."[8] Elder Ashton demonstrated that these were not mere words to him, but a deep and personal conviction. President Thomas S. Monson recalled that just two days before Elder Ashton died, he came to President Monson's office on Church business. "Elder Ashton leaned on the arm of Elder M. Russell Ballard of the Twelve, using a cane with his other hand. It was hard for him to breathe, but he was about the Lord's work."[9] Elder Ashton died February 25, 1994, at the Salt Lake City hospital. He was seventy-eight.

Bruce R. McConkie

Born: July 29 1915, Ann Arbor, Michigan
Sustained to First Council of Seventy: October 6, 1946
Ordained Apostle: October 12, 1972
Died: April 19, 1985, Salt Lake City, Utah, at age 69

B ruce Redd McConkie was born July 29, 1915 in Ann Arbor, Michigan, the first child of Oscar W. and Margaret Redd McConkie. It was a difficult birth and as the doctors worked to save the mother, the baby was laid aside, thought to be still-born. Only after someone heard a tiny cry did they turn their attention to him. A year later the family returned to southern Utah, where young Bruce grew up on a farm. One day, his father felt prompted to run into the orchard. There he saw a galloping horse racing toward him and felt he needed to stop it. Only after doing so did he discover that the horse was dragging his son and that he had saved Bruce's life. When Bruce was a teenager, the family moved to Salt Lake City. Upon graduation from high school, Bruce served a mission in the eastern states. Returning home, he entered the University of Utah, and in 1937 he married Amelia Smith, a daughter of Joseph Fielding Smith. They would have nine children. Sadly, their first child, Bruce Jr., lived for only a few weeks. Obtaining a law degree in 1939, he was employed for two years as assistant Salt Lake City attorney and city prosecutor. During World War II, he served in the armed forces as a security and intelligence officer, returning to civilian life with the rank of Lieutenant Colonel. Following the war, Bruce decided to forego the legal profession and went to work on the editorial staff of the *Deseret News.* Less than a year later, he was called to the First Council of Seventy, which position he would hold for twenty-six years until called as an Apostle. As the October 1972 general conference drew near, President Harold B. Lee informed Bruce that he was being called to the Quorum of the Twelve. Bruce replied, "I know. This is no surprise to me. I have known it for some time."

As a General Authority, Elder McConkie was famous for his gospel scholarship as displayed in his sermons and writings. Well-known to Church members are his encyclopedic *Mormon Doctrine,* his three-volume *Doctrinal New Testament Commentary,* his six-volume Messiah series on the life and ministry of Christ, and his final work, *A New Witness to the Articles of Faith.* Some have been critical of Elder McConkie's limited references to the writings of others, but he was a believer in personal study and in drinking directly from the fountain head. Concerning his writing of the Messiah series, he explained, "I read the standard works from cover to cover, as though I'd never read them before, and elicited from them everything that had anything to do with the promise of a Messiah. Then I organized and wrote *The Promised Messiah.* "[1] He then went on to explain how he repeated this same process for each of the following volumes. With the exception of the Prophet Joseph Smith, he seldom researched what other Church leaders said, relying upon his own understanding of the scriptures. "I would never quote another man," he once observed, "unless I could first square it with the scriptures, and if he said it better than I could."[2] Elder Boyd K. Packer expressed his feelings that, "if ever there was a man who was raised up unto a very purpose," it was Elder McConkie and his contributions to the preparation and publication of the LDS Scriptures.[3]

Yet Elder McConkie was a man of humility who was open to suggestions and could admit to his errors. Robert Matthews, who served on the LDS Scripture Publication Committee, recalled that they would sometimes discuss the wording of the chapter headings written by Elder McConkie. "He was always open and non-defensive and never did I see him use the weight of his office to decide a point. He would often say in a friendly way: 'If you fellows want to change the wording, you may do so.' We rarely did, and only with his concurrence."[4] When the Revelation on the Priesthood [D&C Declaration 2] was released, he said at a BYU devotional, "Forget everything that I have said [or others have said] . . . that is contrary to the present revelation. We spoke with a limited understanding and without the light and knowledge that now has come into the world."[5]

An imposing figure at 6'5" and feeling that it was his duty to preach and exhort rather than tell jokes and stories, Elder McConkie was often seen by others as an austere man. But his wife claimed they did not know the real person. While he possessed a reserve that kept many from truly understanding him, around those who knew him well, he had a great sense of humor, even to being a prankster. His children remember him as a gentle, sensitive, and affectionate father. None of them remember him demanding that they learn the gospel, yet gospel discussions were a part of their growing up. He was described as having a warmth of soul and as sensitive to others' feelings, taking opportunities to compliment and bolster others. He was also known as a very forgiving man who did not hold grudges, even if he was criticized for his doctrines. His secretary of thirty-two years recalled, "In all the years I worked for him, he never said an unkind word to me. I have never known a more Christ-like man."[6] His wife saw him as a man who tended to do things in excess. When a daughter introduced him to rock hunting, he took to the hills, resulting in a yard full of rocks. When he saw a TV special on fitness, he changed from walking to becoming a jogging fanatic. It seems he was a complex man with both a public and a private persona.

In January 1984, Elder McConkie was diagnosed with a form of cancer that is generally fatal within a few months. His life would be extended to fourteen months. With faith that he could be healed, he continued in his apostolic work while submitting to medical treatment. Toward the end, when he was too sick to work, he would fully dress and lay down on his bed. To stay in his pajamas would have been for him a sign of giving up. As the April 1985 general conference drew near, Elder McConkie had a strong desire to address the Saints. Against his doctor's advice but with the faith and prayers of his family behind him, he attended the opening session and gave what would be his final talk. In his closing testimony, he declared,

> I testify that he is the Son of the Living God and was crucified for the sins of the world. . . . This I know of myself independent of any other person. . . . I am one of his witnesses, and in a coming day I shall feel the nail marks in his hands and in his feet and shall wet his feet with my tears. But I shall not know any better then than I know now that he is God's Almighty Son, that he is our Savior and Redeemer, and that salvation comes in and through his atoning blood and in no other way.[7]

The following week, Elder Packer visited the McConkie home and gave Elder McConkie a blessing in which he said it was time for him to submit to the will of the Lord. Elder McConkie turned to his wife and said, "Amelia, do you know what he just did? He sealed me unto death." When Elder Packer left, Elder McConkie put on his pajamas and got under the covers. Amelia, later observed that "this was his way of saying he was submitting. He later told me didn't want anyone fasting or praying for him, that it was all up to the Lord. He desperately didn't want to die. He had been so sure he would live. For him, it was the ultimate test of obedience."[8] On April 19, just five days after his going to bed, he died at the relatively young age of sixty-nine.

# David B. Haight

Born: September 2, 1906, Oakley, Idaho
Sustained Assistant to the Twelve: April 6, 1970
Ordained Apostle: January 8, 1976
Died: July 31, 2004, Salt Lake City, Utah, at age 97

D avid was born September 2, 1906, in the small town of Oakley, Idaho. As banker, bishop, and state senator, David's father, Hector Haight, was a prominent member of the community. Sadly, he died suddenly in his home when he was only forty-six years of age. At the time, young David was nine. David would also lose a sister and a brother in that same year. Just three years previous, a three-year-old brother had died, and two years after his father's sudden death, David's mother took seriously ill and remained so for many years. Consequently, David and his sister Helen, being the oldest children at home, took charge of the household, Helen doing the indoor chores and David doing the outdoor farm and house work. That he took his responsibilities seriously is seen in his winning an award for having the cleanest yard in town.

He also enjoyed playing the violin and organized a high school dance orchestra. In later years David liked to tell of his high school's first football team, of which he was a member. The team had twelve players who wore inexpensive jerseys with their tennis shoes, and was coached by a chemistry teacher who was the only one at the school who had seen a football game. Their first game was against Twin Falls, state champions the previous year. David recalled, "Our problem was to get rid of the ball—it was less punishing." Toward the end of the game, one of David's teammates intercepted a pass and unbelievably ran for a touchdown. The final score was 106 to 6. Referring to this game, David would later teach, "In all things success depends upon previous preparation."[1]

From Albion State Normal School in Idaho, David earned a teaching certificate as a way to earn money to attend Utah State University, although he earned most of his money working on crews extending electrical service into rural Idaho. Graduating with a business administration degree, he moved to Salt Lake City, where he met and married Ruby Olson. They would become the parents of two boys and a girl. David eventually went to work for Montgomery Ward, working his way up to district manager in California. When World War II broke out, he entered the Navy. Rising to the rank of commander, he oversaw the logistics and tactical operations of distributing supplies in the Pacific, which performance earned him an official military commendation. Returning to Montgomery Ward, he was sent to Chicago, where he supervised 165 stores. But in 1951, at the age of forty-five, he decided to enter business on his own, acquiring several hardware stores in Palo Alto, California. During this time he served as stake president and as Mayor of Palo Alto for two terms until called to preside over the Scottish Mission.

Following his mission, David became an assistant to the president of BYU. He also served as a member of the Priesthood Missionary Committee and then as a Regional Representative. In 1970, he was called as an Assistant to the Twelve. Then in January 1976, Elder Haight was called to meet with President Spencer W. Kimball in the Salt Lake Temple, at which time he was called to the Quorum of the Twelve. Concerning the meeting, Elder Haight wrote: "I knew I was in the presence of greatness and had no question that he was a prophet. I was surprised and humbled. I have never coveted a Church position, but I had made up my mind a long time ago that I would accept the calls that came from the Lord. When I thought of all the great men in the Church, I wondered why I had been chosen, but at the same time I did not question the prophet."[2] Elder Haight was a gentle man of great warmth and compassion. President Thomas Monson illustrated this compassion by telling of the time he and Elder Haight went to a mortuary for the viewing of a prominent man who had passed away. As they were leaving the crowded room, they passed a room where another viewing was taking place with only a few people in attendance. Elder Haight entered the room and said to the grieving widow, "Hello, I'm Elder David Haight of the Quorum of the Twelve. I came from across the hall to extend to you my condolences and my sincere prayer for you in your bereavement."[3] The widow was comforted, said President Monson.

As an Apostle, Elder Haight was ever mindful of his responsibility as a witness of the Savior. Speaking at general conference in October 1989, Elder Haight told of a recent and marvelous incident in his life. On January 6, 1989, he had suffered a very serious aortic aneurism that necessitated emergency surgery. When the aneurism occurred, he fell into a state of unconsciousness that lasted for several days. He recounted,

> I was now in a calm, peaceful setting; all was serene and quiet. . . . [I] was conscious of being in a holy presence and atmosphere. During the hours and days that followed, there was impressed again and again upon my mind the eternal mission and exalted position of the Son of Man. . . . I was shown a panoramic view of His early ministry. . . . There followed scenes of His earthly ministry to my mind in impressive detail, confirming scriptural eyewitness accounts. I was being taught, and the eyes of my understanding were opened by the Holy Spirit of God so as to behold many things.

Elder Haight went on to describe the events of the Last Supper and of the Savior's suffering in Gethsemane, the Savior's betrayal and mock trial, His Crucifixion and resurrection, as they were shown to him "over and over again." "I cannot begin to convey to you," he said, "the deep impact that these scenes have confirmed upon my soul. I sense their eternal meaning and realize that 'nothing in the entire plan of salvation compares in any way in importance with that most transcendent of all events, the atoning sacrifice of our Lord. It is the most important single thing that has ever occurred in the entire history of created things; it is the rock foundation upon which the gospel and all other thing rest,' as has been declared."[4]

Speaking of this event at the funeral of Elder Haight, Gordon B. Hinckley said, "That traumatic and remarkable event occurred fifteen years ago. How marvelous has been his influence, how wonderful his work during those 15 years."[5] At the time of his death on July 31, 2004, Elder Haight was one month away from turning ninety-eight years of age. He was the oldest living Apostle of this dispensation, being the first to celebrate his ninety-seventh birthday.

*James E. Faust*

Born: July 31, 1920, Delta, Utah
Sustained Assistant to the Twelve: October 6, 1972
Sustained to the Presidency of First Quorum of Seventy: October 1, 1976
Ordained Apostle: October 1, 1978
Set apart as Second Counselor to President Gordon B. Hinckley:
   March 12, 1995
Died: August 10, 2007, Salt Lake City, Utah, at age 87

James Esdras Faust was born July 31, 1920, in Delta, Utah, one of five sons born to George A. and Amy Finlinson Faust. The family later moved to Salt Lake City where George was an attorney and district court judge. In high school, young James lettered in football and track, and later in track at the University of Utah. Following two years of college, he was called on a mission to Brazil. In those days it was a discouraging mission with very few baptisms. Elder Faust said of those years, "We didn't accomplish much except for the changes in ourselves. I feel it was one of the most productive and valuable times in my life."[1] But they were laying the foundation for a future work. He later observed, "At the time, our labors were unfruitful and difficult. We could not envision the great outpouring of the Spirit of the Lord which has come in [Brazil] and its neighboring countries in South America, Central America and Mexico in the intervening years."[2] Elder Faust would return to Brazil in 1975 to preside over the work in South America as an Assistant to the Twelve, and in 1998 he would receive the rare distinction of becoming an honorary citizen of Sao Paulo, Brazil. After returning from his mission, he served in the military during World War II, married Ruth Wright (whom he had known since high school) completed a law degree from the University of Utah, and went on to a distinguished twenty-four-year career as an attorney.

Looking back upon his earlier years, Elder Faust often reflected upon significant incidents through which he was taught lessons that greatly influenced the remaining years of his life. One such incident occurred when he was quite young and had forgotten to put his pet lamb safely away for the night. When a storm arose, he could hear the frightened lamb bleating, but did not want to leave the safety and comfort of his own bed and go out into the stormy weather. The next morning, he discovered that a dog had also heard the lamb's bleating and had killed it. Elder Faust recalled that what hurt even more was his father's rebuke: "Son, couldn't I trust you to take care of just one lamb?"[3] Young James resolved that very day that in the future he would never neglect his responsibilities should he ever again have occasion to be a shepherd. In later years, as he became a spiritual shepherd over the Lord's flock, he would remember and honor that resolution.

Another important lesson came when he was enlisted into the military during World War II. Applying for officers' candidate school, he was summoned before a board of inquiry. He recalled that many of the questions were directed toward his religious standards. Did he smoke? Did he drink? Though fearful of offending the officers questioning him, he answered the questions straightforwardly. Then he was asked if he thought that the moral code should be relaxed during times of war. Elder Faust said that wanting "to make some points and look broad-minded . . . the thought flashed through my mind that perhaps I could say that I had my own beliefs, but I did not wish to impose them on others. . . . In the end I simply said, 'I do not believe there is a double standard of morality.'"[4] Thinking he had blown his opportunity, he was surprised later to find that he had been accepted to officers' candidate school. From this came another important lesson. "In all my long years of life," he said at general conference, "I have tried not to hide who I am and what I believe. I cannot recall a single instance when it hurt my career or I lost valued friends by humbly acknowledging that I was a member of this Church."[5] Upon returning from the war, fearful that the years were passing him by, he decided not to return to the University of Utah, where he had started his studies eight years earlier. To do so would require another three years of intensive study and poverty. He informed his father that he thought he would just get a job or start a business and move on with his life. His father, a no-nonsense man when it came to matters of importance, replied, "What can you do?" Elder Faust recalled that the question was so brutally honest that it hurt, but he had to admit to his father and to himself that he could not do much. So he reluctantly returned to college and earned a law degree, which would not only benefit him and his family, but would also enable him to effectively serve the kingdom of God in the coming years.

Prior to his call as a General Authority, Elder Faust served as a bishop, high councilor, stake president, and regional representative. Concerning his call as an Assistant to the Twelve, he said, "President Lee told me I could leave my name on the door of my law office. But I told him I had been called, was putting my hand to the plow, and I didn't want to ever look back."[6] Yet, in his thirty-five years as a General Authority, his legal expertise would be drawn upon often in issues of importance to the Church. He also worked hard to build bridges between the Church and other religions. His wife remembered a time when they attended a community event in which a leader of another church ranted against the LDS Church. Elder Faust listened patiently. Afterward, he went up to the man and said, "Now, Reverend, if you feel that way, we must be doing something wrong. I'd like for us to have lunch together so that you can let me know what your concerns are."[7] They did and became good friends thereafter. President Hinckley wrote of him, "as a member of the Twelve . . . I never found a time when he wasn't on the right track, and that's why I asked him to serve as my second counselor."[8] President Monson eulogized, "There was no chink in his armor; there was no guile in his soul; there was no flaw in his character. President Faust loved the Lord with all his heart and soul and served Him with all his might to the very end of his mortal life."[9]

In his later years, President Faust suffered from a series of health complications that culminated in the crippling of his body, but his mind remained bright and alert. He died at the age of eighty-seven from causes incident to age. At his funeral services, the Mormon Tabernacle sang as the closing hymn, "This is the Christ." The text of this hymn was written by President Faust; thus it was his final testimony to the world.

> This is the Christ. . . . the holy Son of God,
> Our Savior, Lord, Redeemer of mankind.
> This is the Christ, the Healer of our souls,
> Who ransomed us with purest love divine.

*Neal A. Maxwell*

Born: July 6, 1926, Salt Lake City, Utah
Sustained Assistant to Quorum of the Twelve: April 6, 1974
Sustained to Presidency of First Quorum of Seventy: October 1, 1976
Ordained Apostle: July 23, 1981
Sustained to the Quorum of the Twelve: October 3, 1981
Died: July 21, 2004, Salt Lake City, Utah, at age 78

Young Neal grew up in a loving but a very modest home. Developing his skills in basketball, he dreamed of playing on the high school team, but by the time he entered Granite High School, his friends had grown significantly taller and he failed to make the team. By then he had developed a serious case of acne which left facial scars that he carried throughout his life. His 4-H project of raising pigs earned prizes, but also it brought cutting remarks from his friends. His self-confidence was further shaken when his high school English teacher gave him a D. When he complained, she said, "Neal, you are capable of doing A work. Until you do, you will continue to get D minus."[1] He went on to earn those

As and become coeditor of the school paper. This began his fascination with the power of words, for which he would become famous throughout the Church.

When Neal graduated from high school in 1944, World War II was raging. Wanting to do his part, he enlisted in the military service and found himself an infantryman in the battle of Okinawa. There he underwent a life-transforming experience. Late one night, enemy fire began exploding around him as the enemy zeroed in on the position of Neal's mortar squad. One shell exploded no more than five feet from his foxhole. As he knelt in his foxhole and pleaded with the Lord for protection, promising to dedicate the rest of his life to the Lord's service, the shelling suddenly stopped. The next night the shelling on their position started again, but almost all the shells were duds or failed to detonate due to landing in soft mud. Neal felt certain the Lord had preserved his life and he remembered his promise to the Lord throughout his remaining years. In 1973, he returned to the spot where his foxhole had been, "which for me, is a sacred spot. Sugar cane has since covered the little plateau, but not my poignant memories."[2] He kept in his office a photograph of that "sacred spot" as a continual reminder of his indebtedness to the Lord.

While in the military, Neal had been able to save money for college. But upon his return home he used the money to serve as a missionary in the Canadian Mission. Unfortunately he found that many members had fallen into inactivity during the war. His children would remind him in later years that as a missionary and serving in the branch presidency, he had baptized two and excommunicated four, for a net loss of two. In his usual humble spirit, he allowed this comment to be included in a biographical article in hopes of giving encouragement to missionaries who were currently struggling and not meeting their own expectations in convert baptisms. Upon hearing that a prepublication reviewer questioned the inclusion of the incident in the article, Elder Maxwell commented that the reviewer must not have much of a sense of humor. Following his mission, he studied political science at the University of Utah. It was at an Institute class that he met Colleen Hinckley, whom he married on November 22, 1950. After graduation, they moved to Washington, DC, where he worked as legislative assistant to Utah Senator Wallace

F. Bennett. His experiences there somewhat dampened his enthusiasm for politics, leading him to later state "that the living of one protective principle of the gospel is better than a thousand compensatory governmental programs—which programs are, so often, like 'straightening deck chairs on the Titanic.'"[3]

Returning to the University of Utah in 1956, he held several faculty and administrative jobs, eventually becoming Dean of Students and then Executive Vice-President. During this time he obtained a MS in political science. He also served as bishop of a student ward. He went on to serve on the YMMIA General Board, as a Regional Representative, and in 1972 was called as Church Commissioner of Education. In 1974, he was called as an Assistant to the Twelve, in 1976 as a Seventy, and in 1981 to the Quorum of the Twelve. A man of keen intellect and deep thought, Elder Maxwell never worried about science or other disciplines challenging the gospel, but felt secular knowledge buttressed the gospel. "In my own education . . ." he wrote, "I found that the basic gospel truths . . . could be harmonized with the great secular truths. [And] those gospel truths which, for the moment, could not be harmonized could . . . be regarded expectantly, for, ultimately, all truths belong to the gospel. Not all theories . . . but all truths."[4] Consequently, Elder Maxwell became a role model, an example of spiritual stability, to those who faced apparent conflicts between the secular and the spiritual.

Among all of Elder Maxwell's talents, he was best known for his gift of language, which was legendary throughout the Church. Speaking at Elder Maxwell's funeral, President Hinckley gave the following tribute: "I know of no other who spoke in such a distinctive and interesting way. When he opened his mouth we all listened. We came alive with expectation of something unusual and we were never disappointed. His genius was the product of diligence. He was a perfectionist, determined to extract from each phrase and sentence every drop of nourishment that could be produced. Each talk was a masterpiece, each book a work of art, worthy of repeated reading. I think we shall not see one like him again."[5]

Elder Maxwells' main focus was on *discipleship*. To be true disciples, he taught, we may be asked to do that which is most difficult for us to do. "Sometimes [therefore] the best people . . . have the worst experiences."[6] In 1996, Elder Maxwell was diagnosed with leukemia. Through aggressive medical treatments he went in and out of remission over a period of eight years until the time of his death. During that period he increased in his empathy toward others in their suffering. President Gordon B. Hinckley said of him, "He has accomplished more in these past eight years [of his illness] than most men do in a lifetime. He comforted, blessed, and encouraged his fellow sufferers. Their oppressive burdens were made lighter by this good Samaritan who bound up their wounds and brought the sunlight of hope into their lives."[7] He succumbed to his illness on July 21, 2004.

## Joseph B. Wirthlin

Born: June 11, 1917, Salt Lake City, Utah
Sustained Assistant to the Twelve: April 4, 1975
Sustained to First Quorum of Seventy: October 1, 1976
Sustained to the Presidency of First Quorum of Seventy: August 28, 1986
Ordained Apostle: October 9, 1986
Died: December 1, 2008, Salt Lake City, at age 91

Joseph Bitner Wirthlin was born in Salt Lake City on June 11, 1917, the eldest of five children born to Joseph L. and Madelinne Bitner Wirthlin. His father was the head of Wirthlin's, Inc., a wholesale and retail food business. Young Joseph had a good singing voice and performed in elementary and junior high school musicals. He was a good student and took his Church duties seriously. His sister Gwendolyn remembered that "I don't have a single memory of his ever having been unkind to me."[1] He grew up with a love for sports and became known as "Mr. Touchdown" as the quarterback at East High School and went on to play halfback for the University of Utah for three years. Though his football career came to an end with a mission call, he never lost his love for the game. In his later years he became a self-appointed chaplain for the Ute football team and was respected by coaches, players, and fans alike. In tribute to him, his football jersey, number 4, was retired by the university. Following his death, his initials, JBW, were printed on the back of each team member's helmet.

After the 1936 football season, and with the world on the brink of war, Joseph's father asked him if wanted to serve a mission. Joseph replied that he did. "Then you must go now," said his father. "If you wait any longer, you'll never go." Elder Wirthlin recalled, "I didn't want to believe him. I wanted to pursue my dream of continuing to play football and to graduate from the university. . . . But I also knew what my father had said was true."[2] Consequently, he served from 1937 to 1939 in the German-Austrian and the Swiss-Austrian missions, heartland of the developing world crisis. Those were difficult times for an American missionary. Years later he observed, "those times of seeming failure may have been some of the most instrumental of my life, because they prepared me for greater things to come."[3] One such preparatory experience took place on a Christmas Eve in the village of Oberndorf, located in the Bavarian Alps. It was here that the carol *Silent Night* was written in 1818. It happened that Elder Wirthlin and his missionary companion came upon a church where the choir was practicing that very carol. Being deeply touched as they made the long walk back to their lodgings in old Salzburg, they spoke of their goals and aspirations. "We determined that we would be even more diligent in our missionary efforts. . . (and) upon our return home, we would serve the Master all our lives through magnifying our assignments in the Church." Elder Wirthlin recalled that he also "expressed my goal to find a girl with qualities of character that stem from a deep and abiding spiritual foundation."[4] At the end of his mission, as he boarded a train in Germany to return home, he watched thousands of Nazi troops board other trains bound for the invasion of Poland. His father's advice proved true. Had he not gone on a mission when he did, the opportunity would have been lost to him due to the outbreak of World War II.

In 1938, Joseph's father was called to the Presiding Bishopric, where he would serve as counselor and then as Presiding Bishop until

1961. Consequently, upon his return home, Joseph managed the family business while also earning a degree in business management from the University of Utah. He would continue as president of the family company until called as a General Authority. Two and a half years after his mission, he met Elisa Young Rogers, who fit perfectly his description of the girl he wanted to marry. For sixty-five years, they would have what Elder Wirthlin called a "perfect marriage." Her later death was Elder Wirthlin's "greatest sorrow" as he confronted the loneliness left by her absence. During their earlier years he served in stake and ward auxiliary positions and was bishop of the Bonneville Ward for nearly ten years. In April 1975, Elder Wirthlin was called as an Assistant to the Twelve. Recalling that day, he said with a grin, "Three hours and thirty-seven minutes after I had met with President Kimball, an earthquake was felt in Salt Lake City. This brought questions to my mind whether the Lord approved of my call. But," he added, "when the quake was over, everything seemed to smooth out, and my confidence waxed strong once again."[5] The following year he was called to the First Quorum of Seventy. Then, on October 3, 1986, President Benson extended to Elder Wirthlin a call to the Quorum of the Twelve. "My first feeling was one of total shock, almost unbelief; then I felt deep humility."[6] A few hours later, when Elisa picked him up to attend a funeral where he was to speak, he told her of the call. Neither of them spoke but simply sat quietly in the car contemplating how their lives were about to change. The following years would see Elder Wirthlin in administrative assignments throughout the world.

Toward the end of Elder Wirthlin's life, a touching scene occurred at general conference. As Elder Wirthlin spoke, his body began to shake and it appeared his legs might give out. Then Elder Russell M. Nelson came and stood by Elder Wirthlin's side with his arm around him, giving him support. When Elder Wirthlin was finished speaking, Elder Nelson helped him back to his seat. Those viewing the incident may have thought, as did this writer, that it was only natural for Elder Nelson, being a physician, to help Elder Wirthlin. But it went beyond medical training. It was the demonstration of a deep bond that began when Joseph Wirthlin, a stake high councilor, trained a new alternate high councilor named Russell Nelson.

It continued over the years as Joseph Wirthlin served as counselor to Russell Nelson when he was stake president and then president of the general Church Sunday School, and then through the years as they worked together as general authorities. Elder Nelson's coming to the podium to support Elder Wirthlin was an outward manifestation of the deep love that had developed between these two brethren over years of dedicated Church service together.

On December 1, 2008, following the Thanksgiving holiday, Elder Wirthlin went to his office to work. That night, at eleven-thirty p.m., he died of causes incident to age. He was ninety-one, the oldest of the living General Authorities.

*Endnotes*

## Abbreviations Used in Endnotes

CES: Church Educational System, The Church of Jesus Christ of Latter-day Saints.

*CHC*: B. H. Roberts, *A Comprehensive History of the Church of Jesus Christ of Latter-day Saints,* 6 vols (Deseret News Press: Salt Lake City, 1930).

CR: Conference Reports of the Church of Jesus Christ of Latter-day Saints.

*HC*: Joseph Smith, *History of the Church of Jesus Christ of Latter-day Saints*, 7 vols (Deseret News Press: Salt Lake City, 1932–51).

*JD*: *Journal of Discourses*, 26 vols. (Latter-day Saints' Book Depot: London, 1854–86).

*LDSBE*: Andrew Jenson, *LDS Biographical Encyclopedias*, 4 vols (Andrew Jenson History, 1901–1936); reprint: Western Epics, Salt Lake City, 1971.

## Thomas B. Marsh

1. *JD*, 3:284.

2. Ibid., 5:28.

3. *HC*, 3:167.

4. *JD*, 5:115.

5. Ibid., 5:207.

6. Ibid.

## David W. Patten

1. *LDSBE*, 1:77.

2. Ibid.

3. Ibid., 1:78.

4. Ibid., 1:77.

5. Lycurgus A. Wilson, *The Life of David W. Patten* (Deseret News: Salt Lake City, 1900), 53.

6. *LDSBE*, 1:80.

7. Lycurgus A. Wilson, *The Life of David W. Patten*, 70.

## Brigham Young

1. Leonard J. Arrington (ed.), *The Presidents of the Church* (Deseret Book: Salt Lake City, 1986), 48.

2. Ibid., 49.

3. *CHC*, 1:370–71.

4. Leonard J. Arrington (ed.), *The Presidents of the Church*, 50–51.

5. Myrtle Stevens Hyde, *Orson Hyde: the Olive Branch of Israel* (Agreka Books: Salt Lake City, 2000), 221–22.

6. CES, *Presidents of the Church* (Salt Lake City: The Church of Jesus Christ of Latter-day Saints, 1979), 61.

7. Leonard J. Arrington (ed.), *The Presidents of the Church*, 43.

## Heber C. Kimball

1. Orson F. Whitney, *The Life of Heber C. Kimball* (Bookcraft: Salt Lake City), 104.

2. Ibid., 132.

3. *JD*, 5:22.

4. Ibid., 1:133.

5. Ibid., 21:299.

6. *LDSBE*, 1:37.

7. *JD*, 12:186.

## Orson Hyde

1. Myrtle Stevens Hyde, *Orson Hyde: The Olive Branch of Israel*, 105.

2. *CHC*, 1:473.

3. *HC*, 7:198.

4. Myrtle Stevens Hyde, *Orson Hyde: The Olive Branch of Israel*, 486.

## William E. McLellin

1. Jan Shipps and John W. Welch, *The Journals of William E. McLellin: 1831–1836* (Brigham Young University Studies: Provo, Utah, 1994), 29–30.

2. Stephen F. Robinson and H. Dean Garrett, *A Commentary on the Doctrine and Covenants*, 4 vols (Deseret Book: Salt Lake City, 2005), 2:227.

3. *HC*, 1:226.

4. Ibid., 3:215.

5. Larry Porter, "William McLellin's Testimony of the Book of Mormon," *BYU Studies*, V. 10, 1970, 486.

## Parley P. Pratt

1. Parley P. Pratt (ed.), *Autobiography of Parley P. Pratt* (Deseret Book: Salt Lake City, 1983, 1985), 20.

2. Ibid., 83.

3. Ibid., 94.

4. Ibid., 292.

5. Ibid., 294.

6. Orson F. Whitney, *History of Utah*, 4 vols (George Q. Cannon and Sons: Salt Lake City, 1892–1904), 4:79.

## Luke S. Johnson

1. Keith Perkins, "A House Divided: The Johnson Family," 57.

2. Elden J. Watson (ed.), *Manuscript History of Brigham Young: 1846–1847* (Elden J. Watson, Salt Lake City, 1971), 72.

3. Darrell Kay Loosle (ed.), *Luke S. and Lyman E. Johnson—Apostles* (Loosle: Provo, Utah, 1964), 15.

4. *LDSBE*, 1:86.

## William Smith

1. *CHC*, 1:40.

2. Roy W. Doxy, "I Have a Question," *Ensign*, December 1986, 65.

3. Lucy Mac Smith, *History of Joseph Smith* (Bookcraft: Salt Lake City, 1958), 184.

4. *HC*, 2:339, 342–43.

## Orson Pratt

1. Elden J. Watson (ed.), *The Orson Pratt Journals* (Elden J. Watson: Salt Lake City, 1975), 498.

2. Ibid., 56.

3. *CHC*, 3:227.

4. *JD*, 4:267.

5. Breck England, *The Life and Thought of Orson Pratt* (University of Utah Press: Salt Lake City, 1985), 217.

## John F. Boynton

1. Lucy Mac Smith, *History of Joseph Smith*, 241.

2. *LDSBE*, 1:91.

## Lyman E. Johnson

1. *HC*, 2:487.

2. Keith Perkins, "A House Divided: The Johnson Family," 57.

3. Orson F. Whitney, *The Life of Heber C. Kimball*, 105.

4. *JD*, 19:41.

5. *HC*, 2:188.

6. Keith Perkins, "A House Divided: The Johnson Family," 57.

## John E. Page

1. *HC*, 3:240.

2. Ibid., 3:241.

3. Leonard J. Arrington, *Brigham Young: American Moses* (Alfred A. Knopf: New York, 1985), 71–72.

4. Ibid., 106.

5. *HC*, 7:582.

6. Elden J. Watson (ed.), *Manuscript History of Brigham Young: 1846–1847*, 81.

## John Taylor

1. B. H. Roberts, *The Life of John Taylor* (Bookcraft: Salt Lake City, 1963), 28.

2. Ibid., 40.

3. Ibid., 449.

4. Ibid., 140.

5. *JD*, 4:34.

6. "John Taylor: A Letter From Exile," *Liahona*, November 1978, 32.

## Wilford Woodruff

1. Matthias F. Cowley, *Wilford Woodruff: History of His Life and Labors* (Deseret Book: Salt Lake City, 1909), 477.

2. *Teachings of the Presidents of the Church: Wilford Woodruff*, 125.

3. Leon Hartshorn, "Wilford Woodruff: Man of Faith and Zeal," *New Era*, January 1972, 32.

4. Matthias F. Cowley, *Wilford Woodruff: History of His Life and Labors*, 530.

5. Ibid., 500.

6. Ibid., 571.

## George A. Smith

1. C. Kent Dunford, *The Contributions of George A. Smith*, Dissertation, BYU Department of Church History and Doctrine, August 1970, 43.

2. Ezra Taft Benson, "Do Not Despair," *Ensign*, October 1986, 4.

3. *HC*, 5:391.

4. Orson F. Whitney, *History of Utah*, 4:36.

5. Preston Nibley, *Brigham Young: The Man and His Works* (Deseret Book: Salt Lake City, 1960), 517.

## Willard Richards

1. *LDSBE*, 1:54.

2. Orson F. Whitney, *History of Utah*, 4:22.

3. Claire Noall, *Intimate Disciple: A Portrait of Willard Richards* (University of Utah Press: Salt Lake City, 1957), 305.

4. Orson F. Whitney, *History of Utah*, 4:23.

5. Ibid.

6. *CHC*, 2:289–90.

7. Ibid., 293.

8. Ibid., 298.

## Lyman Wight

1. *LDSBE*, 1:95.

2. Ibid., 96.

3. *CHC*, 2:435.

## Amasa Lyman

1. *HC*, 7:236–37.

2. *CHC*, 5:270–71.

3. Albert L. Lyman, *Amasa Mason Lyman* (Melvin A. Lyman: Delta, 1957), 254.

4. Dean Jesse, "Steadfast and Patient Endurance," *Ensign*, June 1979, 46.

5. Albert L. Lyman, *Amasa Mason Lyman*, 269.

## Ezra T. Benson

1. *Ezra Taft Benson, 1811–1869,* http://www.boap.org/LDS/Early-Saints/ETBenson.html.

2. John Henry Evans and Minnie Egan Anderson, *Ezra T. Benson: Pioneer, Statesman, Saint* (Deseret News: Salt Lake City, 1947), 85.

## Charles C. Rich

1. *JD,* 19:250.

## Lorenzo Snow

1. Eliza R. Snow, *Biography and Family Record of Lorenzo Snow,* 10; as cited in CES, *Presidents of the Church* (The Church of Jesus Christ of Latter-day Saints: Salt Lake City, 1979), 139.

2. LeRoi C. Snow, "Devotion to a Divine Inspiration," *Improvement Era,* June 1919, 656; as cite in CES, *Presidents of the Church,* 140.

3. Eliza R. Snow, *Biography and Family Record of Lorenzo Snow,* 7–9; as cited in CES, *Presidents of the Church,* 130.

4. Leonard J. Arrington (ed.), *The Presidents of the Church,* 171.

5. LeRoi C. Snow, "An Experience of My Father's," *Improvement Era,* September 1933, 677; as cited in CES, *Presidents of the Church,* 136.

6. Leonard J. Arrington (ed.), *The Presidents of the Church,* 175.

## Erastus Snow

1. Orson F. Whitney, *History of Utah,* 4:44.

2. *LDSBE,* 1:106.

3. Ibid., 1:111.

4. *CHC, 5:106.*

5. "Funeral Services of Apostle Erastus Snow," *Millennial Star*, Vol. L, no. 24, July 2, 1988, 419.

## Franklin D. Richards

1. *LDSBE*, 1:115.

2. Orson F. Whitney, *History of Utah*, 4:315.

## George Q. Cannon

1. Jerreld L. Newquist (ed.), *Gospel Truth*, 2 vols (Deseret Book: Salt Lake City, 1974), xv.

2. Ibid., xvii.

3. Ibid.

4. Ibid., xviii.

5. Ibid., xxv.

6. Preston Nibley, *Brigham Young: The Man and His Works*, 534.

7. B. H. Roberts, *The Life of John Taylor*, 416.

## Joseph F. Smith

1. Joseph Fielding Smith (comp.), *The Life of Joseph F. Smith*, 164; as cited in CES, *Presidents of the Church* (The Church of Jesus Christ of Latter-day Saints: Salt Lake City, 1979), 160.

2. Joseph F. Smith, *Gospel Doctrine* (Deseret Book: Salt Lake City, 1971), 518.

3. Joseph Fielding Smith (comp.), *The Life of Joseph F. Smith*, 226–27; as cited in CES, *Presidents of the Church*, 152.

4. *Teachings of the Presidents of the Church: Joseph F. Smith* (The Church of Jesus Christ of Latter-day Saints: Salt Lake City), 210.

5. Joseph F. Smith, *Gospel Doctrine*, 522.

6. CR, October 1918, 2.

## Brigham Young Jr.

1. Dean C. Jesse (ed.), *Letters of Brigham Young to His Sons*, (Deseret Book: Salt Lake City), 34.

2. Ibid., 52–53.

3. *LDSBE*, 1:126.

## Albert Carrington

1. Brigham D. Madsen, *Exploring the Great Salt Lake* (University of Utah Press: Salt Lake City), 189.

2. Ibid., 815.

## Moses Thatcher

1. *LDSBE*, 1:129.

## Francis M. Lyman

1. Albert R. Lyman, *Francis Marion Lyman: Apostle* (Melvin A. Lyman: Delta, 1958), 38.

2. Ibid., 37.

3. Ibid., 179.

## John Henry Smith

1. Jean Bickmore White (ed.), *The Diaries of John Henry Smith* (Signature Books: Salt Lake City, 1990), 572.

2. Ibid., 241.

3. Ibid., 258–59.

## George Teasdale

1. *LDSBE*, 3:790.

## Heber J. Grant

1. Leonard J. Arrington (ed.), *The Presidents of the Church*, 224.

2. Ibid., 225.

3. Ibid., 230.

4. Ibid., 231.

5. CR, October 1936, 3.

## John W. Taylor

1. *LDSBE*, 1:154.

2. Kenneth W. Godfrey, "The Coming of the Manifesto," *Dialogue*, Vol. 5, no. 3, Autumn 1970, 23.

3. *CHC*, 6:400.

4. *LDSBE*, 3:389–90.

## Marriner W. Merrill

1. Bryant S. Hinckley, *The Faith of Our Pioneer Fathers* (Bookcraft: Salt Lake City, 1956), 183.

## Anthon H. Lund

1. *LDSBE*, 1:162–63.

2. Ibid., 164.

## Abraham H. Cannon

1. Dennis B. Horne (ed.), *An Apostle's Record: The Journals of Abraham H. Cannon* (Gnolaum Books: Clearfield, 2004), 61.

2. Davis Bitton, "That Your Children May Know," *Ensign*, November 1973, 46.

3. Brian H. Stuy (ed.), *Collected Discourses*, 5 vols (B. H. S. Publishing, 1987–1992), 171–72; as cited in Davis Bitton, *George*

*Quayle Cannon: A Biography* (Deseret Book: Salt Lake City, 1999), 409.

4. "Discourse by President Wilford Woodruff," *Millennial Star*, Vol. 58, no. 47, November 19, 1896, 742.

## Matthias F. Cowley

1. *LDSBE*, 1:170.

2. Henry A. Smith, *Matthew Cowley: Man of Faith* (Bookcraft: Salt Lake City, 1956), 23.

3. Ibid., 28.

4. *LDSBE*, 1:154.

5. Henry A. Smith, *Matthew Cowley: Man of Faith*, 29.

## Abraham Owen Woodruff

1. Gerry Avant and Douglas Palmer, "'A love story, a drama, a miracle,'" *Church News*, July 24, 1993, 3.

2. "Editorial: Death of Apostle Woodruff and Wife," *Millennial Star*, Vol. 66, no. 25, June 23, 1904, 392.

3. Gerry Avant and Douglas Palmer, "'A love story, a drama, a miracle,'" 3–4.

## Rudger Clawson

1. *LDSBE*, 1:175.

2. David S. and Roy Hoops, *The Making of a Mormon Apostle: The Story of Rudger Clawson* (Madison Books: Lanham, New York, 1990), 26.

3. Ibid., 56.

4. Nephi Anderson, "Rudger Clawson," *The Juvenile Instructor*, December 1900, 775–76.

## Reed Smoot

1. *LDSBE,* 1:179.

2. *CHC,* 6:393.

3. Ibid., 397.

## Hyrum Mac Smith

1. CR, October 1974, 18.

2. Hyrum M. Smith and Janne M. Sjodahl, *The Doctrine and Covenants Commentary* (Deseret Book: Salt Lake City, 1976), v.

3. Joseph Fielding Smith, *The Life of Joseph F. Smith* (Deseret News Press: Salt Lake City, 1938), 474.

4. Ibid., 417.

5. *LDSBE,* 3:780.

6. John P. Hatch, *Danish Apostle: The Diaries of Anthon H. Lund: 1890–1921* (Signature Books: Salt Lake City, 2006), 677.

## George Albert Smith

1. Robert K. McIntosh, *An Analysis of the Doctrinal Teachings of President George Albert Smith* (Master's Thesis, Brigham Young University, 1975), 22; as cited in CES, *Presidents of the Church* (The Church of Jesus Christ of Latter-day Saints: Salt Lake City, 1979), 193.

2. CR, October 1906, 46–47.

3. Leonard J. Arrington (ed.), *The Presidents of the Church*, 255.

4. CR, October 1945, 31–32.

5. Ibid., October 1947, 5–6.

6. "Elder Tells of President Smith's Concern For His Lamanite Brethren," *Church News*, April 11, 1951, 11.

## Charles W. Penrose

1. "School Thy Feelings," *Hymns*, no. 336.

2. George D. Pyper, *Stories of Latter-day Saints Hymns* (Deseret News Press: Salt Lake City, 1940), 158–59.

3. "Oh, Ye Mountains High," *Hymns*, no. 145.

4. *CHC*, 6:362.

## George F. Richards

1. Lucile C. Tate, *LeGrand Richards: Beloved Apostle* (Bookcraft: Salt Lake City, 1982), 5.

2. CR, October 1946, 139.

3. Ibid., 140.

4. Lucile C. Tate, *LeGrand Richards: Beloved Apostle*, 226.

5. Edward L. and Andrew E. Kimball, *Spencer W. Kimball* (Bookcraft: Salt Lake City, 1977), 208.

## Orson F. Whitney

1. *LDSBE*, 1:658.

2. Ibid., 659.

3. Ibid., 660.

4. Bryant S. Hinckley, *The Faith of Our Pioneer Fathers*, 211–13.

5. Orson F. Whitney, *The Life Story of Orson F. Whitney* (Zion's Printing and Publishing: Independence, 1930), 263.

6. *LDSBE*, 3:793.

7. Orson F. Whitney, *The Life Story of Orson F. Whitney*, 326.

8. Ibid., 272.

## David O. McKay

1. Llewelyn R. McKay (comp.), *Home Memories of David O. McKay* (Deseret Book: Salt Lake City, 1956), 6.

2. "Peace Through the Gospel of Christ," *Improvement Era*, March 1921, 405–6.

3. Jeanette McKay Morrell, *Highlights in the Life of David O. McKay* (Deseret Book: Salt Lake City, 1966), 37–38.

4. David Lawrence McKay, *My Father, David O. McKay* (Deseret Book: Salt Lake City, 1989), 39.

5. David O. McKay, *Cherished Experiences* (Deseret Book: Salt Lake City, 1955), 102.

6. "Memories of a Prophet," *Improvement Era*, February 1970, 72; as told by Arch L. Madsen, President of Bonneville International Corporation.

## Anthony W. Ivins

1. "History of Anthony W. Ivins," www.onlineutah.com/ivins_anthony_w_history.shtml, 5.

2. CR, October 1978, 126.

3. "History of Anthony W. Ivins," 7.

## Joseph Fielding Smith

1. Joseph Fielding Smith Jr. and John J. Stewart, *The Life of Joseph Fielding Smith* (Deseret Book: Salt Lake City, 1972), 65.

2. Joseph Fielding Smith, *Doctrines of Salvation*, 3 vols (Bookcraft: Salt Lake City, 1954–56), 1:v.

3. Leonard J. Arrington (ed.), *The Presidents of the Church*, 340.

## James E. Talmage

1. *Aaronic Priesthood Manual 1*, Lesson 1, "Priesthood" (The Church of Jesus Christ of Latter-day Saints), 2–3.

2. John R. Talmage, *The Talmage Story* (Bookcraft: Salt Lake City, 1972), 184.

3. Ibid., 226–28.

## Stephen L. Richards

1. Sheri L. Dew, *Go Forward With Faith* (Deseret Book: Salt Lake City, 1996), 86.

2. Gordon B. Hinckley, "President Stephen L. Richards: 1879–1952," *Improvement Era*, June 1959, 417.

3. CR, October 1935, 94.

4. Matthew O. Richardson, "The Christis Legacy," *LDS Living Magazine*, 2008, 25–27.

5. Francis M. Gibbons, *David O. McKay: Apostle to the World, Prophet of God* (Deseret Book: Salt Lake City, 1979), 401.

## Richard R. Lyman

1. Edward L. and Andrew E. Kimball, *Spencer W. Kimball*, 209.

2. Ibid., 346.

3. Albert R. Lyman, *Francis Marion Lyman: Apostle*, 194.

## Melvin J. Ballard

1. "Sketches from the Life of Margaret McNeil Ballard," 3; as cited in M. Russell Ballard, "Margaret McNeil Ballard's Legacy of Faith," *Ensign*, July 1989, 19.

2. Bryant S. Hinckley, *The Faith of Our Pioneer Fathers*, 226–27.

3. CR, April 1986, 15.

4. M. Russell Ballard, *"Thinking Straight,"* New Era, March 1985, 46.

## John A. Widtsoe

1. John A. Widtsoe, *In a Sunlit Land* (Deseret Book: Salt Lake City, 1952), 79.

2. Widtsoe to Susa Young Gates, October 30, 1931, Susa Young Gates Collection, Utah State Historical Society; as cited in Allen K. Parrish, *John A. Widtsoe: A Biography* (Deseret Book: Salt Lake City, 2003), 484.

3. John A. Widtsoe, *In a Sunlit Land*, 156.

4. "Life of Apostle Extolled in Impressive Rite," *Deseret News*, December 6, 1952; as cited in Allen K. Parrish, *John A. Widtsoe: A Biography*, 664.

## Joseph F. Merrill

1. "Sketch of New Apostle" *Church News*, October 10, 1931, 3.

2. A. Lowell Merrill, "He Helped Us Develop a Love for the Gospel," *Church News*, February 13, 1952, 4.

## Charles A. Callis

1. CR, April 2001, 61.

2. Vaughn J. Featherstone, "Secret of the Second Mile," *New Era*, May 1990, 4.

3. *Teachings of the Presidents of the Church: Harold B. Lee* (The Church of Jesus Christ of Latter-day Saints: Salt Lake City, 2000), 52.

4. Harold B. Lee, "Speaking for Himself—President Lee's Stories," *Ensign*, February 1974, 15.

5. Richard F. Bennett, "Elder Charles A. Callis," *Ensign*, April 1981, 51.

## J. Reuben Clark Jr.

1. CR, April, 1986, 48.

2. Ray Hillman (ed.), *J. Reuben Clark: Diplomat and Statesman* (Brigham Young University Press, Provo, Utah, 1973), 13.

3. Ibid.

4. Spencer W. Kimball diary, April 9, 1951 (entry); as cited in Michael D. Quinn, *Elder Statesman: A Biography of J. Reuben Clark* (Signature Books: Salt Lake City, 2002), 147.

5. CR, April 1951, 154; as cited in Michael D. Quinn, *Elder Statesman*, 148.

6. Marion G. Romney diary, April 9, 1951 (entry); as cited in Michael D. Quinn, *Elder Statesman*, 149.

7. Marianne C. Sharp letter to J. Reuben Clark, 19 April 1951; as cited in Michael D. Quinn, *Elder Statesman*, 151.

8. Spencer W. Kimball to J. Reuben Clark, August 28, 1958; as cited in Michael D. Quinn, *Elder Statesman*, 426.

## Alonzo A. Hinckley

1. Bryant S. Hinckley, *The Faith of Our Pioneer Fathers*, 232–33.

2. "Speakers pay tribute to Apostle Hinckley," *Church News*, January 9, 1937, 3.

3. Ibid., 6.

4. Bryant S. Hinckley, *The Faith of Our Pioneer Fathers*, 235.

5. "Speakers pay tribute to Apostle Hinckley," 3.

6. CR, October 1949, 43.

## Albert E. Bowen

1. Albert L. Zobell Jr., "Albert E. Bowen: 1875–1953," *Improvement Era*, September 1953, 652.

2. "Elder A. E. Bowen: Funeral Service," *Church News*, July 25, 1953, 4.

3. "Beloved Friend and Apostle," *Church News*, July 25, 1953, 2.

## Sylvester Q. Cannon

1. Winfield Q. Cannon, *Sylvester Q. Cannon: Tall in Character and Stature* (The Winfield Cannon and Wanda Canon Trust: Provo, Utah, 1998), 77.

2. "Development of the Church Welfare Program," www.history-ofmormonism.com/2009/07/07/welfare.

3. Ibid.

## Harold B. Lee

1. Leonard J. Arrington (ed.), *The Presidents of the Church*, 347.

2. L. Brent Goates, *Harold B. Lee: Prophet and Seer* (Bookcraft: Salt Lake City, 1985), 137.

3. Harold B. Lee, "The Way to Eternal Life," *Ensign*, November 1971, 17.

4. CR, October 1962, 83.

5. L. Brent Goates, *Harold B. Lee: Prophet and Seer*, 349.

6. Spencer W. Kimball, "A Giant of a Man," *Ensign*, February 1974, 86.

## Spencer W. Kimball

1. Edward W. Kimball, *Lengthen Your Stride* (Deseret Book: Salt Lake City, 2005), 383.

2.  Edward L. and Andrew E. Kimball, *Spencer W. Kimball*, 195.

3.  Ibid., 1.

4.  Edward W. Kimball, *Lengthen Your Stride*, 215.

5.  Ibid., 222.

## Ezra Taft Benson

1.  Mark E. Peterson, "President Ezra Taft Benson," *Ensign*, January 1986, 10.

2.  Ibid., 7.

3.  Ibid.

4.  Leonard J. Arrington (ed.), *The Presidents of the Church*, 434.

5.  Ibid., 435.

6.  "President Ezra Taft Benson: The Sure Voice of Faith," *Ensign*, July 1994, 15.

## Mark E. Peterson

1.  Thomas E. Monson, "Mark E. Peterson: A Giant Among Men," *Ensign*, March 1984, 6.

2.  "News of the Church," *Ensign*, March 1984, 75–76.

3.  Ibid., 76.

## Matthew Cowley

1.  Henry A. Smith, *Matthew Cowley: Man of Faith*, 31.

2.  Ibid., 42.

3.  Ibid., 54.

4.  Ibid., 65.

5. "Matthew Cowley Funeral," *Church News*. December 19, 1953, 5.

6. Henry A. Smith, *Matthew Cowley: Man of Faith*, 122.

7. Ibid., 152.

8. Ibid., 169.

## Henry D. Moyle

1. "Associates Pay Tribute to President Henry D. Moyle at Tabernacle Service," *Church News*, September 28, 1963, 4.

2. Ibid., 5.

3. Ibid., 6.

4. Ibid.

## Delbert L. Stapley

1. "Apostle Praised for Service," *Church News*, August 26, 1978, 3.

2. Ibid.

3. Ibid., 14.

4. "News of the Church," *Ensign*, October 1978, 57.

5. Ibid., 58.

6. Thomas E. Monson, "Preparation Precedes Performance," *Ensign*, September 1993, 71–72.

## Marion G. Romney

1. "President Marion G. Romney Turns Eighty," *Ensign*, October 1977, 86.

2. "President Marion G. Romney: All is Holy When He Kneels," *Ensign*, July 1988, 73.

3. Ibid., 75.

4. Ibid., 76.

5. Ibid.

6. Gerry Avant, "Leader's life yielded abundance of stories," *Church News*, May 28, 1988, 5.

7. Ibid.

8. Lee Warnick, "Honoring a 47-year ministry," *Church News*, May 28, 1988, 3.

9. "President Marion G. Romney: All is Holy When He Kneels," 75.

10. Ibid., 78.

11. Lee Warnick, "Honoring a 47-year ministry," 4.

12. Ibid.

## LeGrand Richards

1. "First Presidency notes loss in apostle's death," *Church News*, January 16, 1983, 3.

2. Lucile C. Tate, *LeGrand Richards: Beloved Apostle*, 231.

3. Ibid., 234–35.

4. Ibid., 145.

5. "First Presidency notes loss in apostle's death," 16.

## Adam S. Bennion

1. Henry D. Moyle, "Adam S. Bennion Appointed to the Council of the Twelve," *Relief Society Magazine*, June 1953, 370.

2. Harold B. Lee, "In Memoriam: Adam S. Bennion," *Relief Society Magazine*, April 1958, 217.

3. Albert L. Zobell Jr. "Adam S. Bennion," *Improvement Era*, April 1958, 241.

4. Harold B. Lee, "Stories from General Authorities," *New Era*, March 1973, 12.

5. Harold B. Lee, "In Memoriam: Adam S. Bennion," 217.

6. Richard Cracroft, "Questions and Answers," *New Era*, November 1983, 11.

7. Harold B. Lee, "In Memoriam: Adam S. Bennion," 217.

8. Albert L. Zobell Jr. "Adam S. Bennion," 240.

9. Ibid., 267.

## Richard L. Evans

1. Marion D. Hanks, "Elder Richard L. Evans," *Ensign*, December 1971, 3.

2. Richard L. Evans Jr., *Richard L. Evans: The Man and His Message* (Bookcraft: Salt Lake City, 1973), 6.

3. Ibid., 5.

4. Ibid., 4.

5. Ibid., 84–85.

## George Q. Morris

1. "Services for Elder George Q. Morris," *Church News*, May 5, 1962, 14.

2. M. Elmer Christensen, "George Q. Morris: 1874–1962," *Improvement Era*, June 1962, 470.

3. "Services for Elder George Q. Morris," 13.

## Hugh B. Brown

1. Edwin Brown Firmage, "Elder Hugh B. Brown 1883–1975: In Memoriam," *Ensign*, January 1976, 86.

2. Ibid., 88.

3. Truman G. Madsen, "Hugh B. Brown: Youthful Veteran," *New Era*, April 1976, 16.

4. Edwin Brown Firmage, "Elder Hugh B. Brown," 90–91.

5. G. Homer Durham, *N. Elden Tanner: His Life and Service* (Deseret Book: Salt Lake City, 1982), 255–56.

## Howard W. Hunter

1. "President Howard W. Hunter: The Lord's Good and Faithful Servant," *Ensign*, April 1995, 10.

2. Mark Scott, "Reflections on Howard W. Hunter in Jerusalem: An Interview with Teddy Kollek," *BYU Studies*, Vol. 34, no. 4, 1994–1995, 9–14.

3. Jon M. Huntsman, "A Remarkable and Selfless Life," *Ensign*, April 1995, 25

4. "President Howard W. Hunter: The Lord's Good and Faithful Servant," 16.

5. Gordon B. Hinckley, "A Prophet Polished and Refined," *Ensign*, April 1995, 33.

## Gordon B. Hinckley

1. Jeffrey H. Holland, "President Gordon B. Hinckley: Stalwart and Brave He Stands," *Ensign*, June 1995, 8.

2. "President Gordon B. Hinckley 1910–2008. In Memoriam," *Ensign*, March 2008, 5.

3. Sheri L. Dew, *Go Forward With Faith* (Deseret Book: Salt Lake City, 1996), 505.

4. Ibid., 506.

5. Ibid., 507.

6. Ibid., 508.

7. CR, April 1996, 89–90.

8. Sheri L. Dew, *Go Forward With Faith*, 448–49.

9. CR, April 2001, 4.

## N. Eldon Tanner

1. Hugh B. Brown, "President N. Eldon Tanner: A Man of Integrity," *Ensign*, November 1972, 14.

2. "President N. Eldon Tanner Dies," *Ensign*, January 1983, 8.

3. Ibid.

4. Ibid.

5. Richard L. Evans, "Nathan E. Tanner of the Council of the Twelve," *Improvement Era*, January 1963, 40.

6. "President N. Eldon Tanner Dies," 9.

7. Ibid., 11.

8. Ibid., 12.

9. Ibid., 11.

## Marvin J. Ashton

1. Breck England, "Elder Marvin J. Ashton: Friend of Prisoners and Prophets," *Ensign*, July 1986, 10.

2. Ibid., 9.

3. Ibid.

4. Ibid.

5. Ibid., 8.

6.  Ibid., 9.

7.  Sheri L. Dew, "Elder Marvin J. Ashton: As Elder Statesman," *This People*, 1984, 22–25.

8.  "Elder Marvin J. Ashton: A Voice of Faith and Hope," *Ensign*, April 1994, 76.

9.  Ibid.

## Bruce R. McConkie

1.  Sheri L. Dew, "Bruce R. McConkie: A Family Portrait," *This People*, 1985–1986, 53.

2.  Ibid.

3.  Ibid.

4.  "Elder Bruce R. McConkie: Preacher of Righteousness," *Ensign*, June 1985, 16.

5.  Ibid., 19.

6.  Bruce R. McConkie, "All Are Alike Unto God," *CES Religious Educators Symposium*, Brigham Young University, August 18, 1978.

7.  "Elder Bruce R. McConkie: Preacher of Righteousness," 19.

8.  CR, April 1985, 12.

## David B. Haight

1.  CR, April 1981, 58.

2.  "Long life well lived," *Church News*, August 7, 2004, 5.

3.  "Elder Haight: An honorable man," *Church News*, August 2004, 4.

4.  CR, October 1989, 73–75.

5.  "We shall miss him," *Church News*, August 7, 2004, 3.

## James E. Faust

1. "Elder James E. Faust: Sharing His Love for the Lord," *Ensign*, October 1986, 8.

2. "Man of balance," *Church News*, August 18, 2007, 7.

3. "President James E. Faust: Beloved Shepherd," *Ensign*, October 2007, 2.

4. Ibid., 3–4.

5. Ibid., 4–5.

6. "Man of balance," 7.

7. "President James E. Faust: Beloved Shepherd," 5.

8. "Man of balance," 7.

9. "One of a Kind," *Church News*, August 18, 2007, 4.

## Neal A. Maxwell

1. Bruce C. Hafen, "Elder Neal A. Maxwell: An Understanding Heart," *Ensign*, February 1982, 8.

2. Bruce C. Hafen, *A Disciple's Life* (Deseret Book: Salt Lake City, 2002), 115.

3. "Elder Neal Ash Maxwell: A Promise Fulfilled," *Ensign*, September 2004, 11.

4. Bruce C. Hafen, *A Disciple's Life*, 166.

5. "Apostle's work continues beyond veil," *Church News*, July 31, 2004, 3.

6. Bruce R. Hafen, "The Story of the Disciple's Life—Preparing the Biography of Neal A. Maxwell," *BYU Studies*, Vol. 42, no.1, 2013, 16.

7. "Elder Neal Ash Maxwell: A Promise Fulfilled," 13.

## Joseph B. Wirthlin

1. Don L. Searle, "Elder Joseph B. Wirthlin: Finding Happiness Serving the Lord," *Ensign*, December 1986, 10.

2. "Mission sets tone," *Church News*, December 6, 2008, 4.

3. Ibid.

4. Joseph B. Wirthlin, "Silent Night, Holy Night," *Church News*, November 29, 2008, 9.

5. "Elder Joseph B. Wirthlin of the Quorum of the Twelve," *Ensign*, November 1986, 95.

6. Ibid.

# About the Author

J erry H. Houck joined The Church of Jesus Christ of Latter-day Saints at the age of eighteen. Since then, he has dedicated his time to education. With a master's and doctorate in special education, he has worked with the Church Educational System (CES) for thirty-nine years, teaching and supervising religious education in such varied places as the Navajo Reservation in the southwest, Western Samoa, and Washington, DC. He has also served in such capacities as a field researcher and writer for the CES Curriculum Department, a member of the Aaronic Priesthood Curriculum Writing Committee, and the chairman of the Church Writing Committee for *Teachings of the Presidents of the Church: David O. McKay* manual. Now retired, he and his wife, Wendy, currently reside in the Salt Lake City area.